THE PLACE OF

Divine Intimacy

Where Relationship With God
Changes *Everything*

CC LITTLEJOHN

Light and Water Publishing

Light and Water Publishing, Alberta, Canada
For inquiries, permission requests, and more, go to: cclittlejohn.com

Scripture quotations marked (AMPC) are taken from the Amplified Bible, Copyright © 1954, 1958, 1962, 1964, 1965, 1987 by The Lockman Foundation. Used by permission.

Scripture quotations marked CSB have been taken from the Christian Standard Bible®, Copyright © 2017 by Holman Bible Publishers. Used by permission. Christian Standard Bible® and CSB® are federally registered trademarks of Holman Bible Publishers.

Scripture quotations marked (ESV) are from the ESV® Bible (The Holy Bible, English Standard Version®), copyright © 2001 by Crossway, a publishing ministry of Good News Publishers. Used by permission. All rights reserved.

Scripture quotations marked (MSG) are taken from THE MESSAGE, copyright © 1993, 2002, 2018 by Eugene H. Peterson. Used by permission of NavPress, represented by Tyndale House Publishers. All rights reserved.

Scripture quotations marked (NASB) are taken from the (NASB®) New American Standard Bible®, Copyright © 1960, 1971, 1977, 1995, 2020 by The Lockman Foundation. Used by permission. All rights reserved. www.lockman.org.

Scripture quotations marked (NIV) are taken from the Holy Bible, New International Version®, NIV®. Copyright © 1973, 1978, 1984, 2011 by Biblica, Inc.™ Used by permission of Zondervan. All rights reserved worldwide. www.zondervan.com. The "NIV" and "New International Version" are trademarks registered in the United States Patent and Trademark Office by Biblica, Inc.™

Scripture quotations marked (NLT) are taken from the Holy Bible, New Living Translation, copyright ©1996, 2004, 2015 by Tyndale House Foundation. Used by permission of Tyndale House Publishers, Carol Stream, Illinois 60188. All rights reserved.

Scripture quotations marked (NKJV) are taken from the New King James Version®. Copyright © 1982 by Thomas Nelson. Used by permission. All rights reserved.

Cover: Special thanks from the author to Kelly Mulner for all your help
Author photograph by Frank Wong
Editing and interior design: Rachel L. Hall, Writely Divided

ISBN: 978-1-7776402-0-0 Paperback edition
ISBN: 978-1-7776402-1-7 eBook edition

The Place of Divine Intimacy: Where Relationship with God Changes Everything / CC Littlejohn —1st ed.

To my children,

Savian, Justus, & Kira

*My prayer is that you
will learn the incredible joy of living
moment-by-moment in the hand-in-hand
company & love
of our Triune God.*

CONTENTS

CONTENTS

CONTENTS

CONTENTS

Contents

THE PLACE OF

Divine Intimacy

Introduction

For as long as I can remember, I have been deeply blessed by a tangible experience of intimacy with God. By this, I mean that I sense His genuine presence and experience His love in my day-to-day life. I find evidence of His care, encouragement, and direction. When I became a Christian around age 7, at the time, I was the only Christian in my family and had limited biblical instruction. Yet from that early age, I experienced God's provision, protection, and spiritual teaching in all seasons, transitions, blessings, and challenges.

My passion for relationship with God—not just Christianity—was formed in a unique way. I was well-acquainted with some who said they were once Christian but were not any longer. A longing grew in me to understand why. The idea that my deeply treasured knowledge of belonging to Father God could ever be lost drove me to consistent prayer. I wanted to have the forever-faith like that of a child, faith that's ever-increasing, and faith that moves mountains. Years later, my pastor defined *faith* as a relationship with God. By the time I heard this definition, I was in my late teens, and I knew my prayers had been answered. Someone can walk away from a belief, a religion, or a church. However, one cannot so easily leave a relationship behind. I had formed a relationship with God that ran deep, and I was certain walking away from it would never be an option.

By my late teens to early twenties, I had a passion for writing and recording my thoughts and experiences of God's life-changing love. Wanting to take seriously the call to be light in this world, I looked for ways to grow in relationships with others and encourage them to find this deeply personal God I knew. Eventually, I found writing was the only outlet that could satisfy my passion to be long-reaching in my attempt to inspire others contemplating for themselves the ideas around the intimate heart of God.

Within my journey, I faced circumstances that further encouraged urgency to pursue these writings on what I felt to be the most important life truths. At 27, just shortly after my first son's birth, I was diagnosed with cancer. A few years later, just before my second son was born, I experienced God's calling to write a book about intimacy with Him. This request was easy to say yes to, for it allowed me to record what I felt to be the best possible gift to give my children, whether I was here with them or not. I set my heart to help them in whatever way I could so that they would know the secret of why we are here: to see the mystery that lies in the love relationship that we have with the Father, His Son Jesus, and Holy Spirit.

Yet as I studied, contemplated, and focused on intimacy, God made it apparent that just as I want my children to experience intimacy with Him, He has a similar passion for every single created person. He wants each of His beloved children to know Him personally in all His great affections. With this glimpse into God's heart, God's passion became my passion. I want everyone to encounter the reality of this love and to learn to live in a daily, deeply connected relationship with our Triune God.

My prayer is that people worldwide would be exactly where God wants them—in a genuine love relationship with Him, living in the pure joy of the fellowship which has the power to transform every area of life. Then, in that love, to join the Kingdom work of spreading the message further and further, by whatever means God invites us to join Him.

May this book be a glimpse and an entryway into the very intimate nature of the relationship God intends to have with each one of us. May it lead us into the journey of living in close, personal connection with our Maker.

Section 1:

THE EXTRAVAGANT MAGNITUDE OF GOD'S INTIMACY

What a blessing that we live in a time where God is inviting us into incredible intimacy. Our intimacy with Him has always been on His heart: it is His very nature, this ultimate longing for connectedness, with us, His created. Yet it is in this very time in history, because of what Jesus accomplished on the cross, that we are invited into the most intimate offering with Triune God. Through God's giving and our receiving of the Holy Spirit, we are empowered to live in close relationship with Him. What favor we have received to come and explore this intricate and generous gift!

> *And I ask him that with both feet planted firmly on love, you'll be able to take in with all followers of Jesus the extravagant dimensions of Christ's love. Reach out and experience the breadth! Test its length! Plumb the depths! Rise to the heights! Live full lives, full in the fullness of God.*
>
> ~ *from Eph. 3:17–19 (MSG)*

Joining the Desire of His Heart

An extraordinary, life-changing invitation is sent to everyone. This invitation is like no other. It is exquisite, it is sealed with a promise of certainty, and it holds the highest significance. For some, accepting it can prove challenging. Yet the value of embracing it has long-standing importance and worth, beyond any of its asking. This invitation is without question the most crucial offering extended to us in our lives.

As Christians, we may have seen the great invitation as one which allows us to be joined into God's family, into forgiveness, into redemption, or the wonder of our ultimate resting place in heaven. However, rather than these incredible blessings being the end place of the invitation, they are the starting place. These individual gems make the way possible so that we may step into the greatest treasure of all.

Unfortunately, we often stop at the point of finding salvation. We can miss the extent of the invitation which calls us to the sacred, holy place of God's heart and into the big picture of His desire. There are no shortcuts, no allowance for half-heartedness, and it is not of our choosing. Instead, the requirement is to work for His desire alone, and that has remained the same since creation. Yet it took Jesus on earth, His death, and His resurrection, to put into motion all the possibilities of His intent. What was broken is now restored, the seemingly impossible is made achievable, and the invitation is out.

On the cross, Jesus accomplished a new beginning for us. He established an open door that cannot be shut, which invites us to join into rich fellowship with Triune God. Among their company, we find a remarkable, intertwined union of the most profound commitment, limitless love, and joined purpose. Jesus welcomes us into this incredible bond of highest friendship. That bond is His core desire. Entering it satisfies the heart of our God when we, His created, seek to genuinely love and live in beautiful, relational connection with the very One who made us.

Making the Lord Our Savior

Some people are blessed to come to salvation in Jesus from a young age, often through the influence of living in a Christian family. Seeds are planted, sound teaching embeds truth, and continual spiritual growth and living are nurtured. However, if this is our story, our faith may be found to be like that of the women of Samaria, whose commitment was based on another person's testimony. It's wonderful that they accepted the woman at the well's witness. Yet each person who has heard another's testimony still needs to arrive at their own encounter, a sacred place of spending their own time with Jesus. Every one of us needs to come to our own standing, not merely standing on our mentor's encounter, but a position where we can say like these women:

> *"We're no longer taking this on your say-so. We've heard it for ourselves and know it for sure. He's the Savior of the world!"*
>
> ~ *John 4:42 (MSG)*

However it happens, something amazing happens when we ask Jesus into our hearts and lives. There in that place, the words and the power of the Holy Spirit do something incredible to bring us to that position as we are led into truth by the very Spirit of God. Sometimes, the testimony or witness of another is enough to get us into this place of beginning to believe. The Samaritan women trusted the story of the encounter. Yet it was in spending time and hearing Jesus for themselves that the story became personal to them. They no longer depended on another's account; now they had a faith-story of their own. They personally knew Him as Savior of the world.

This is the point when belief grows stable and lasting faith forms. Our beloved Lord's heart desires an individual, personal, sincere relationship with every one of us. It is what will make us complete in His fullness. He, then, "through his mighty power at work within us, [will] accomplish infinitely more than we might ask or think" (Eph. 3:20, NLT).

The Virtue of Trust

Before we can experience intimate bonding with Triune God in complete, integrated, incomparable encounter, we must meet a prerequisite. The prerequisite is a concept with which we are familiar. Yet in practical, daily action, it can prove to be exceedingly difficult. However, our Maker, the One who is entirely aware of what is fully needed, says it is required. Triune God —Father, Son, and Holy Spirit—already exists. They are in perfect unity with each other. They know that for their love to enter our lives successfully, we need to put forth another type of virtue first.

What is this virtue? It is the complex but essential component of trust. For us to enter into His love, God requires our trust. And trust is a beautiful place God calls us to. Through it, He promises incredible possibilities, freedom, and straight paths. Through trust, God extends His invitation to intimacy. He asks us to abandon our old company, fear, and determinedly embrace our new friend, trust.

Choosing trust enables us to enter into perfected love. Whereas fear and love are almost incompatible, trust and love are inseparable in nature and company.

There is no fear in love. But perfect love drives out fear.

~ 1 John 4:18 (NIV)

In love, we trust in the One we have come to know, and we have faith what He says is true. As well, we choose to trust and to believe the best in Him, just as He has chosen to believe in us and move us into our best. In this beautiful relationship founded on the virtue of trust, God can move us into all that He wants for us.

Perhaps not surprisingly, the measure of trust we extend to Him will often reflect the measure of intimate connection we are equally able to experience from Him. Freely abandoning ourselves to trust, we find ourselves in the place of living in that perfected love, free to enjoy the close, intimate bond with the Triune God as they desire.

Encountering the Person Truth

Authenticity is essential for progressing into true intimacy, especially when it comes to the Divine. From the beginning, across generations, nations, and cultures, the human heart has quested after the answer to the question, *What is truth?* We are wired to desire truth and equipped to seek it. Consequently, we look for something in this world that is solid and firm—for something that always inspires good, right motives, pure heartedness, and a clear conscience.

Our very souls are deeply engraved with the need for truth. We need to find the truth to satisfy our desire for a universal solution and a set of standards to measure our lives against. We need something dependable, something true, because life can be so full of uncertainty. People look for a truth that does not fight over semantics but willingly pours out unity and peace, convincing us of its consistency and goodness. We search for a truth that has meaningful insight and that holds tightly both matters for this life and the eternal.

Scholars throughout history have asked, *What is truth?* They often conclude their studies unable to solve the mystery beyond anything but conceptual, abstract virtues such as love, decency, and beauty. Yet Jesus came into the world not only displaying these qualities beyond what anyone had ever seen, but He also went much further by proclaiming words that can finally settle one's heart on the matter of *What is truth?*

Jesus says,

I am the way and the truth and the life.

~ *John 14:6 (NIV)*

Jesus holds the title of being The Truth! Our desire for knowing something to be certain, unchanging, and good to the core rests in Him. When we encounter and accept Him, we are blessed to hold what is true. Three key elements open us to all sorts of possibilities in the spiritual realm. One is truth. First comes a desire for it, followed by a search, and in the end, we come to a person. For to commit to and accept Jesus as the way the truth and the life, is the cornerstone and foundation to build a sincere relationship with the Divine.

Faith: Commitment of the Heart

After truth, faith is an additional essential element to unlocking the mystery of intimacy with God. Truth leads us to the person, Jesus, and faith comes in committing ourselves to Jesus. Faith believes what we have learned about the One we cannot see and takes up sureness and hope in all the truth He stands for (see Heb 11:1). When we view faith through the lens of intimacy, we find faith is all about relationship with God. That perspective can transform the virtue in our minds. While it is seemingly almost unattainable to some, faith is not something like a belief or feeling that needs to be forced to be embraced. It is not really even a mind-made decision that weighs all that has been learned of the person Truth and then commits to it through reason. Instead, in the end, faith is a pure, solid commitment from the heart to follow forever what you know to be absolute Truth.

Arising as it does from the most innocent, uncomplex, wholesome part of us, faith surrenders with a powerful, childlike humility, and it believes all the wonder found in Jesus (see Matt. 18:2–4). Faith is a place of movement of our heart when it says Yes to His heart of love for us. Faith becomes essential to our connection with God, for it is this very thing that makes Him happy.

To enter into the unseen hope that we are living for, we must have faith. It allows our minds to find the remarkable space of believing that which our hearts lead us to. When we approach Him with faith, our love pleases God. It shows that we acknowledge His existence, trust Him, and believe He loves us enough to interact with us in very real ways.

So then, may we enter this relationship with Truth—who is Jesus—with all our hearts, filled with childlike faith that completely trusts. From that place, we encounter relationship, bless the heart of God by our commitment, and we find ourselves under pure, genuine love.

Intimate Encounter Creates Passion

As we explore and encounter God's intentions, a deep foundation of incredible love builds within us. When we begin to understand the wonder and beauty of God's desire for intimate connection with us, an unrelenting and persistent seed of passion for our First Love forms within our hearts. This seed is somewhat like faith: it is not something we must create or somehow muster up. Instead, it is the natural result of the desire to know the One who first loved us (1 John 4:19). The seed is planted at our first encounter of true knowledge of the Most High. From the moment we became aware of and experienced the genuine, trustworthy love obtainable only through our Creator, the seed of passion continues to grow. Through it, the unblemished affection and attachment of God infiltrate our reality.

Even though we cannot create passion through self-will, there are ways our spirits learn to grow in intensity in living for God. At times, almost by accident, perhaps in raw moments of pain, periods of intense gratitude, or in desperate need to have God come through for us, we find ourselves entirely honest and real before God. This place is full of concentrated connection. It's where we know that we need Him and that He not only knows, understands, and cares for us but also is prepared to help. He is before us, ready to support us with full acceptance and amazing, generous love. As our hearts respond to such intense moments of His interceding on our behalf, passion, a sense of thankfulness, and worship can penetrate the depths of our being. This passion that builds intimacy is not forced, falsified, or even complicated. Rather, it is a pure result of admiration of the One who has loved us. This is passion that comes from our very depths. Those of us who worship Him will find ourselves doing so from "[our] very being, [our] spirits, [our] true selves, in adoration" (John 4:24, MSG).

The Element of Time

It is God's deep desire that we would be so blessed to fully see and understand the wonder of His longing for intimate connection. He wants our eyes to be open to the love He has for us. Yet this takes time! It takes time to know someone, especially someone as complex and awesome as God. It takes time to come to the awareness that we are truly known. So, it is essential to be alert and work towards an accurate perception of the One we meet. However, like any good thing, the relationship cannot be rushed. God lives outside the restrictions of time, so He inherently has all the time in the world for us. However, He needs us to take time with Him, to surrender our schedule, to open up opportunities for revelation. In those moments, He can show us just what our spirit needs.

Living in the place that satisfies, in the intimacy God designed us for, requires intentionally, continually striving to find the beautiful place that includes Him in all of our moments in each increment of each day. Perhaps this way of living is the very dwelling place, the residence of spiritual living the Psalmist longed for (see Psalm 84). Imagine residing in the most satisfying places, living moment by moment with our God, purely delighting in His company. As we extend our hand to Him with our time, He lovingly extends His hand back to us with the most treasured gift. The gift is that He, too, gives us His time, His moments, and when we join with Him, we become inseparable from His most excellent companionship and presence.

Time is the virtue component, the essential element that allows truth, faith, and passion to grow. Time builds deep, unshakable roots of trust. There is no roundabout way to establish intimate relationship. It cannot be rushed: time is the ingredient for its growth. When we embrace this concept, God blesses us with the beautiful knowledge that He simply wants us to enjoy the journey with Him, as He enjoys it with us.

Genuine Desire for Another's Company

We underestimate God's delight in simply being in our company. An intimate, faith relationship is defined by friendship. "All things have been created through him and for him" (Col. 1:16b, NIV). When we step away from our need to achieve, accomplish, and attain in daily life or even in ministry, when we focus on being purely "made for Him," we show that we aren't in it for what we can do for Him, or Him for us, but that He enjoys our company. We believe that the accomplishment is His desire. Yet, high ambitions often get in the way of what God is after. In the busyness, the best gets crowded out.

God desires from us our genuine desire for His company. That makes the friendship. He designed us to want real camaraderie with another. If we are really blessed, we may even experience it with a few others. We experience it with people who don't want anything from us: they just want us because to be with us makes them happy. It is the same with our Lord: it is a picture of purest, sincerest attachments. It is a bond built out of delight in another and the unsaid pledge to keep that friendship as the highest treasure.

True intimacy experiences this, prioritize this, lives for it. From the garden in Eden, where humankind walked with God, to King David, to Jesus' time on earth, to us here and now, friendship is the secret to all.

> One thing I have asked from the LORD, that I shall seek:
> That I may dwell in the house of the LORD all the days of my life,
> To behold the beauty of the LORD.
>
> ~ Psalm 27:4 (NASB)

God is searching for people who authentically work to see Him as a real, alive, relational Being, and who want to be in His company. The invitation to this relationship is amazing. Once we experience it, our heart-need is met, and we find there is no other place we would rather be.

To See Jesus

Intimacy calls us to the highest relationship with Jesus. It requires trust, encounter, faith, passion, and time. Yet there is a question to this intimacy that many will encounter in their walk: How can I see Jesus? A child or new believer may ask it this way: Why can I not see Jesus?

This is a fair question of the One who calls us to the deepest relationship of trust, encounter, faith, and passion. Oddly enough, we have seen what it looks like in the lives of the disciples who physically saw, walked, and lived day by day with Jesus. They witnessed first-hand Jesus' beautiful dependence on the Father.

Yet, they also faced staggering doubt in times of separation from Jesus—on the boat in the storm, praying without seeing power or results, and of course at the crucifixion where they all fled. However, when Jesus talked of leaving, He promised that though He was to go away, something better was coming. They (and we) were to be opened up by it, to a new way of living and seeing. For after Jesus left the earth and sent the promised Holy Spirit, this created the astonishing opportunity for us to see with spiritual eyes open and to experience Jesus' company, wisdom, power, and presence continually.

So why can't we see Jesus? Well, we can. It's as though what was removed in the physical form of Jesus' presence in this world was transferred into a constant availability for encounter: an omnipresent fellowship with God, for all believers, that would never leave. Seeing, experiencing, and remaining in Jesus is made possible through the Holy Spirit for those seeking the relationship.

Of course, this all is impossible on our own. Yet it is possible through His gift of the Holy Spirit who leads us into all truth (see John 16:12–14). Connected and one, Jesus and the Holy Spirit are in perfect unity. As we accept the Holy Spirit, we also receive the continual Presence of Jesus.

Shared Vision for the Kingdom

As the Holy Spirit leads us into all truth, remarkable things begin to happen. Intimacy starts pouring into our field of spiritual vision. Our focus, purpose, and sight begin to tune in to the things of our God—Kingdom things.

So, we might ask, How can we see God? As we step into our new birth and the new life of God's Kingdom, our eyes open. Jesus explained it this way: "Take it from me: Unless a person is born from above, it's not possible to see what I'm pointing to—to God's kingdom" (John 3:3 MSG). Without this new birth, seeing God remains impossible. It is in the spiritual dimension, not the physical dimension, that this kind of seeing occurs.

What is required for this new birth? That question has a simple answer, but it includes a complicated task. We need to come to the place of being full of love for God. The absolute, beautiful perfection of Jesus on earth exemplifies this place of love. In a similar position of surrender, we must be willing to lay down our lives in great love, just as He did. Delivered from our old way of living, we step into the rebirth of Spirit-filled, Kingdom-focused living. This involves not only seeing God but completely joining with His ambitions. Doing so transforms our vision and purpose, and our rebirth joins us in a more profound relationship with our God.

Not surprisingly, Jesus, as the object of our affection, the source of intimacy, is the answer to it all. The required seeing and believing come from being connected to what He represented in life and death. "Everyone who looks up to him, trusting and expectant, will gain a real life, eternal life" (John 3:15, MSG). This encounter with Jesus, this seeing and stepping into Kingdom life for here and eternity, can do nothing less than transform us. Our vision and purpose align with His to match the great, unseen heavenly purposes.

The temporarily painful task of laying our life down opens us to new life. That new life makes the empty way of the old life appear weak and lifeless. What incredible treasure exists in intimately joining and believing in Jesus, in whom we find full, Kingdom of God living.

Ritual and Relationship

Transforming ourselves into possessing a Kingdom of God focus is, at its core, a matter of immersed intimacy. Some suggest that we enter the Kingdom of God through rituals of repenting, baptism, and living a transformed life by following rules. However, without sincere delight and desire for comradeship with God, even these best actions are not enough on their own. While they have the power to introduce in-depth nuances to Kingdom of God living, that power only comes if it is hand-in-hand accompanied by a sincere passion to see God.

But never mistake religious requirements as a replacement for the genuine heart-delight and sole desire for the intimate company of Triune God. It is His want, as well as our very own core design, for a shared life. To enter the Kingdom is to enter His heart: it is to live and to be ready to give, sacrifice, fight and do whatever it takes to see Jesus.

We do repent: we certainly want to be holy and pure like the God we love. We are baptized: we believe the action deeply bridges us into the sharing of Christ. We place ourselves freely under the laws with allegiance to the One we love. Yet, in all of this, we enter the Kingdom of God with nothing less than a pure, intimate connection. A sincere joining of hearts, in unity and synchronization of Kingdom of God purposes, is the picture of strongest devotion.

Though we know that we must obey the heart of God, may we never lose sight that it is His company we are after, just as it is what He is after. Far above any ritual, religious spirit, or even the most sacrificial of deeds, may we not confuse the act of obedience alone to be love. It can only be a demonstration of our love. Intimacy is love shared, a fight for, and striving after our inmost desire for the Almighty's company. It is a life that lives sincerely to obey and enters with love into the Kingdom of God, working towards a continually greater capacity and dwelling space for a close-knit, wonderful relationship.

Authentic Search

I feel like I need to share that in all reality, even after spending years writing this book on our relationship with God, I still have much to learn. Intimacy with God is my passion. I love pursuing it, understanding it more, and it brings me a lot of joy. But it is so beautifully complex that I will always be growing in my understanding of it. I am not an expert.

When I read entries in this book, it's like I'm learning the same principles all over again. I'm challenged to refine my passion, believe my true identity, face a lie, or pursue meeting my potential better. Some of these entries come out of my own experiences, observations, and struggles. Others come from decades of discussions with others. (Given the chance to discuss it, relationship with God is my favorite conversation topic!) But overall, what I've learned the most, is the pursuit of intimacy is a journey God brings to completion. It is His divine power alone that can bring us to the place of divine intimacy. All we need is to genuinely ask for it and sincerely seek it out.

When we embrace the realities of our Maker's extraordinary character, nature, and passion for us, we step into wisdom. The Almighty's grip of affection holds us with genuine, personal intimacy. Its highest worth is undeniable to any who has experienced it. However, even though His love is freely available to all, like any valuable treasure, it is wrapped. An authentic experience of relationship with God is no simple matter. Its pursuit cannot be entered with half-hearted strength, weak devotion, or divided attention, for the sacred award of the gift is too valuable. The heart of God and His deep, mighty purposes could never be easily exposed or be given to one weak in want. For love to be accepted and given requires a genuine desire for the relational encounter. Our heart's sincerity is transparent before God. Our individual capacity to seek Him is known by Him alone. Once found, the reward is so valuable that it has the power to transform every inch of our lives.

If we are determined to prioritize understanding this love, we can be reassured that it takes no more strength than that of a child. In this place of mystery, authentic intimacy with Triune God is built. The encounter leads us to the confidence we need to find our true identity as people profoundly loved. This incredible love drives us to a pure-hearted passion to increasingly know God, and that is the place of extravagant, ultimate living, pursuing this mystery. We will find ourselves on a journey of joyous wonder and excited anticipation as we set out to discover God's love and desire for us.

> *"When you come looking for me, you'll find me. Yes, when you get serious about finding me and want it more than anything else, I'll make sure you won't be disappointed." GOD'S Decree.*
>
> ~ *Jer. 29:13–14 (MSG)*

To Be Known by Another

Truly knowing someone and truly being known is a life reward and heart desire beyond measure. It is often an unspoken inner need, or an intriguing desire not entirely understood. Yet, the necessity of being known exists in our spirit, even if we are unaware of its presence. To experience this God-intimacy, that we are, in fact, wonderfully and abundantly known, ignites a consciousness within us that leaves a mark of deep impression. As we become aware that He looks right into our hearts, emotions, longing, and fears, we begin to understand that He wants to be involved in every circumstance, thought, and motive. Jesus enters into the realm of our space, not attainable by any other being, and satisfies the need in us which is only met by the Divine. God cannot possibly be distant or aloof: that is not conceivable of The One who says He chooses to dwell in us. The reality of His closeness is more real than the actuality of all we see in the physical realm. The barrier to intimacy has been crossed in that God sees every detail about us:

> *From where he sits*
> *he overlooks all us earth-dwellers.*
> *He has shaped each person in turn;*
> *now he watches everything we do.*

> ~ *Psalm 33:14–15 (MSG)*

We are not merely one person out of billions who have lived. We are unique, known, shaped, and fully understood by our Creator. We are not only made by Him with thorough detail and care, but we each are handcrafted with intentionality. He continues to bless us by extending gifting, purpose, and passion to us.

In the haven of His affection for us, we find an extended invitation, an intimate bidding into Divine belonging, closeness, and camaraderie of the Almighty. There we begin to see ourselves as known, and we even begin to know ourselves honestly. What a great position to find ourselves in, the sacred place of beginning to understand just how much we are loved. It produces a mighty resolve within us that desires to share, reciprocate, and pour out this same beautiful love.

To Know Another

Stepping into the position of being known draws us into the place of desiring to know the One who alone truthfully sees us. Part of His heart's desire is that we would work towards knowing Him as Triune God. He designs us with a powerful pull in our spirit that draws us to the unveiling of the mystery of Him who loves us so deeply. Knowing everything about us, He, too, has a desire to be truly known. "God's eye is on those who respect him, the ones who are looking for his love" (Psalm 33:18, MSG). To know God is to know His love; it is who He is. The Father sent Jesus to earth, which was the greatest step of conveying God's revelation to the world—it was an in-depth exposure of His nature, goodness, and ways that set forth immediate and future encounters. The statement, "We look at this Son and see the God who cannot be seen" (Col 1:15, MSG), shows us the invisible God was made known.

While He wants us to know Him through faith, our visual impression of God, and what we think we understand to be true of Him holds remarkable importance. Through the Word and our encounters, the accuracy of this picture holds incredible influence on our ability to be loved by Him. It shapes the way we see and experience God. Traits, such as His availableness to us, the goodness of His nature, and His limitless abilities, build our understanding of the faithful Almighty. As we seek to know Him, He likely eagerly awaits our response. What will we do with the One whose character and nature we are discovering? How do we respond to what Holy Spirit reveals to us about God? Will we extend ourselves to Him who has offered us such lavish love?

The authentic search for knowledge of the Holy One will never leave us empty-handed, even though our search will likely continue for eternity. He holds such beautiful complexity, incredible goodness, and wonderful mystery. Blessed are those who seek to discover our loving King.

Transformed by Love

When we are intensely aware of our sin, we are in what feels like a delicate position of vulnerability. In that state, connecting intimately with God seems difficult, if not impossible. However, in that place, love wants to transform us, not condemn us. After all, we were in sin when the love of God initially called us out to salvation and the transformative journey. The question stands: Will we be brave, bold, and honest enough to seek His authentic love that forgives, absolves, and then transforms?

The untruth is prevalent: it is a legalistic view that sees sin as a place of intense exposure and liability before the Most Holy. It presents a powerful falsehood that in His presence, we will face harsh criticism and disapproval. Yet, our ever-present and all-knowing God does not live in disappointment with us or in frustration over the sin we battle. Rather, He sees the battle has the potential to draw us deeper to Him, to bring workings in our heart to produce the fruit of intimacy.

We must know and believe He is always victorious in battle. He battles for us and has a beautiful extension of grace for us in every struggle. In Him, there is unfailing strength for us by what Jesus founded in the new covenant. Under the new covenant, we are not bound by rules, failing of rules, or lists of expectations (see Gal. 5). Something far more dominant binds us: all-consuming love. Grace is the new way, and with it comes perfected love that leads to all sorts of freedom. Not permission to sin, but permission to live under His overcoming love that transforms our hearts to live His will. To see our sinful nature and our need for forgiveness is an influential tool that God uses to compel us into His deep love. As we experience His acceptance and mercy, there is a beautiful transformation of our desire and personhood to a place where the power of sin loses its hold. There, living in the ability to obey becomes almost uncomplicated, nearly effortless, and even non-negotiable within ourselves, for we have encountered love.

Understanding the Heart

Triune God does not tolerate us: they adore us!

It is crucial not only that we know and have an accurate image of God's nature and character, but that we have a good understanding of Triune's heart towards us. In the beginning, the Trinity together said, "Let us make mankind in our image, in our likeness" (Gen. 1:26 NIV). We were created from the start with a sealed love, a belonging, and an unbreakable connection to the Divine. As we search to know Him, He is delighted to be known. As our relationship grows, we become increasingly aware of just how well we are already rightly known. Over time, we grow to understand more about this love.

Two particular events from my early childhood set the stage for me to know the Lord in a personal way. The first event was a simple game a girl in my neighborhood and I played in my backyard under a large birch tree. We were daughters of a good, loving, all-powerful king. That made us princesses. End of the story: that was the game.

I don't know where the game came from or whose idea it was. There wasn't much detail to it. All I know is I loved playing it, and the memory of it has stuck with me for years, even though I probably only played it a few times. It brought into my mind the reality that I have a Father who is the King. And He adores us.

The second story is less pretty. There was a time I felt rejected by some peers in my neighborhood. Hurt, I ran away to a secret place in my backyard where no one could find me. In this lonely place, I found the unseen presence of someone good who comforted me. Years later, I would recognize that this was Jesus, my best friend by my side.

Both childhood events were foundational for me to discover the very intimate, caring, good God I now know. These moments of understanding the heart of God drew me into wanting to know Him more. I believe every person, when they look back, will find God revealing His heart in their story.

Throughout the Bible, we see examples of how God goes to countless lengths to help us realize His deep delight in and desire for a genuine, intimate connection with us. He refers to His people as His beloved. In that name, we realize His affection and favor is fierce, concentrated, and real. The Holy Spirit seals love and light on each one of us who comes to Him. This love extends fully: indeed, God makes an analogy of us as "the church" as His bride. The bride receives a solid commitment, tender admiration, and profound care, with her forever future promised and secure with God.

A key is that even though we may know the truth from His word in our mind, it must go deeper. We need to allow our personhood to altogether embrace relationship with Him by permitting these truths that our mind knows to land with completeness in our hearts. For this to happen, we must place our spirit under the Holy Spirit. In this place of surrender, these warm, compassionate, stunning truths of God's deep affection and favor for us will speak and transform us into a position of truly living as His bride and beloved.

How valuable it is to take the time to accurately find His heart of love for us and understand the honor He extends us in believing the immense fullness of delight we bring Him.

Walking With Hearts Locked Together

The most astonishing reality in this world is that the God who created the universe loves us. A careful look at the detailed, meticulous consideration God takes in us, His creation, and at how He delicately intertwines His heart with ours is nothing other than incredible. The human heart' has a profound need for love, acceptance, and belonging. There is no place it could ultimately be filled other than before the living God. The demands on us in the relationship are clear: full devotion, commitment, surrender, and diligently following His ways. Yet in His calling to us for righteousness and total dedication, He remains absolutely aware of our weaknesses and failures, of the flesh we are born into. We often scorn these fleshly battles in which God's plan is interwoven with our need to depend on Him daily. There is a day-to-day requirement to spend time with Him, join Him in the fight, and be in an intimate lock of hearts by necessity, desire, and dependency. These very battles often move our spirits to obey what seemed impossible: to "pray without ceasing" (1 Thess. 5:17). We pray, speak, and interact relationally with our God in the struggle. The result is a rich oneness.

God's design for us was to have our daily bread, remain in Him, and know we can do nothing without Him. To bear fruit for His glory to please our Father, one victorious way alone, by being with Him. What other love requires a confession of desperate desire for another, a commitment to die to oneself, and a need for togetherness every step of the way? Where or in what else could we possibly find a living that leads one to the fullest of life? In the intimate affection of the Trinity, we step into an incomparable fellowship that allows human freedom to live wholeheartedly and completely in abundant life.

Section 2:

TRULY SEEKING
TO KNOW GOD –
A PREREQUISITE
OF INTIMACY

We are faced with many presumptions about who God is, and we find varying and even competing ideas concerning Him. So, it is vital for us to honestly seek to understand the truth about Him. The good news is that we can come to know Him well if we genuinely search after His authentic personhood. If we want to know Him, we must look into who God shows and says Himself to be, beyond the world's many differing opinions. We owe it to God, our Creator, and we owe it to ourselves to authentically consider who He is and what He extends to us in relationship. When we recognize the immense value of this life-long journey, we continue to seek to know our God, and we are blessed with assistance from the Most High.

> *Ask the God of our Master, Jesus Christ, the God of glory—to make you intelligent and discerning in knowing him personally.*
>
> *~ Eph. 1:17 (MSG)*

The Need for an Accurate View of Who God Is

It is implausible to think that one could trust someone they know nothing about, let alone enter into an intimate, life-long relationship with that person. Before we commit ourselves to anyone through a pledge or promise, we must be practical: to the best of our ability, we must learn about who they are. Intimacy may begin with an unplanned or unexpected encounter. However, for it to remain, one must move towards understanding who the other person is.

Comprehending who God is to us and who we are to Him is vital to form a relationship with Him. Even though much of God's nature is beyond human understanding, we can begin to know Him more as He presents Himself as full of virtue, kindness, and strength (see Psalm 36:7). As we search out the truth, we find our connection to God through His personal involvement with and deep fondness for us. Throughout the Bible, we see key elements of God's disposition and character. He is reliable and unchanging. His nature remains constant, and He displays endless abilities. Yet this all-powerfulness of God is paired with His traits of loving passionately, pursuing fiercely, and always being steadfast in goodness.

It is wonderful to look at God's nature through the lens of intimacy. Through it, we realize that He is not an aloof, distant deity that holds these admirable traits but our personal, connected Maker. We are blessed to be in relationship with One who has such great character. If we do not work to know this God whom we are accepting or rejecting, our lives will never meet the potential of all they could be. To live life to its fullest, we must evaluate the promises of having an amazing, intimate connection with our Maker. His invitation is for the best of all friendships, the most powerful connection, the deepest of knowing, and the purest, lasting bond.

What we find when we seek out who God is will never disappoint, for He is most undoubtedly worth the search.

Dependable and Available

This was probably my biggest misconception of God: I pictured Him loving, able to help, and caring, yet busy with all the cares and prayers of the whole world. As a kid, I understood that adults have important things to do and, as loving as they may be, don't necessarily have all the time in the world to spend with kids. So, as an adult, the idea that God is outside of time forced me to disassemble my false view of God and align it with the truth.

God is not busy, overwhelmed, or unavailable as we humans sometimes are. He is outside of time and space. He is peaceful, in control, and always available.

Our relationships with others have a powerful impact on our view of God. Associating our relationship to God with our human relationships can work for the good and the bad. When our interactions with others determine how we believe interactions must be with God, we put limits on God that never should be placed on Him.

No wonder God wants us to love one another well. He knows that how we treat each other ultimately, though indirectly, impacts how we see Him. True to His nature, the love of our God is far beyond anything we can imagine. It is entirely pure, good, and unmovable. One of the limits we place on God includes comparing His dependability and availability with our earthly interactions. Unlike any human relationship, it is on Him alone that we can depend to always be there for us. He promises to be with us in every moment.

God does not live within the time and place constraints we are accustomed to. He has limitless time for each of us. The undivided availability of the Divine allows for deep intimacy and connectedness. The idea that we each have the potential to be alone with the God of the whole universe seems inconceivable at first. But surely, grasping that God is outside of time dramatically changes not only how we see God but how we experience Him. Removing false impressions of a preoccupied, distant, aloof God, we find a focused, attentive, approachable Father. Once we remove our perceptions of time constraints from our understanding of God, we are freed up to have faith to reach out in the smallest crisis and with every need and experience. We are assured, knowing God is right there with us and has the time for us. In our heart's desire to give Him our moments, the reality is that He gives us His undivided attention in all minutes, in every moment.

And be sure of this: I am with you always, even to the end of the age.

~ Matt. 28:20 (NLT)

Power to Experience Love

Understanding the privilege of having alone time with God has transforming power when we apply that understanding to worship and prayer. Picture the Creator of the world, His eyes fully focused on us with love and admiration, hearing each word we say. Does that image not change our perception of challenging times? We can be assured we are under divine care in those moments. With underlying knowledge that each of our words is held and heard, we enter the potential to pray, believing the Lord of the universe holds our words personally and that ours is not just another of a billion prayers, but our prayer is uniquely heard and weighed. Our hopes, disappointments, and struggles are not merely identical to all other prayers breathed by countless others before us but are uniquely important to Him. Does this understanding not transform how we view God?

Perhaps this idea of God wanting such a close connection with us as individuals seems foreign. Why would the God of the universe, who has everything and needs nothing, desire closeness with us? Yet we find that our God, who is glorious, majestic, and excellent, desires to personally and intimately connect with us. It is so strange to us, but perhaps that is why we find hints regarding God's heart on the matter again and again in scripture.

John the disciple wrote: "Our fellowship is with the Father and with his Son, Jesus Christ. We are writing these things *so that you* may fully share our joy" (1 John 1:3–4, NLT). The very idea of fellowship, camaraderie, or friendship with God was presented with a foreshadowed promise of joy. This understanding of the depth of God's love for us was a passion of Paul's, which he says brought him to his knees in prayers. In a desperate plea, he prayed that we would grasp how lovingly committed and devoted our Father is to us: "May you have the power to understand… may you experience the love of Christ, though it is too great to understand fully" (Eph. 3:18–19, NLT).

Let us pray and worship under the intimate love-banner of all His offerings, knowing it is His heart for us to be under His covering of love. This is who we are. This is who God truly is to us, personal and present. May we invite these truths to powerfully transform us.

The Focus of His Love

God's thoughts about us began even before the creation of the world. His deliberations came with purpose and pleasure. The apostle Paul explains it this way: "Long before he laid down earth's foundations, he had us in mind, had settled on us as the focus of his love, to be made whole and holy by his love" (Eph. 1:4, MSG). This explanation holds such significance, for it makes a case for a God with a concentrated, set, pure desire. We find God planned to produce a life in which we can experience His amazing, perfected love. Furthermore, we find His heart's desire for us to be set apart for Himself. In being set apart for Him, we can be made fully alive, fully complete.

When God is introduced at creation, we witness a relational God who takes great pleasure in the fellowship within the Trinity. As He brings the wonders of the world into being, we see Him as the mighty, powerful, able-to-do-anything God. When He created humankind, He did so intentionally. Though He lacks nothing, He had a longing for companionship and a plan for closeness with us. Indeed, He made us in His own image. His purposes were filled with meaningful intentions for His created to be loved, made holy and whole. What pureness of heart and resolve are exemplified in Him! If we ever question His character, motives, or reasoning, we should remember we have a glimpse from before time began of His creation, aim, and plan. We are the divine, heavenly Father's very own offspring. Without question, His heart is that of a parent, fiercely protective, providing the very best, and leading His children in the right direction. We are ever sealed as "the focus of His love." This is our almighty Father's heart for us, since the very beginning and forevermore.

Unbreakable Bond of Creation

As we look at the beginning of time, we can attain an understanding of who we are to God. Because we are created by the Maker, the Designer of the whole world, our worth is significant. We have a personal and inescapable bond with God. No one can undo His connection of our beings, even if one deliberately attempts to disengage. This unbreakable connection between Creator and created sets a tie between us for eternity. This tie never changes and can never be undone. Immediately following the creation account is a description of the Garden of Eden. It provides an early glimpse of a God longing for perfect connection and fellowship with man. This beautiful place created for people impresses on us His perfection and glory and His care and delight to bless us with the best.

Humankind's created purpose is one of friendship with the Alpha and Omega in face-to-face relationship. Yet the devastating interruption to this perfect connection, at the fall of man, still overshadows our view of God. Perhaps knowledge of the consequence Adam and Eve received for their sin, their expulsion from the Garden, interferes with our ability to surrender to the intimate bond with God we are invited to experience in the present.

However, let's revisit the story through the lens of intimacy. We find that beyond God's deep sadness and firm consequences over disobedience, He also displays an unstoppable, unyielding love: He did not abandon Adam and Eve. He remained faithful towards them while also having a big picture plan for all of mankind through Jesus. God remained full of love and goodness, even when we were in sin. He dependably cares for us no matter what, and He consistently keeps His word. Both are significant traits that humankind needs to depend on forever to survive and meet the criteria our heart's desire in a healthy intimate relationship.

Our God is always loyal. He takes care of us. He is always trustworthy and honest to keep His word. How wonderful to find ourselves in a secure, forever-bond of intimate connection with Him.

In Control Even in Adversity

The story of creation provides us deep grounds for understanding God is always in complete control and is never caught off guard in times of adversity. He is full of mercy and has had a perfect plan for us from the start —a divine strategy to completely intervene in any circumstance on our behalf, including the initial fall. From the beginning until the end, "God is our refuge and strength, an ever-present help in trouble" (Psalm 46:1, NIV). Since the onset of our formation, we find He not only provides pleasant, inconsequential things of life, but most importantly, He gives what our hearts desperately need in the form of a rescue-producing love.

A redemptive plan always existed. It set a stage for building a true relationship established on trust in Him, even in uncertainty. Within the crisis of sin, the God of the Bible offers direction, boundaries, and discipline. At times, they can feel uncomfortable, but they are all gems in that they hold great potential for helping build closeness to the Divine in us. As we study scriptures and seek to understand the mystery, we find that behind all the direction, limits, and our own failures, there is one anchor of strength that can endure the relationship. Only one thing can produce the true repentance seen in a sincere change of path, and that is love: the love of our God and a genuine love for our God. In love, our souls' depths can return to the spiritual Garden to live life in the full. It is in the place He provided in love that we can re-establish unity with Triune God.

It is only in Christ that this promise is found. Jesus makes us right in our relationship with the Father, creating intimacy like no other—it is who He is. Triune God's plans always faithfully look out for us, help us, and tend to us, especially in times of adversity. They are always loyal and forever in control for us, in all circumstances.

God All-Powerful

God is ruler over all things. God is able, all-powerful, and nothing is too difficult for Him. Whereas we find situations that seem impossible, the scriptures declare, "Everything is possible with God" (Mark 10:27, NLT).

How does His trait of omnipotence affect our relational interactions with the Almighty? God's unlimited power can stir much emotion. His omnipotence, though, is linked to His complete goodness. Without these characteristics being hand-in-hand, the all-powerful side of God could be unbearable. However, we have a God who is powerful and holds the deepest love for us. With His unfailing affection, we have the assurance of care, protection, and provision. Where we need intervention, help, or strength, He can bring anything and everything to pass that is within His good and perfect will to do. Now we ought to be aware that the later part of this "within his will" stuff can at times upset us when our will is not His will. When hardship comes, the enemy is quick to suggest that Our God didn't come, and therefore can't, implying His inability. Alternatively, the enemy suggests He didn't intervene because He won't, suggesting God is unkind.

We need to trust that the Father works in a particular direction, even if it seems opposite to our requests or desires. We must trust He is doing a beautiful, deep, Kingdom work that holds great purpose, beyond our understanding or desire. It requires the strongest of trust to believe the promise that within His purposes, "God causes everything to work together for the good of those who love God" (Rom. 8:28, NLT).

God's almighty power is ruled by His heart of love in all things. Within an intimate God-encounter, His love and goodness can settle us with profound peace in His omnipotence. What joy this can bring when seen through the right lens!

If God is for us, who can be against us?

~ Rom. 8:31 (NIV)

God All-Knowing

In addition to God being deeply personal, available, and all-powerful, He also holds the unhuman trait of being all-knowing or *omniscient*. Nothing is hidden, secret from, or missed by Him, even in our innermost thoughts (see Psalm 139:2). God is deliberate and always attentive. Oddly, even though this close God-watch is uncomfortable for some, being seen and understood is one of our deepest desires. We long to truly know another and to be truly known. In our modern world full of distant and remote relationships, this powerful desire is commonly unfulfilled. God intentionally created our intense longing to be known. There is only One who can possibly meet this desire. Only He can provide exclusive intimacy: even the best of earthly relationships cannot compare. No other single connection could ever measure up to Triune God's doting affection and attention. Humans can't possibly be as conscientiously attentive or connected to another human as the Trinity is to us given its all-powerful, always present, and all-knowing nature.

Scripture is laced with detailed descriptions of our observant, aware, and involved God. From the mundane details of our lives to important and urgent concerns, each component of our situations and circumstances are under His watch. So, under the lens of an all-knowing God, paired with His extreme affection, we find intense attentiveness. There is no burden, trouble, doubt, struggle, or defeat that does not pass without His knowledge. Neither is there any circumstance we face that catches our God by surprise. He is aware of every deep hope, longing, wish and desire within us. In short, a beautiful trait exists in this all-knowing relationship that we cannot receive through anyone else: understanding. He understands! He knows and measures our hearts' attempts and comprehends our weaknesses. He sees all of who we are, and still, without wavering, He likes us, and He loves us.

God All-Loving

God is love. Only the One who is so fully accompanied by love in His nature, actions, and approach to us can be referred to as being *love*. God's love is dependent on nothing. Even if we choose to ignore, reject, or even to just not believe in Him, He still loves us like no other being possibly could. "Nothing in all creation will ever be able to separate us from the love of God that is revealed in Christ Jesus our Lord" (Rom. 8:39, NLT). He is our Creator, and we are His created. Our actions, efforts, and best attempts to gain His love are unnecessary, for His love is not something to be captured. Although our obedience is His delight as it can demonstrate our love for Him, His love for us is unaffected by it. Just as we have acceptance and right-standing with God because of Christ and our salvation is received as a gift, so God's love is given and needs to be received freely. It certainly is not something that we could ever earn or buy. Rather, it takes us to a crossroads: Will we choose to accept, trust, and believe the love?

Perhaps part of our responsibility is to realize our value to God. We need to allow His loving embrace to hold us in all its perfection, security, and wonder. Accepting it will enable us to be entirely comfortable with ourselves despite our faults, to be encouraged by our intrinsic worth, and empowered by the deep affection and love our God has for us. As a testimony to the truest love and deepest intimacy, we should live in this relational blessing with confidence.

If we allow Him, He will become our closest friend, dearest companion, and the One who constantly walks with us. If we make Him our life, He will become our heart's joy, delight, and purpose. Who could love us so faithfully other than the One who is known as love Himself (1 John 4:16)?

God, Perfect in Goodness

Knowledge of His perfect goodness is essential to our intimate relationship with God. We all encounter people who have mixed motives, who act with injustice, and who are corrupt. Seeing others act with malicious self-motivation or simply selfishly can cause us to lose faith and trust. We might

ask: Is there good in the world? On a simpler level, we are likely aware of
our own weaknesses and failures—our own lack of goodness. Should we give
up believing in good because of that? No. There is purpose there in the
place that confronts us with the truth that even in our best attempts to do
good, right there beside the good is often our own self-agenda. The good is
stained with the filth of desire for our own gain. "Our best efforts are grease-
stained rags" (Isa. 64:6, MSG).

Honestly confronting our own weakness makes being invited into the
presence of the One who alone is truly good even more refreshing. There is
no question of motive, character, or sincerity here. God is just, He is
incapable of doing wrong or evil, and He alone is perfect in love and
righteousness. From the creation story, we see God is capable of anything,
and He does everything without any difficulty. He holds complete power and
knowledge yet is pure and rich in unshakable goodness. In all our other
relationships, including the people closest to us, our associates,
acquaintances, possibly even in our spiritual leaders, we will likely have times
we must face a lack of goodness in the people around us.

*My failure is that even when I am working towards doing good,
self-ambition may creep its way in to my thoughts. Sure,
sometimes I can say it's temptation. It wasn't my thought, and I
reject it. But sometimes, the thought is mine, and what do I do
with that? Over time I've concluded awareness is key – I must
honestly confront my own behavior. Recognizing the thought or
action that doesn't align with God's direction, disallowing it, and
going His direction is my goal. At times, my good acts are like
"filthy rags" that are soiled with mixed or self-advancing motives.
But I also know He, who is perfect in goodness, calls on me to
make that same goodness my goal and genuinely reflect it.
Therefore, I rely on and trust His Spirit in me makes this all
possible. Doing good for His Kingdom becomes increasingly
achievable as I spend time with and in Triune God. In their
company, I am drawn into the transforming power of their most
good nature.*

The harsh reality is this: "No one is good—except God alone" (Luke 18:19, NIV). Perhaps the benefit to it all is that our inability to truly be good can draw us to sincerely explore God's character, to discover and then learn to rely on the depth of His goodness. By the empowerment of the Holy Spirit, we can move in the other direction. By spending time with Him, there is hope for authentic goodness to seep into us and transform us from the inside out. Connected, we are continually drawn closer to the One who is perfectly good.

So, in the grip of wonder, in the intimate company of our very good God, may His goodness sink so deeply into us that it heals us and alters our very nature to reflect all that is good. May it become contagious in us.

Holy Spirit Empowers Us to Know Him

In all truth, we are incapable and ill-equipped to succeed at living out a fully intimate walk with God, along with being even more than a bit undeserving. But it is in the place of accepting our limited abilities that we position ourselves as well-ready to encounter His love that He so freely and wonderfully gives! As with the free gift of salvation, we are offered limitless help to encounter this love. The key to intimacy is in accepting the promised gift of The Holy Spirit. This gift holds high value.

It is almost unattainable to human understanding that the God of heaven would bless us enough to dwell in us through the presence of the Holy Spirit. An unexplainable mystery, exceptional in grace, our Father's offer of presence is incredible in its generosity. It offers a step back into the Garden of favor and wonder of God; it is an invitation into His most intimate place where full living and fullness of life is offered. It is by His Holy Spirit in us that the completeness of the love-mystery unlocks. With his richest deposit placed in us, we are strengthened through His Holy Spirit to understand the love. Without the indwelling of the Spirit, we would be unable to attain the full measure of the Father's affection for us. For it is our beloved Holy Spirit who alone can enable us with power in our inner being to know love and to experience completeness. Not only is it the Spirit's responsibility to empower us to know the love, but scripture says it is within

His ability to do so, with "glorious and unlimited resources" (Eph. 3:16, NLT). This truth changes everything.

Therefore, may we journey onward with fierce determination to discover our God's very intimate heart and ask the Holy Spirit for the help we need to truly understand "how wide, how long, how high, and how deep his love is" (Eph. 3:18, NLT).

God's Names for Us

The very idea that God designed us to operate under the amazing, generous gift of His indwelling Holy Spirit provides multiple new possibilities of intimacy with Him. To know God more, we can look at His colossal love by exploring the descriptive titles and names He gives us throughout scripture. While He was on earth, Jesus gave titles to His followers that revealed deep affection. He referred to those who follow Him as His *brothers* and *sisters* and as *friends*. Those titles seal the truth that we are His family, the ones He loves to spend time with. Camaraderie and community set the stage for being a believer in Jesus.

These descriptions provide an incredible picture of close relationship with the Divine. They show how God identifies with and relates to us, and they invite us into the secure place of belonging. The picture of commitment, tender admiration, and affection is further enhanced when Jesus references the church (the people who love God) as *the bride of Christ*. Surely, He gives us only the best in this invitation, confirming His deep commitment to us, offering an unbreakable bond, closeness, and promise of companionship.

These tender titles weren't the end. Jesus called us to be His *co-workers* to join Him in Kingdom plans (1 Cor. 3:9, NIV). He blesses us with this title/position because He sees the best in us and believes in our potential to join in His purposes if we would only step up to follow Him.

The intimacy with God was reinforced to the deepest level of inhabiting love with these words. "For we are the temple of the living God. As God has said, 'I will live with them and walk among them, and I will be their God, and they will be my people" (2 Cor. 6:16, NIV). What incredible invitation and honor He places on us when He calls us His temple, His people, His loved ones He dwells with. We see the fullness of God's delight in us His created with this offering of presence. These names and titles form our identity and reveal much of our beloved Triune God's nature and goodness.

Glorious God

God invites us to explore His character. It brings Him great pleasure to unravel the mystery of His disposition and heart to those who sincerely seek Him. What favor He gives us to reveal so much of who He is.

At first glance, the varying and sometimes seemingly contradictory traits of God can be confusing. We are first presented with the unstoppable, mighty, powerful God of the Old Testament. Then in the New Testament, we find Jesus in beautiful humbleness, as the sacrificial Lamb of God. Examined closely, the contrast of these traits seems to present an incohesive and unintegrated depiction of God. Yet taken together, the full encounter is with One whose personhood is nothing short of amazing in His power, goodness, love, and deep intimacy for us. He has made Himself known; our Glorious God has revealed Himself. From Master and Ruler to Savior and Friend, He has brought awareness of His temperament to make Himself understood and known in even His most complex traits.

This is His delight: that we enter into the place where we understand the God who loves us with intensity. Unified in all His roles and individuality, we find the One who is perfect in love. "Greater love has no one than this: to lay down one's life for one's friends" (John 15:13, NIV). Our Lord's love runs so deep in His veins and we are so intently valued by Him that if we take even the smallest look at God in honesty, we are quickly struck with an awe of this purest form of love. With earnest searching, we find He welcomes us into His very own family and has great pleasure in doing so (see Eph. 1:5).

To step into our designed identity, we must search out and understand His full character. Because He loves intimacy with us so much, it delights His glorious heart to reveal Himself to us more and more. May we come to understand His glorious nature so that we can discover our true value as those the King rejoices over, those He truly delights in.

Our New Role in Knowing God

As God makes Himself known to us and we acknowledge His incredible value, our life's purpose and direction transform. When God reveals Himself to us and we experience His glory, our hearts are changed. We develop a desire and need to glorify Him in return and then to reveal His wonders to others who may not know Him or at least not know Him fully. Jesus knew this need and invited us to be in such proximity with Him that we would join in the work of revealing the Father. He calls us His *branches* (John 15:5), His *personal witnesses* (Acts 22:15), and *workmanship* (Eph. 2:10). He calls us *salt* and *light* (Matt. 5:13,14) and says we are *chosen and appointed to bear fruit* (see John 15:16 NIV).

What possibly could satisfy our need for purpose to the extent that the positions and functions these titles represent? They present us with amazing belonging in His Kingdom work. There is an intended purpose for which He calls us into these roles. Although God is fully capable of accomplishing all the Kingdom work of transforming lives all on His own, He knows that we will grow in our relationship as we join with Him.

For us to carry out these roles, we must continually seek His guidance and intensely trust Him. After we encounter Him, He does not want us to proceed in trivial living but rather to grow in continuing connectedness with Him. His invitation is an ongoing, "Come, follow me" (Matt 4:19).

What favor He gives us, that we would be invited to so closely joined to Him in His purposes. He has set our life so that we need to seek Him daily, moment by moment, for how we should play a part in what He is doing. When we are connected to Him, we are empowered to succeed in Kingdom work, so we look to Him as our source of help. In Kingdom endeavors, we are blessed to know we've invested in the great work of helping others understand and know our beloved God.

What an invitation to have Him transform our lives that they will serve to beautifully testify to His incredible greatness.

The Truth Will Face Opposition

The more we seek God and learn about Him and His nature, something interesting happens: we want more. It is incredible to discover the core of God's heart, the intensity of His love, and His beautiful character. However, with the gained victory of God-awareness comes the need to be watchful, for we will face the enemy's attack on God's character. Ever since the garden experience, lies, half-truths, and misconceptions about God have been relentlessly placed before mankind. They should never be taken lightly. Without careful cross-examination, they hold the potential to be detrimental to the most sacred relationship.

Many aspects we discover of the Divine's nature, and many of the truths we begin to cherish about the One we love will be tested by the enemy who intends to completely dissolve love. We will find the goodness, pure intentions, trustworthiness, and most of all, the love of our God for us challenged again and again.

Yet, we are certainly not without hope, for the One who is in us and who is for us is far greater than the one in the world (see 1 John 4:4). Taking up our armor daily, equipping ourselves with prayer, and trusting the One who is greater keeps us strong. Certainly, we have been promised victory and help with the King of all kings on our side. In any relationship, great power comes in taking up wisdom through assuming the best of intentions in another. With God, this approach is nothing but reasonable as we most certainly cannot understand all of His ways. Once we are certain of God's nature and character, we can clearly see who we are in all the goodness that He has called us to. Convinced of who God is and who we are, we become powerful warriors in the battle for Kingdom agenda.

We have been raised as an army of passionate warriors for His cause of love. What a beautiful assignment. By studying His very heart and personhood, we are blessed into incredible intimacy with the Divine. Now with truth and love, may we protect all that we have learned.

Ask—For He Has Himself to Give

"To know and be known - that's all I want."

I read these words at the university I attended. They were written in white on a giant black chalkboard in a massive auditorium. Some random student left it, like a message to others. Perhaps it was a cry for help. Those words stuck with me as a life-truth I felt must be written on every heart. How the heart longs for such a connection. Yet even blessed as I have been with genuinely great people in my life, I realized over time this full "knowing" can only be possible by one person alone - God!

"God looks down from heaven on all mankind to see if there are any who understand, any who seek God" (Psalm 53:2, NIV). At the beginning of our relationship with Him, we discipline ourselves to know God. He says: "ask, seek, knock" (See Matt 7:7). He wants to know: do we truly want Him? Bit by bit, we search after God, perhaps at first out of merely a feeling of what we ought to do. But as we search, God opens the most wondrous of doors, and He answers with the most beautiful, sweetest of words that captivate. As we look, and as we listen, our heart finds its most earnest of desires. We were created for this deepest and most wonderful of loves.

Seeing we were serious about knowing Him, He fills us with understanding. Even though we did not comprehend what we were searching for, this taste of His goodness makes us seek more. All He wants to know is this: Are we serious to seek Him? Because blessed are those who do. He has the richest of treasures to give and the highest of experiences or desires: He has Himself to give.

But why "cast your pearls before swine" (Matt. 7:6, NKJV)? Why share your heart with someone who could care less? We reveal our secrets to those we trust. We share ourselves with those we love and disclose ourselves intimately only to those we believe deeply care for us. And so, we have this utmost of richest experience only when we want to be in love with God because He gives us the full capacity to know His love for us. If we as mere humans have a natural guard on our hearts which allows us to open ourselves up only to those that genuinely care and want to know us, why would we expect any less from God?

> The eyes of the LORD range throughout the earth to strengthen those whose hearts are fully committed to him.
>
> ~ 2 Chron. 16:9 (NIV)

May we commit to ask, seek, knock, and know all we can of our magnificent God. It is a joy to seek to know Him. May He find us with hearts fully committed to the search. It is a blessing to know that we are truly known, for He alone knows us like nobody else.

Section 3:

GOD MEETS OUR DEEP-SEATED NEEDS

Our hearts are on a search for meaning. We know we were designed for a life of significance. Yet what in all life's ambitions can truly satisfy? Even the best of the good things in life don't seem like enough. Yet if Jesus is the answer and His Presence is what we truly seek, we will never be disappointed. Embracing the offer of divine love settles our most profound, deep-seated desire. Our strongest longing is met with the unmatchable affection of the extravagant, personal love of God.

I will see you face to face and be satisfied.

~ Psalm 17:15 (NLT)

Our Hearts' Search for Satisfaction

My heart has had longings. Everyone's does. Some of my dreams and hopes have come true, and of course, I have also had disappointments. Both play a role in how God meets the deep-seated need of my heart. The disappointments drew me to Him, and with Him, I experienced the realness of His love. In disappointments, He was by my side, caring for me and whispering His promise of always working for my best, no matter what comes.

Fulfilled longings also play an important role. These powerfully highlight that it is God alone who fills the deepest desires of the heart. Even in the biggest joys of life when I received what I thought I wanted the most, I have found an undeniable pattern. Though getting what my heart hopes for brings great joy, and I am thankful when I do, it brings a raw awareness that any dream come true is never enough. Building a marriage, family, home, and life plan can each be a blessing, a great gift from God. However, even when life hands us the best, it's still not enough to meet the deepest need. There is still a longing that remains.

What I have found is that my relationship with God alone truly satisfies me. This has been my experience, and it reflects how we were designed: to walk in intimacy.

The heart constantly searches. Sometimes its search is ongoing. Its focus may shift over various occurrences in life, and we may not be sure precisely what we are looking for. We may look for fulfillment in the next optimal experience, perhaps in a holiday, a vacation, or a celebration. Sometimes we think fulfillment will come through a big event, like a move, a birth, or a promotion at work. We hope we will be satisfied after reaching a new goal, ambition, or learning something new. However, once one of those life-markers has passed, while the event in and of itself may have been special, this thing, whatever we are looking for, persists unsatisfied.

The heart remains resolved in its search for something that truly fulfills. It is as if it knows that what it needs is something greater than what's offered in this world, something more significant and permanent, something that provides peace and completion. Part of our design includes our innate desire to search for something of the highest worth, something significant and true. But at our core, we are designed to be at rest, not to be on a constant search.

If we believe that there is a Maker, we can trust our inner being was purposefully designed to find fulfillment within the Maker's plan. At the core of our design is His plan for intimacy, where we are loved by God and love Him. Experiences, successes, and gains—whatever they are—don't have a chance to compete with an intimate connection with God. Without that connection, we cannot be content, for the design is not complete without it. If His Kingdom plan and desire for us is to live in intimacy with Him, why would we accept anything less?

> The kingdom of heaven is like a merchant looking for fine pearls. When he found one of great value, he went away and sold everything he had and bought it.
>
> ~ Matt. 13:45–46 (NIV)

Giving over all else is worth it to find this blessing. So, do we value ourselves enough to go all in and seek what we greatly need and what is freely given?

May we know the Almighty who is the only One who satisfies the deep-seated need of our heart!

A Rich, Satisfying Life

It is a high priority of God to see us achieve this life that satisfies. It is a delightful place where our lives and wills have beautifully aligned to join with devotion to His desire. It is intuitively in us to seek this life that satisfies. We are designed to pursue a peacefulness in which our Spirit is living full, here in this time, here on this earth. To be content in life, pleased, fulfilled—this is what taking residence in the rich and satisfying life looks like. It is only in living in an intimate relationship with God that we can reach the end of our lives and have said of us as it was said of Abraham that we have lived "a long and satisfying life" (Gen. 25:8, NLT).

Will we resolve to surrender our agendas, goals, gains, all other purposes, and pursuits, and have an unyielding determination to be satisfied in God alone? To accept this gift of life, and allow Him to bless us with heart-filling love that transforms everything? To do so does not mean we won't face troubles, for circumstances can be difficult. Will we allow Him to transform the vision we have for our lives so that we see through the lens that reveals that in all situations, God has been drawing us closer to Himself?

May we be able to live in such a way that when we look back, it is with genuine contentment, knowing we set our minds and goals in the direction set out by our Father. Jesus Himself said His very purpose is to "give [us] a rich and satisfying life" (John 10:10, NLT). He was dedicated to helping us understand the lengths and depth of His love, to live for this love, to live in this love, and to live reproducing this love. He knew if we could believe, trust, and learn to live in His love, we would be Spirit-filled and completely satisfied, as those lacking nothing. Therefore, may we full-heartedly pursue the love that leads to the satisfying life Jesus set out to give us.

Purified Pursuits That Satisfy

We choose what we pursue. As we decide what to focus our time on and determine our life's vision, God would love nothing more than for us to align our core with His solid truth. Ultimately, He knows there is only one genuine, honorable pursuit that will satisfy our hearts' deepest need: to live loved by Him and to be so filled up in this love that we, too, would love others and follow His desired path for our lives.

Yet, there are barriers that threaten this focus and distract us along the way. A simple search for the word *satisfy* in the New Testament reveals that we will be challenged by this world to live for our own interests, for ourselves, and our flesh nature. Or in modern terms, we will be tempted to pursue what we think will make us happy at the moment. However, its promise to genuinely satisfy is false. Instead, we are called, again and again, to live in freedom in His love rather than to use freedom to satisfy our sinful nature. "So you must live as God's obedient children. Don't slip back into your old ways of living to satisfy your own desires" (1 Pet. 1:14, NLT).

As we are strengthened in His love, resolve to follow Him, and begin to dream, work, and endeavor as followers to build His Kingdom, we are on the right path.

There is another barrier to living a truly satisfying life which may be a little less obvious. When the goal of building the Kingdom, or "God's work," becomes more important to us than our relationship with Him, this too, though so good in intentions, will nonetheless also compromise the beautiful life that satisfies.

For we can accept all the right theology, we can obey, we can serve, we can give our everything to and for God, but if we have not love, we have nothing (see 1 Cor. 13). It is impossible to be truly satisfied if we miss the intimacy mark with Jesus, which fuels us for living a life of giving and serving well.

We must always keep Him sealed on our hearts as our first love. It is possible if we learn to remain in this love that we can be fully satisfied each day by living purposefully in His utmost desire, as ones deeply loved.

So, may we bask in the Presence that gives life. May we allow Him to "satisfy us each morning with [his] unfailing love" (Psalm 90:14, NLT).

Presence Fills Desire for the Eternal

A longing fulfilled is of great worth; it satisfies something profound in us.

How lovely is your dwelling place,
O LORD of Heaven's Armies.

I long, yes, I faint with longing
to enter the courts of the LORD.

With my whole being, body and soul,
I will shout joyfully to the living God.

~ Psalm 84:1–2 (NLT)

With Triune God's generous offer of Presence, we have the blessing to enter this holy place here and now. Often, we picture entering God's court, dwelling, and reality later—not now—when we're in heaven. But this verse is a reminder we can have His presence, His intimacy, and a connection with Him here on earth now. Just as the Psalmist experienced, God can meet the deep-seated need of our heart: we do not need to wait to be satisfied. We can have a current connection with the Divine. He exists in the present and offers to fill our hearts with affection and closeness.

Psalm 84 shows we can live in the Lord's house, or in other words, we can be in His presence here on earth. The Psalmist speaks of this place of our heart where we are in deep connection with our God moment to moment. Once we enter that place, an unstoppable need to praise and worship Him can overwhelm us. We may shout out for joy because of His faithfulness and love. To be in a state of intimacy means the very life we live, we live with joy for His glory, and in a sense, always sing his praises (see Psalm 84:4.)

As we walk with the Lord in life, may our senses be awakened to the reality of His closeness. For He loves that we look to Him to satisfy us. Experiencing the reality of Triune God is an honor that refreshes and encourages us like nothing else. To dwell in His courts of presence fulfills a longing of great worth.

He meets our eternal desire with the gift of Himself, even here, even now.

A Place of Worship: God's Gift to Us

Our Lord loves when He finds extreme, faithful commitment in His followers. From the beginning, He expressed His desire for loyalty in the commandments (see Deut. 5:8–9a). God knew that it was only in worship of Him alone that we could ever have our soul's deepest need met. Worship (which is almost commanded in the Christ-following life) is not there because God is egotistical or in need of approval. He is already perfect in every way and does not need to be built up. We need worship because it fills in us something that aches to be filled: it's the need to acknowledge there is something of great worth in the world, so wonderful it is worthy of our full honor, attention and admiration. We are designed to worship; it is practically a basic need. If we fail to worship the one thing we were designed to, we will worship our stuff, success, achievements, accomplishments, loved ones, images, ideas, even ourselves, all in vain. However, as we worship the One who loves us perfectly, as we reflect on His revealed glory, His pure love, His gift of Himself, then we are truly filled and satisfied. The Psalmist writes: "Worship God if you want the best; worship opens doors to all his goodness" (Psalm 34:9, MSG). What else could possibly compare? What experience, possession, answered prayer or desire could compete with the depth of satisfaction that comes from connecting with our first love, God?

Worship is God's gift to us in the intimacy puzzle. When true worship is present, it draws a picture of a sincerely connected, fine-tuned-in-love surrender, which bursts with affection and adoration. We were purposed for this. Jesus knew in this heart-design need that we would find deep contentment when we are connected to, walking with, and worshiping our God. This worship is Triune's mysterious gift to us. It is a place to pour out our pure heart of love to the Divine.

Worship with the Purest Intent

> *They will be my people, and I will be their God. And I will give them one heart and one purpose: to worship me forever, for their own good and the good of all their descendants… I will never stop doing good for them.*
>
> *~ Jeremiah 32:38–40 (NLT)*

We can find ourselves feeling we have too many obligations, responsibilities, and things we ought to be doing. We can imagine many things God has purposed us for: teaching, praying, helping, serving. Yet scripture says we have *one* purpose: to forever worship God.

All acts of love or service we do in true intimacy pour out to God. They may be songs, prayers, ambitions, or actions. If they please, honor, or bring Him glory, then they serve as worship. However, if they are done out of routine, obligation, or any wrong motive which removes the heart's ambition to worship and bless God, without love, they are nothing.

May we come to our God to worship without a self-agenda, with the wonder of being able to authentically touch His heart, only desiring to bless Him and to live in sincere love and conversation with the Father, as we saw Jesus did on earth. Knowing our purpose rests in always seeking to honor the Lord, we set our hearts on the one purpose of worship above all else.

Unfortunately, much of even our most earnest coming to God has underlying self-motives. These motives can be rather innocent, such as the desire to learn, grow, or even just experience His amazing presence. These are good things, but there is a deeper place of love that comes to simply *be* with God. It is a place from which we express adoration and reverence, in which we are in deep awe over His love, and from there, we seek to be with God and endeavor to bring a heart-offering in our best attempt at the same love He gives us. This place has great potential of blessing our hearts' deepest needs by loving our God well with the purest intent. As we give of ourselves, He, in perfect generosity, is already working to bless us back.

The sacred dwelling place of worshipping God! It has shown up for me in such a variety of different areas. I love singing the hymns of old that I sang when I was young, with just my simple voice lifted to God. I still have worship songs on my heart that I sang back in my days of being in the church choir. There is no experience quite like that of being surrounded by other believers, singing in harmony. The lyrics stayed with me, and they come out at times in praise, even though I learned them two decades ago. Then there are very recent songs from talented musicians who write lyrics that move my heart into the state of praise. Worship comes whenever I am struck by awe about how amazing my best friend Jesus is. It comes with breakthrough or an answered prayer. Worship comes in times of battle or complete brokenness. In all seasons and situations, praise remains such a sacred place of encounter for me, of fulfillment like no other. There I feel like I can simply be with God and lift up my full adoration.

Rhythm of the Spirit's Filling—Randomness

What allows us to be filled with the flooding of His Spirit in one moment and feel empty at others? When we are in a place of full intimacy with God, we feel Him by our side. Worries, cares, and concerns do not matter. Yet such moments seem to come without rhyme or reason. They seem nothing of us and entirely of God. But they are more valuable than gold, so it is worth spending time to reflect on the experiences, to break them down, and try to uncover their mystery. The pure in heart will see God (see Matt. 5:8).

Do we seek the answer like a hidden treasure? God wants to give it only to the One who truly wants it. Are we willing to ask God to destroy whatever is in our life that may be standing in the way of the filling of the Spirit, or are we afraid to let go? Would that hinder Him anyway? His Spirit is sovereign and does as it may. It is all about God, not about us or our holiness.

Maybe intense Spirit-filled times are simply His blessing of love. Perhaps we just need to accept them, enjoy them, embrace them, and thank Him? For more often than not, these times cannot be broken down. Yet we should do all that we know to do, to encourage more great moments of living in God by fine-tuning our minds, faith, and perspective.

May our asking of God not be too little. Just as our heart desires closeness, so does His heart, so may we create space to allow God to meet us in our asking. Yet whether we are feeling filled, flooded, or burdened, may we remain in living, obeying, and loving our God. Just as Paul said, we are in a race, so may we train and discipline ourselves and run with purpose every step of the way (see 1 Cor. 9:24–27).

Praise God we have the promised Holy Spirit in us, who empowers us to run this race that genuinely satisfies our hearts' deep desire in all seasons of life.

Rhythm of the Spirit's Filling—Cause and Effect

While at times they seem random, deep connecting moments with God can at times be traced to a form of cause and effect. We were created with a free will —our choices of how we live have direct effects on our experience of God. By faith, we open all sorts of doors with God. Jesus had a lot to say about living and genuinely believing in this intimacy-mystery between ourselves and God.

In Jesus' time, we see the intimate connecting of people who believed Him. Results come from their belief: requests are granted, people are saved, healed, and delivered. Jesus said it Himself as He healed: "Because of your faith, it will happen" (Matt. 9:29, NLT). When we come to a place where we process the world, our thought, and emotion through the lens of the knowledge that God loves us and everything He has revealed through His word is real, it has the power to change the way we live. This faith and belief hold such power to transform our hearts' attitudes, which influence our behavior, which changes the core of our lives. God cannot fully meet our hearts' deep-seated needs until we resolve to believe and know His love, care, and good plans for us.

Perhaps surprisingly, our resolve can be measured. If we honestly look at our hearts and see how much we trust God in the matters of His love, we can assess how successful we are at believing Him. Our belief in Him then relates to how we connect with Him. Trust is a powerful element. It requires an abandonment of self-protection. In trust, self-protection is replaced by relying on another to care for us in whatever situations or circumstances we face.

To allow God to meet the deep-seated need of our hearts, we need to take on the perspective of belief and trust. In this place, the Holy Spirit can fill us in a way that leads us in incredible rhythms of powerful closeness.

Guard the Gems

Whether our experiences of intimacy with God come to us in an unexplainable manner or as a result of discipline, unfortunately, there are times that our relationship will be under attack. We can expect a battle against this most sacred bond. As it is our treasure, we need to stand our guard faithfully. There is power in being aware that our intimacy with God will be confronted. By acknowledging that our enemy will aim at our relationship to bring destruction, we face it with honesty.

We need to understand what surrounds us and our thinking. How we see God and how we see ourselves are essential components that determine our spiritual walk. Self-awareness is vital to fighting the battle. In its absence, our relationship will be challenged. Somehow the freedom that comes with the love of God allows us to become aware of what is taking place in our soul, mind, and heart, but this awareness ought to take place in the realness of His presence. Perhaps it's that being in the presence of His infinite grace and acceptance allows us to fully admit the extent of our undeserving status and sin. In His true fatherly concern, we find the place to confess the deep desire of our heart. Together with the One worthy of praise, we can reflect with genuine thankfulness.

In God's guidance, we find an accurate and godly perspective of our circumstances. To understand—no matter the size of our faith—we always have permission to ask the Lord, "show us how to increase our faith" (Luke 17:5, NLT). Once we have taken the time to assess the situations that surround our hearts, we can be ready to battle for the rebuilding of truths. Jesus has so wonderfully satisfied our soul, and we must guard the gem of that certainty.

Off-Track Assessment

Rather than going through repetitive routines of spiritual disciplines that can become too ordinary, we have to invite God in. Perhaps that is where a genuine connection with Him begins: somewhere between practicing discipline and inviting God in, we experience His presence. "We are made right with God through faith and not by obeying the law" (Rom. 3:28). This *faith* comes in being in a relationship with Him.

We want God. So, what can cause us to become distant from our first love? Disciplines can become mere exercises rather than connection. Our focus can veer too far ahead to future events, rather than staying in the moment of the present. We can allow distractions to become so powerful that they drown out our focus on His voice. Perhaps warfare waged against us has successfully dulled our connection. We know God desires we remain in sweet fellowship. Has something become more important to us than Him? Or have we taken our eyes off God and placed them back on ourselves, leaving behind who we are in God?

We must be aware of the battle and carefully guard that which is most valuable. When we take time to look, we have a great capacity to know what is truly going on in our own hearts. "Examine yourselves to see if your faith is genuine. Test yourselves. Surely you know that Jesus Christ is among you" (2 Cor. 13:5, NLT).

May we examine ourselves and see where the enemy, the world, or sin in our hearts has allowed us to get off track. For the relationship that meets the deep need of our heart is surely worth protecting. In perfect love, He, with all of Heaven's Army, is always ready and able to help us in each and every battle. And the best news is that the One who loves us is always victorious!

Contentment and Simplicity

Once we have walked in the Christian life for a while, we develop a more solid, deep-rooted faith. However, we have a tendency to complicate relationships. Often, we find ourselves lost: our deep-seated needs are unmet because we lose the art of simply being with God, which is a beautiful place of contentment. There is a place where we are emotionally filled by God and satisfied in the present moment, just by remaining in His presence. As with Mary's time at the feet of Jesus, we need to make a place for enjoying the utmost of honored company we have found ourselves invited into. In slowing down, seeking His presence, and surrendering again, we regain perspective, and our lives feel joy-filled.

Happiness is a gift from God that cannot be bought, earned, or self-created. Contentment is a place that does not require more, has no demands, and no need for change. We find joy in placing our hope in the One we trust our lives to. "Better is one day in your courts than a thousand elsewhere" (Psalm 84:10, NIV). An essential beauty comes with our soul's delightful embrace of this simple idea that is so incomprehensibly complex: the Creator of the world desires companionship with us!

As followers of Jesus, may we realize we are under Kingdom time. With its fast-paced demands, the world deludes us into feeling rushed even when we meet with the Most High. But under Kingdom time, we have all the time in the world. Time belongs to Him. He tells us we have time to simply be with Him, to not feel rushed. We can bask at His feet, for He has much love to lavish on us and much to say to us if we will only pause to listen.

Our Most High God delights in our company so much that He resides in us through the Holy Spirit. We find friendship meets the heart's deep need in the simple company of togetherness. The great complexity and simplicity of amazing Presence bless us with great contentment.

Perfection: No Substitute for Presence

Ambition for excellence is a noble pursuit. "Be perfect, therefore, as your heavenly Father is perfect" (Matt 5:48, NIV). This aim can fuel our drive to be all we can be for God. Our Lord delights in this ambition, and He will challenge us and bring us surprising new revelation in it. He loves us exploring, finding, and striving to improve and perfect our God-given gifts, talents, and calling. We can anticipate that God always has more to teach us. He will help us grow and use us for His glory.

These times of growth are precious and exhilarating, but they must not be mistaken for or used as a substitute for our heart's most authentic longing to simply be with God. They are a gift from God, but may we never tire of simply being in His presence. At times, He just loves being with us. Unfortunately, complicating our relationship with God seems to come more naturally than just being with Him. Yet when we are simply with God, we allow Him the opportunity to speak to us, open our eyes to His beauty, and awaken our senses to His real presence.

We are blessed to have received encouragement from belonging to Christ and comfort in the love and fellowship with the Spirit (Phil. 2:1). These are products of being with our Maker, in His company. They fuel us to love others and work together with believers with one mind and purpose. But if we skip the God-fellowship, we will fail to be excellent in His Kingdom work. This is not a punishment but a natural consequence that protects our hearts' purpose to live in intimacy.

May we carve out time to simply *be* before the Lord. To talk with Him, be with Him, love Him, and be loved by Him. Our achievements, accomplishments, and abilities will never satisfy us to our deepest core. We are designed incredibly and without apology by a Maker who purposed us to have Him alone. He fills our hearts and souls.

Remain in Love, Our Daily Bread

Once we find this place of new perspective and of simply being with God, a flood of joy comes. We need to set our sights on remaining in this place, for Jesus commands us to stay in His love. "I have loved you even as the Father has loved me. Remain in my love" (John 15:9, NLT). With this promise that Jesus has loved us in the same manner as the Father loved Jesus, we are assured He will provide for us, protect us, and guide us spiritually. As we remain steadfast under His affections, He meets the deep-seated need of our heart by giving us joy in the knowledge of unchanging certainties. Our life has been built on a rock-solid foundation of the sure truths of God.

These assurances of grace and goodness are endless, so when storms and chaos hit, we remain in Him. We trust in His complete loyalty. Our heavenly Father, who loves us with perfect acceptance and extends to us forever-belonging, makes these realities that cannot be shaken or destroyed. The promise of remaining in His love gives us all we could possibly ever want. Everything our soul longs for—forgiveness, redemption, sanctification, restoration, and renewal—is ours simply by remaining in Him.

This may all seem all too common in our Christian life, but these certainties must be remembered, and we must remind ourselves of these realities. We cannot fill up once for a day, a month, or even a four-year degree on these truths and walk away. Jesus prayed: "Give us this day our daily bread" (Matt. 6:11, NKJV). But we do forget. So to endure in His love, we must remain in His truth; to endure in His truth, we need to remain in the Word.

May we never try to fill up and move on, but rest and find comfort in His daily spiritual food. Intimacy remains in this simple place as we depend on God. It is no accident that we are called to this daily bread, for it keeps His beloved treasure close to His heart, in that we must then remain in Him. For this place alone satisfies our soul. It is a life daily embedded in treasuring God-realities.

Friendship Like No Other: He is Enough

It can be an awakening, a revelation, or an epiphany to see that all along what our heart has been searching for is God. The Almighty purposed us to search for, find, and be satisfied in Him alone. However, that revelation is only the beginning. What follows is the incredible challenge of living day to day in the truth that God is enough—always enough—which requires us to trust what He says.

We must believe we are immensely valuable and important to Him and that He alone is sufficient to satisfy our heart's need for significance. When we believe, His Word continues to work in us, and our actions line up with His asking.

God alone can meet our hearts' deepest needs. This truth reassured something else fundamental to me. God designed me with a big heart. My nature is to want the best for every person. Yet, I am painfully aware that many people (some I love the most in life) don't have the things our world values most. Disappointments come in marriage, family, sickness, job loss, and all sorts of crushing hardship. But it delights my heart to know every person in this world has access to the best. I have seen significant loss. It is a possibility for any of us at any time. I've experienced it personally. But I also honestly believe the thing we need most in life cannot be taken from us. The heart's deepest need is met in a relationship with Triune God, and this best thing ever is freely accessible and unchangeable for every person. This brings me incredible joy. No matter what life hands any person, we all can get in on what's most important - the relationship that once accepted offers intimacy with the Divine.

There is a divine promise that only Jesus can give: He is truly good, and His love will endure forever. Jesus, the image of God in the flesh, is truly beautiful, flawless, faithful, and the best person we could ever hope to have a friendship with. He is what we need, and His devoted character meets the deepest desires of our hearts.

So, may we stand in the truth that He alone satisfies and gives us significant living for the Kingdom of God. May we never stop abiding in His company that holds power beyond measure that enables us to accomplish great things. Let us live with this truth forever sealed on our core—He alone satisfies. He is enough. He is the answer to the deep-seated need of our hearts.

Section 4:

THE POWER OF LOVE
THAT
FORGIVES AND RESTORES

To be brought near to Triune God through the gift of Jesus is incredible. The thoroughly thought-out, complete design of His love, sacrifice, and ultimate offering of intimate affection bridges over every sin, wound, and offense. There is no further need for any additional sacrifice. He promises to bring us into His presence without any record of fault.

> *That's salvation. With your whole being you embrace God setting things right, and then you say it, right out loud: "God has set everything right between him and me!"*
>
> ~ *Rom. 10:9–10 (MSG)*

> *But sin didn't, and doesn't, have a chance in competition with the aggressive forgiveness we call grace. When it's sin versus grace, grace wins hands down.*
>
> ~ *Rom. 5:20–21 (MSG)*

In the Beginning, a Planned Gift

In the beginning, there was perfect unity between God and man. Life between God and man meant closeness, connection, and enjoying each other's company and space. Intimacy was natural, expected, and good. This is how God designed life and meant it to be from the start. There was no sin, so there was no need for the notion of forgiveness. Once sin entered, the consequence—as it still is in any human relationship—was that union was significantly compromised.

Yet we can be encouraged, for this change did not take God by surprise, and He had a beautiful plan for the future. The central theme of the Bible is the incredible love strategy set perfectly in place by Triune God, which brings restoration to the broken relationship. It's described as a mysterious plan that fulfills His own good pleasure (see Eph. 1:9, NIV). God knew the heart-wrenching results that would come from the entry of sin. In omniscient anticipation of all that would unfold in the Garden, He had a plan to reach each of us who would confess the inadequacy of our own efforts to fix the breach in our relationship with Him.

His heart is so genuinely intimate. He wants to know if we love Him enough to desire to have our broken relationship repaired, and He gives us the choice to accept or reject His offer. He presents His plan to each of us at some point, and hopefully, we realize the distance between us can only be traversed and overcome by the blood of Christ (see Eph. 2:13). When we come to the end of ourselves and admit our inability to repair the gulf through our own human efforts, God meets us. As we confess our desire for a true and intimate relationship, all possibility opens up. We simply have to do this for perfect reconciliation: to "rely on what Christ Jesus has done for us" (Phil. 3:3, NLT). That was God's initial intimate plan from the beginning.

No Other Sacrifice

It may seem strange that the solution to our separation problem was to be fixed through a violent crucifixion. The solution is difficult for many to accept. But perhaps this mysterious plan is a significant piece of the intimacy puzzle. What Jesus did displays His heart's extreme commitment to us. His sacrifice demonstrates how valuable we are to Him and is a huge component of the mysterious love He has for us and that He wants us to understand fully.

What an amazing gift, available to rich and poor, imprisoned and free, young and old, man, woman, and child. This was the best gift He could have given to lavish His love on us, for it is incomparable in how it meets our soul's need. God could have made it so we would have to earn forgiveness and reconciliation. He could have made us work hard, complete difficult tasks, sacrifice, toil, or slave away. Our reconciliation could have been dependent upon a measure of our grievance over our sin. He could have required us to do impossible tasks, give up everything we have, or even face our own cross.

Yet instead, we find in scripture, "He is so rich in kindness and grace that he purchased our freedom with the blood of his Son and forgave our sins" (Eph. 1:7, NLT). So remarkable is His love that He blesses us with forgiveness and reconciliation at His own cost and ultimately brings complete restoration.

Jesus makes a bridge for us to unity with Triune God. He loves to be near us, so He draws us to Himself with absolute love through self-sacrifice, Him for us. He desires to have us seated with Him in solid, flawless, sealed friendship, fully forgiven. This is the truth, this is the solution, all through Jesus. Nothing else will ever compare.

Intimacy Allows Vulnerability and Truthfulness

In this place of lavish love, we find complete acceptance that allows us to be vulnerable and truthful with ourselves and God, and we have permission to sincerely share our hearts. We can feel safe to share our real questions, lay down our burdens, and admit our joys, dreams, and struggles.

In a truly intimate relationship, we are convinced the other cares. Therefore, we trust that they are willing to help, see the best in us, and despite our failures, they believe in our potential. In a safe relational place, we can share struggles, failures, and shameful acts without hesitation. Often these are battles we felt we could never share, but as we do, we experience love, acceptance, and deliverance that could never have been known in the absence of the struggle.

Coming to our first love in complete vulnerability to confess the depth of our soul's foolish sin is a powerfully intimate act. The truth is, the One who knows all about us already sees our sin. He knows absolutely everything there is to know about us (see Psalm 139). There is no hiding from God. He knows how damaging our sin is. He knows how harmful sin is to intimacy if we remain in it. Because He is so aware of the freedom and victory He's made available to us, God desperately wants us to pour out our hearts and confess our sin to Him. He delights in the intimacy built by the honest baring of a soul. He is always there, ready to help.

> *If we confess our sins, he is faithful and just and will forgive us our sins and purify us from all unrighteousness.*
>
> ~1 John 1:9 (NIV)

In Triune God, we have a place that beckons us to honest living. There, when we confess our weaknesses and entrust Him with all our vulnerabilities, we find pure freedom, healing for our soul, and deep intimacy.

Denying Sin Erodes Intimacy

The unfortunate alternative to being vulnerable and confessing one's sin is repressing it. Repression leads to increasing darkness that slowly erodes intimacy.

We might wonder: do we all sin? Some believe they live a *pretty good* life with the idea that it pleases God. Yet what we don't realize is that this disillusion is self-protective. It's an ingenuine attempt to safeguard relationship. God doesn't ask us for self-sufficiency, human effort, and flawless living (as if it were even possible). God asks us for honesty, humility, trust, and repentance again and again. The truth remains: "All have sinned and fall short of the glory of God" (Rom. 3:23, NIV). He knows the deepest darkness of our hearts and sees that even in our good deeds, we are often motivated to benefit ourselves. But if we are ever confused as to whether we have truly sinned, Jesus sets the bar to an impassable height. That drives a significant point home.

You may say to yourself, *I think I'm good. I have not murdered or committed adultery. I obey the rules, and I love people.* But the truth is when you are angry with someone, Jesus sees it as sin and as serious as murder. He considers lust comparable to adultery. He says, in effect, "I know you love those who love you, but you miss the mark when you don't love your enemies and those who hate or hurt you." We all sin. But Jesus assures us He is here for that very purpose (see Matt. 5:22,28,44–45, NIV).

The bar is high because He is perfect in love and goodness. Until we sincerely see our sin, we can't completely experience the fullness of His love, and our hearts cannot be flooded with the love of His most intimate gift. Jesus extends the richest offering for unconditional love, acceptance, pardon, and forgiveness, despite our sin. He loves to lavish us with love through this treasured gift that builds relationship. He gives us something no one else could possibly ever give: the gift of complete forgiveness.

The Incomparable Gift

God knew if we would accept something He alone could give that the gift had incredible potential to build relationship. Foreseeing how His love poured out would satisfy our soul's need for affection, He designed it such that He alone, through Jesus, could meet our most profound need.

We tend to believe that we provide for our own needs. Yet this self-sufficiency is an illusion: it is God who provides. We can easily settle for what's second-best in our relational life by looking to people to completely satisfy all our emotional and relational needs. However, their attempts will never compare to what we can have when we are connected to our Savior.

When it comes to health, monetary provision, protection, achievements, and growth, we can believe that we are in control. Perhaps, we think, it is chance, our decisions, and our choices that impact these elements of life, not Divine oversight.

But when it comes to our need for forgiveness for our moral failures, we have nowhere to look but to God. There is no excuse we can give to cover them, and there is no acceptable pardon to seek outside of God. And our Lord knows this. So, He wants to give us something that no one and nothing could give other than Him. The inevitable result of sin is death, but the generous, flourishing, breathed-out gift of God to us through Christ is life. Now *that* builds relationship, *that* creates intimacy.

> But God is so rich in mercy, and he loved us so much, that even though we were dead because of our sins, he gave us life when he raised Christ from the dead. (It is only by God's grace that you have been saved!
>
> ~ Eph. 2:4–5 (NLT)

He gave His life so that He could provide us with the gift that is priceless, incomparable, and worth everything.

The Sacrificial Gift Cannot Be Taken Lightly

This is a purposefully unusual gift: you can't sincerely accept it and then just walk away. First, in our constant battle against our sinful nature, we will need this gift again and again. Second, because the gift is too big, too precious, and completely sacrificial, there is no possibility of receiving it lightly and then just moving on from it. Forgiveness is a gift that demands reflection and relation. By nature, it requires acknowledgment of the sacrifice and love behind it.

The relationship offered through this gift is key. It is not simply a belief or idea we accept that rescues us, but a mutual relationship, trust, and acceptance. This incredible gift from the One who loves us is essential not only for our forgiveness but also for our spiritual health. Through Christ's blood, it replaces distance from God with proximity. It reconciles the separation humanity underwent in Eden. The most profound need, the wisest desire, the most earnest wish is met in this gift from God to us.

What good will it be for someone to gain the whole world, yet forfeit their soul?

~ Matt. 16:26 (NIV)

Deep down, we know there is nothing so valuable, nothing we could wish for that could be more essential than to be right with the loving God from whom we are separated. It was designed as the most valuable and demanding of gifts: it requires contemplation and to be held in utmost seriousness, so that will see the full, true heart of the greatest divine love behind it. It was intimately designed this way. Triune God gives us that which will mean the most to us for life: the forgiveness that bridges us back into right standing with the One who gives us perfect love.

Love Tested

The power that exists in the act of forgiveness is amazing. It holds a profound expression of genuine, committed, and unyielding love. It is necessary in any ongoing interaction in this world. By definition, the need for *forgiveness* implies someone has been wronged, hurt, offended, or mistreated. If love is absent from the relationship, there will be a permanent state of resentment, anger, bitterness, even hatred towards the offender. In the absence of love, there is no desire to fix what's broken.

Yet forgiveness can break through these strong, powerful emotions with something even more forceful—love. It is almost as if forgiveness allows something that could not be present in the same way if the Fall never happened. Love that passes a test is a deeper, stronger love than love that is never tested. We can love, and indeed deeply love, someone who is always good, never disappoints, agrees with us on every matter, and is always perfect in reciprocating our love. But test this love a bit, perhaps with less-than-ideal reciprocation or a few minor disappointments, and we have to make a choice: will our love grow stronger, or will it weaken? Place that love under further testing of hurts, insults, or offenses, and it will either wilt under pressure or grow resilient and beautiful.

This testing was not God's plan or in His nature, for He is perfect and never insults or offends. Our human nature cannot make an equal claim. Before the Fall, forgiveness was not an issue. But God in His perfectness brings good even out of bad. He can use our wrongdoing to transform our relationship with Him into one even better than before the wrong. Intimacy is built and solidified out of forgiveness. It demonstrates a love that will not give up, give in, or be allowed to remain in disappointment. Rather, it displays a love that is persistent in hope and strong in perseverance, and most certainly a love that would never fail (see 1 Cor. 13:4–8).

Love, Not Rules, Keeps Us in Place

It is almost incomprehensible how deep the intimate gift of forgiveness goes and just how much freedom it opens up for the person who accepts it. To be declared and hold the title of being *righteous* is amazing. To be called *righteous* means that purely because of Christ, even though we continue to fail, fall, and sin, God sees us through Jesus' sacrifice as virtuous, good, justified, and blameless. In Christ, we are not only seen as decent but as honorable and upright.

Even when we act with the best of intentions, we still fall into sin. So, being called *good* by the only One who is truly good simply because we accept and trust His most beautiful gift is a mystery. Through intimate relationship, the One who is holy trusts us with a gift of full pardon and extends unlimited freedom to us. We get to make choices regarding how we live and what we do. We are no longer under the boundaries of the law's requirements. We live in freedom, yet we are only complete in the righteousness of Christ and free to live for Him by His Spirit (see Gal. 5). In how we respond to unconstrained freedom and in our reciprocation of intimacy, God sees what's genuine in us.

Christ takes the emphasis off sin and condemnation, eliminates it, and lavishes us with love in its place. What do we do with this incomprehensible gift? With freedom at our fingertips, unlimited by rules or condemnation, God tests our hearts to see not if rules keep us in check but if love holds us. Do we make decisions that please Him? Do we follow Christ not out of fear of condemnation but out of love in response to His promise of unlimited love and pardon? His desire for us is that we pursue good and right living because we love Him and want to delight Him. The one who obeys Him is the one who loves Him (see 1 John 5:3, John 14:21).

I Am Righteous

"I am righteous." Those were the words in a worship song at church. I sang them, I knew the Bible supported them as truthful, and I was struck that I struggled to believe them. So, it came down to honestly confronting this belief - or lack of belief. By recognizing the lie, I decisively rejected it, took the thought captive, and aligned it with the truth.

He calls us righteous. He made the way for us. I felt Jesus whisper that not accepting this beautiful truth minimizes all that He took on the cross for us to bring us into perfect, right standing with Him. It's not about my feelings, understanding, or the challenge to grasp it. Rather, it is about simply believing the truth. Under the redeeming blood of Christ, each of us can say with confidence: "I am indeed righteous."

To say of oneself, "I am righteous," even as a believer under the redeeming blood of Christ, can be difficult. Why? For that is what we are. Christ and the Bible declare it as reality. Even though we continue to sin, sometimes on a daily basis, as God's people, we are set free from the law of sin and death and now live in the Spirit (see Rom. 8:2).

Yet, we may struggle with the idea that we are righteous. Our hearts are aware of our sin, and we have likely failed to fully grasp the depth and purity of Christ's forgiveness. We need to accept our Father's incredible love, His perfect plan, and the redemption bought for us. Then we can stand firm in the forgiveness and righteousness secured for us. When we accept it, we must be confident in the gift of the title of righteousness. It frees us from the guilt, shame, and condemnation that the enemy would love to use to disgrace us.

Power and potential come with our ownership in being called righteous. Righteousness produces much good and more spiritual fruit than we ever possibly could on our own if we remained trapped under the weight of sin.

> So I died to the law—I stopped trying to meet all its requirements—so that I might live for God. My old self has been crucified with Christ. It is no longer I who live, but Christ lives in me. So I live in this earthly body by trusting in the Son of God, who loved me and gave himself for me.
>
> ~ Gal 2:19–20 (NLT)

We are free indeed, living in freedom and under perfect love.

So, may we stand in freedom and shun lies that cause us to fear anything in life, death, or judgment. Living in fear is no longer for us. Under Jesus, we are sealed in love and righteousness.

Holy Spirt Leads Us into the Transformed Life of New Identity

We need to actively remember that Jesus' sacrifice bought our forgiveness, salvation, and freedom. As we enter the place of examining our hearts before Jesus, we must acknowledge that His sacrifice was essential to establish the certainty of our value to Him. We must be solid in understanding the truth that there "is no condemnation for those who belong to Christ Jesus" (Rom. 8:1, NLT).

But it is also important to be still in that place and ask the Holy Spirit to guide us. Scripture reveals that the Holy Spirit teaches, trains, rebukes, and corrects. So, may we enter asking Holy Spirit to direct our time and to silence the enemy. The enemy would love to pile on accusations of our inadequacies to trap us in destructive habits of false guilt. He is, after all, the great accuser and the father of lies. Yet, if we are guided by the authority of the Holy Spirit, we can praise God that any rebuke from Him comes with kindness and gentleness. Conviction from Holy Spirit comes not with shame and dismay. His conviction comes in a way that inspires us to repent and change.

If we ask with sincerity, we can trust He will provide us with wisdom, truth, and discernment concerning where our hearts are out of His will. As our loving Father, He will show us how to find His way to change areas in our lives that are out of alignment. Romans 7 and 8 explain that we now live in the Spirit. We will continue to sin because we still have our flesh nature in this world, but in Christ, we are made fully new, and He has put His beautiful Spirit in us. That is who we are, and that is how God sees us.

While the flesh will still battle, our true identity is in Christ. We can keep our flesh in check by looking not so much at our actions but at the heart behind them. Our response to sin can be gauged by the direction of our hearts. If our heart-attitude reveals repentance over the desires or actions of foolish flesh, we can be at peace, knowing the love of God is being deeply engraved in our very being.

Love: More Powerful in the Light of Sin

Perhaps sin and love don't need to be separated. Maybe the purpose of sin is that it highlights God's deep love. For one to say, "I love you because you are good, accomplished, or successful" is one thing. That is easy. Yet if one says, "I see your heart's inner motives, and each struggle you have against selfishness, petty frustration, and pride, yet I still love you so much," a sense of deeply secure love is established. God loves us not for our goodness, abilities, talents, or successes; He loves us simply because He made us. Seeing all we are, He is aware of our sin and failures, yet in Christ, we stand without condemnation or shame. He believes the best in us and provides what we need to bless us to be all we can be. He sees our potential to become our newly identified selves through His Spirit working in us. His love coexists with His grace and forgiveness, and through it, He honors us with value, self-worth, and security.

Under such love and mercy, we have much potential for growth. Sin, shame, and guilt turn our hearts towards regret, frustration, and disappointment. However, Christ's love, sacrifice, and calling can turn our hearts to true repentance and change. The call to intimate connection with God brings conviction as a result of a heart broken over sin, which ultimately has the power to alter our direction. The potential with Him is endless; the power with such intimate love is great. Perhaps this is why the following words are classified by many to be of utmost importance:

> *I passed on to you what was the most important and what had also been passed on to me. Christ died for our sins, just as the Scriptures said. He was buried, and he was raised from the dead on the third day, just as the Scriptures said.*

> *~1 Cor. 15:3–4 (NLT)*

He Sees All and Loves Completely

We are not without sin, but we do not live in darkness because we have fellowship with God (see 1 John 1:5–8). We have nothing to accomplish, achieve, or attain before we can live out the fullness of life, fellowship, and life in the light that He offers through the gift of His Son. We simply need to accept that Christ accomplished salvation for us and offered His life in the full as a gift. We only need to trust in His forgiveness, and we can live free from the burden and weariness of guilt. We need to live in a constant state of depending on God's grace and trusting in His unquenchable love for us as His children.

This is a state of being where we stop trying to be "good enough" and instead completely rest in Jesus' gift. He is enough and has delivered us from ourselves; He is completely sufficient to make us right with God. When we rest in the promise that through the cross, Jesus has made us perfect, our intimacy with God is built, trust is solidified, and love is secured. He works His holiness into our lives.

How amazing that God sincerely sees us in the perfect righteousness of Christ Jesus. As Father to His children, when He looks through His love at our hearts, He sees even what we think He doesn't see. In His omniscience, He sees all and yet loves and accepts us completely. He also sees our potential in Him to be all He wants us to be. He will continue His perfect work in us until it is complete. This is so powerful because where we see weakness, He sees potential and future completion. He sees us in the perfect righteousness of Christ Jesus. Where else can we find such a deep love that always sees the best in us in all our potential?

The Lie that Christ Died for the Lovely

As Christians, we are taught that Christ dies for all of us, for we are all sinners. Through His death, we receive the undeserved gifts of forgiveness, justification, and redemption. We know that Jesus said He came for the sick and the sinners. However, if we go about living in day-to-day ease, the enemy can plant a lie that we might somehow allow to creep into our thinking: Christ died for the lovely. Who could these lovely ones be? Likely, they would include the child, the lost teen, the broken-hearted, the dying, or the helpless: those who look like they deserve love.

However, give us the cruel, the abusers, the lowest of low or worst of sinners—if we get a glimpse of or experience the ugliness of their sin, the depth of their wickedness (perhaps especially if we personally know someone who was wounded in their path)—it can feel less obvious that Jesus actually came for *them*. Yet in case there is any debate over whom Jesus came to save, Paul shares this truth:

> *This is a trustworthy saying, and everyone should accept it:*
> *"Christ Jesus came into the world to save sinners"—*
> *and I am the worst of them all.*
>
> ~ *1 Tim. 1:15 (NLT)*

We don't often focus on Paul's history of leading the fight to murder Christians and persecute the church. Despite (or perhaps because of) his cruel sins, God chose to demonstrate the limitless wonder of His grace through Paul. God was very purposeful in this, Paul explained, so that "Jesus could use me as a prime example of his great patience with even the worst sinners. Then others will realize that they, too, can believe in him and receive eternal life" (1 Tim. 1:16, NLT).

We must remember to battle the subtle lie of the enemy. As we show grace, others can begin to believe in the most amazing of all grace, the undeserved love of God in Christ Jesus.

How deep the intimate love flows from the One who created us!

Incredible Promise Holds Us to the End

All glory to God, who is able to keep you from falling away and will bring you with great joy into his glorious presence without a single fault.

~ Jude 1:24 (NLT)

What tremendous and incredible promise He gives. Our Savior has great joy in presenting us to the Father, flawless and blameless in Him. When it is all said and done, we have a promise of full acceptance and completion. All who trust Jesus have this great hope knowing we will be in His presence free from any accusation when our life is all wrapped up in the end. We are honored to live in His Spirit now, and we wait with anticipation and faith to receive the full righteousness promised to us (see Gal. 5:5). Our God is here to protect us, love us, and free us. Scripture tells us that "unfailing love and faithfulness make atonement for sin. By fearing the LORD, people avoid evil" (Prov. 16:6, NLT). His love does even more than merely atone for sin. It helps us to make changes and to avoid evil and the things that hurt us.

What an intimate, secure love our Lord extends to us who love Him and genuinely trust what He has done for us. He will never again remember our sins. Our sins have been forgiven such that there is absolutely no need for any further sacrifice (see Heb. 10:17–18). Perhaps the most beautiful part of it all is that we have incredible, undeserved, unlimited access to His presence where He loves us, cares for us, and tends to our hearts broken from sin.

And since we have a great High Priest who rules over God's house, let us go right into the presence of God with sincere hearts fully trusting him. For our guilty consciences have been sprinkled with Christ's blood to make us clean, and our bodies have been washed with pure water.

~ Heb. 10:21–22 (NLT)

This is love. This is intimacy. This is the complicated, delicate, and wonderful mystery of forgiveness.

Section 5:

BEAUTIFUL EMBRACE
OF
TRUST AND SURRENDER

Trust and surrender. The words convey complex ideas that can provoke all sorts of emotions, such as hope and peace but also concern and even fear. Trust is essential to our relationship with God. If we can discover the place of trusting the goodness of Triune God, we can also attain a stance of surrender that feels safe and hopeful. The Lord is the One who is in control. Yet He is completely good. So, in the sanctuary of relationship with God, we can have faith in His good plans for us and know that He directs our paths. As we align ourselves with Him, we find in authentically trusting Him through deliberate surrender, He will take us to great places.

> *But if you see that the job is too big for you, that it's something only God can do, and you trust him to do it… well, that trusting–him–to–do–it is what gets you set right with God, by God. Sheer gift.*
>
> *~ Rom. 4:4–5 (MSG)*

Trust Leads to Surrender

Intimacy cannot be separated from two beautiful, complex virtues: trust and surrender. Both are honorable virtues that go hand-in-hand as part of one's relationship with God.

To trust is to believe in another. We place belief in a person based on what we know of their character, strength, motives, and ability. When we trust a person, we believe that they work for the best on our behalf, for those we love, and ideally for all humankind. To trust is to be confident in an individual's honesty, to believe that they will come through and do as they say. It involves believing in an individual's merit: that they embody goodness, are dependable and have pure intentions. Hopefully, we have had many people in our lives we could trust.

However, due to humanity's struggle with sin, the expectations we have in others' trustworthiness are not always met, and trust can be broken. The love we give and receive is far from perfect. If we have had our trust broken repeatedly, our capacity to trust others may be frail. As difficult as trusting can be, the alternative not to trust anyone is an ominous option.

In relationships where we have trust, we surrender, in a sense, our hearts, emotions, and selves to the other. There we enter a safe place where we allow ourselves to become vulnerable and beautifully known. In the same way, as we trust God, that trust confirms that we believe not only in His good character and nature but in His care and plans for our lives, loved ones, and humanity. If we decide not to trust God, there is little else left in life to put our hope in.

Yet when we decide to trust God, we find the secret to life that frees us to be vulnerable, to be known, and to be in the perfect, safe place of genuine love. "The fulfillment of God's promise depends entirely on trusting God and his way, and then simply embracing him and what he does" (Rom. 4:16, MSG).

Surrendering Control

I felt like I had surrendered. Over the years, I made an agreement with the Lord: I will do whatever you ask. But as I started writing about surrender, I was surprised to find it challenging. I knew surrender was an essential part of the Christian life and beneficial to moving us into the best God wants for us. I was happy with every area of my life I had surrendered - knowing it was so much better than if I had done things my own way. But I also found it almost terrifying to think about what God could ask of me next, for I felt like God had asked for more than a few really difficult things.

The Lord has moved me to a deeper place of trust through this season. A lot came from looking back. Remembering His faithfulness in the past strengthened me to commit to surrender again in the future. Trusting His goodness, His all-knowingness, and seeing how He had worked for the best even in difficult seasons moved me to not fear yielding and to strive with all I've got to live in a position of continual surrender. The One with the purest of motives, who is the most trustworthy and in charge of it all, He watches over me. These truths moved me to say, surely, I can trust Him with my complete surrender.

If trust is an essential quality of our relationship with God, where does the concept of surrender enter? *Control* is the near opposite to *surrender*. In our humanness, we like control. If we feel we are in control, we generally feel good; we feel safe. When we are in control, we have a say in how things in our life look and what we do. Letting go of control is not comfortable. Yet holding on to control makes it impossible to surrender ourselves before God.

In a person-to-person relationship, *relational surrender* occurs when we relinquish elements of control to another, as we invite that person to directly influence our space. Surrender of control to another can come in small or great ways. In a trusting relationship, we see surrender to various degrees. We willingly give time, energy, and effort to the other. To the degree we trust the other, we become more honest and increasingly vulnerable as we share life with them. Trust, which goes hand and hand with surrender, allows us to feel safe to do so.

With God, we present ourselves, invite Him to fully consume our space, and give Him all our time, energy, and effort. When this is hard, we must be vulnerable with Him about it and look to His strength and His Spirit to lead us. Why do we have to give full abandonment? In the intimate embrace of God, we discover a secret (one we keep from ourselves) that helps unlock trust: we are actually not that trustworthy. As we begin to trust God, we simultaneously discover our own smallness, unreliability, and incapability to be in control.

Surrender is found in the intimate place of genuine trust that it is God, not us, who it is all about. He alone sees the full and end picture. He alone is truly good and works for the genuine best for us and for all people.

Trust to Enter What God is Doing

The desire to surrender control comes when we discover the truth regarding our position and God's position. We must understand that the ability to direct situations, events, and our very lives rest in Him alone. Thankfully He is a very good God who is full of love and can be trusted. However, we must not become so comfortable in His goodness and love that we would forget who it is truly all about. Jesus alone is supreme over all creation. He is indeed first in everything.

It's essential to remember we are the created ones. This perspective helps us learn to trust God, relinquish our control, and surrender to His good and perfect will. We are called to rule, create, govern, and operate in our God-given positions and gifting. In His love, God created us as purposeful beings. He entrusts us with responsibility, influence, and capabilities. Behind all that remains the essential, big picture: everything is fully, wonderfully, and purposefully from, for, and about God. He is in control.

So, where we have been given such favor through giftedness, abilities, and the sacred invitation into the Kingdom itself, which is the eternal working of God, may we maintain proper perspective. Jesus is the beginning, supreme, first, and fullness, the one who completed the reconciliation and made peace with everything on the cross (see Col. 1:18–20). What allows us to step into our proper place is the acknowledgment that He has always held the right and honor to forever hold all control, with all the responsibility, power, and blessing that comes with that control. When we acknowledge His rightful position, we are more easily able to surrender and trust. In recognizing our own smallness wrapped up in all His greatness, we find, as Abraham did, that this life, our obedience, our trust, and surrender "is a God-story, not an Abraham story... Abraham entered into what God was doing" (Rom. 4:2–3, MSG).

May we, too, enter our role in the Almighty's story and trust Him as He intimately leads.

Surrendering to the Source of Truth

Trusting and surrendering to God can be one of the most difficult things we ever do, but through trust and surrender, we are led to the most beautiful of places. Living a life apart from trust and surrender can never lead us to the life of close intimacy we desire.

We can't escape trust. We are always trusting in something. What we put our trust in operates our will, determines what we live for, and influences our obedience. If we are not trusting God, we are still trusting but have shifted our trust to an unreliable source, which we'll later regret. God is the powerful truth He says He is. When we don't trust Him (even in small things), we place our trust in another informant for direction. That "other," since it is not God, can only offer a lie.

Take, for example, worry or fear. We know God's word speaks to us to embrace courage, hope, and strength. But at times we accept a lie instead, and we do not trust God. It may seem trivial at the start: how could our agreeing with one small lie matter in the grand scheme of things? However, believing another source for our "truth" begins a slippery slope toward unbelief. We may have trusted ourselves, another, the world's view, or God's very own enemy. The father of lies is, after all, the great deceiver, always ready to offer an alternative to the truth. Is it a sin to worry? We know this to be true. However, worrying would perhaps be considered a lot less serious than the sin of trusting in another over God as our source of truth.

My husband jokes I have the worry gene. This may be true. I am good at it. I am also a mother of three, so that gives me a free pass to worry.

We laugh at that, in our culture - a parent's permission to worry. I did. But I have felt God challenge me over the years. The fear, the worry, imagining the worst, were anything but from Him. Speaking truth and having hope for the best are important.

Then I had this revelation. Our world tells us it's normal to worry, but Jesus says, "Do not worry." When I worry, I believe - or agree with - a lie from the enemy of God. Now that's a big problem! That's got to change. It's my job to reinforce truth in my life, words, and actions, not give in to lies.

So, do I still worry? Yes, at times. But I take the issue seriously and do my best to see the lie at hand and fight it. By embracing courage, hope, and strength, I make a greater effort to protect and stand in truth. I choose to believe the One whose name I trust: He will never abandon my children or me.

The truth must be vigorously protected. If we stand in Him who is the truth, we have a safe place to trust. So, we decisively surrender to God as the source of truth. He will not disappoint us. When we actively seek intimate knowledge of Him and seek to truly know God, we more easily and freely trust Him.

> *Those who know your name trust in you, for you, O LORD, do not abandon those who search for you.*
>
> *~ Psalm 9:10 (NLT)*

Fear of Surrender

What purpose could there be in God requiring such abandonment from us? Surely, He knows we are aware of the scriptures that tell of His people and the fierce trials they faced. Just the mention of *trust, surrender,* or *submission* to God has the power to stir vulnerable, broken, or fearful feelings. Perhaps we have sought to surrender before and still have scars reminding us of the cost of obedience. Maybe our experience with surrender was not a choice, but rather from hard circumstances that we know God allowed. We may be fearful of what God may ask of us if we surrender and agree to do all that He requests.

The scriptures say that to be productive, we must be like a wheat kernel that falls to the ground (see John 12:24). Through the loss of life, we gain our real and best life. We must take up our cross. We need to redesign the images that come to mind when we contemplate surrender, replacing pain, brokenness, and hardship with the vibrant, exhilarating, abundant life He promises, where we live in the perfect place of His will. May God in His power bless us with the truest images of all that surrender brings!

Truth is powerful, and seeing it from the Kingdom's perspective is important.

> *Notice how God is both kind and severe. He is severe towards those who disobeyed, but kind to you if you continue to trust in his kindness. But if you stop trusting, you also will be cut off.*
>
> ~Rom. 11:22 (NLT)

We should, therefore, have no fear of surrendering. Instead, we should fear having the wrong perception of the One who so deeply loves us. Guarding the truth that He is trustworthy and kind is key to remaining in the safe place of His kindness.

May we walk in beautiful, intimate connection, embraced by His love and kindness, where all fear is cast out and replaced with the foundation of trust.

God is Trustworthy with Our Surrender

So, if we know the truth of who Jesus is and decide to trust Him, when will we step faithfully to a place of surrendering to Him? *Surrender* brings all sorts of emotions to mind. We know we ought to surrender easily and freely. Our heart's deepest desire is to be close to God and live as He desires, yet it seems that our very hearts fear abandoning our selves. To not surrender to God suggests that we don't trust Him, and how could it be that we would not trust the One we so deeply love? Surely, we know surrender is required, commanded, and essential to remain in His will so that we can be all He intends us to be.

Throughout scripture, we witness difficult, wearying submissions. Consider Abraham's sacrifice of Isaac, Paul's placement in chains, and of course our beloved Savior's crucifixion. The difficult situations they had to face to comply with God's will stir concern in us. Yet, in the testimonies of these journeys, the surrender each offered, which at first seems incomprehensible, always held worthwhile results. As we, God's people, surrender, bow, and make ourselves willing to face all sorts of loss, trials, and hardships, powerful Kingdom work is accomplished for the ultimate glory of our beloved.

If we avoid surrender, we sacrifice our prized possession. No surrender means no trust. No trust interrupts the intimate connection we are honored to enter with God. Interestingly, when we do bow our physical position, and surrender our heart, we are often given a gift of clarity, wisdom, and we find ourselves in agreement with our God. Becoming aware of our weaknesses as we contemplate our frailty in the face of sacrifice opens doors to His power and strength. "Our God is not human, that he should lie" (Num. 23:19, NIV), nor is He the least bit frail as to fail. He is pure without any wrong motive. He is the essence of what it means to be trustworthy.

Free Will and the Wild Card of Surrender

The enemy would love for us to believe that a surrendered life is a one-way ticket to a difficult life. We know that intimacy—the relationship we have established with the King of kings— moves us to lay our lives down in trust. We believe Him for the best in whatever may come. But we must deal with the complex, God-given trait of free will, something most people appreciate and yet some struggle with.

As we in our humanness desire control, the ultimate control God gives us is to choose Him, to choose surrender: these are part of our making. But if "choosing" God were automatic, if it could be mathematically predicted that our choice meant we were automatically entitled to a life of peace and ease, would that not alter and negate the motive of love through which God wants to be chosen?

Just as a rich individual would not want to be married for their money alone, so God does not wish us to surrender to Him for the promise of mere blessing. We, too, who love our God, have a jealous, protective love for Him. We are willing to face hardship simply because He asks, but also to prove our love for Him and hope that others witness genuine love, too. To choose God for His blessings only is different than choosing God knowing the possibilities for adversity and His requirement for us to give Him our all.

Oddly enough, whatever it is that we fear losing in surrender turns out to be fool's gold compared with the unsurpassable joy of trusting in the Lord. As we surrender, the intimacy with God that our hearts were designed to attain is there for the taking. In the face of hardship, the wonder of this gift becomes even more powerful. There is simply this truth: when we sign up with God, it's a wildcard where it will take us. But He gives our lives purpose, and He promises we will have the best of company along the way.

Hope Within Surrender

To receive all God intends for us, surrender is required. While we may encounter great struggles within the yielding, we need to be hopeful and not expect the worst but hope for the best. That hope brings us back to the theme of trust. We trust for the ultimate best and hope for the good.

Hope is a powerful tool. Though it's often underestimated, it ranks in importance with faith and love. It is an act of trust to surrender to the unknown plans of God. In surrender, there is always risk. However, there is also promise for strength, power from on high, and the fruit heaven will bear. In surrender, we take on the perspective of the big picture beyond immediate circumstances. A Kingdom view of life understands the favor and promise for all those who love God. We can know with certainty every detail in our lives will work for the forward-moving good of God's perfect purpose.

Beyond visible physical circumstances, there is an unseen heavenly world where battles and forces work in our individual situations for reasons that might remain unknown on this earth forever. Yet all this exists under the shelter of the wings of the One who loves us. His promise is firm and forever for us and our good, whether we see that good in this life now or in the life to come. "'I know the plans I have for you,' declares the LORD, 'plans to prosper you and not to harm you, plans to give you hope and a future'" (Jer. 29:11, NIV). When we practice hope, there is power for endurance through any suffering we face here because we know it is building a reward in heaven far greater than we can anticipate. May we take courage to surrender with trust and hope in Him who is most certainly and forever for us and not against us.

Avoiding Entitlement

To know we have a Heavenly Father who is affectionate, nurturing, and available is a matchless and wonderful gift. The moments we approach Him —when we ask, believe, and trust—build the beautiful relationship in which we live out our nature as heaven's children who depend on their true Father.

Being so comfortable with our Father to the point that we easily approach Him and ask for help, tell Him needs, and request His intervention is a beautiful thing. However, we need to maintain a strong sense of who is in control. Just a short distance away from the revelation of ease, the attitude of entitlement within us can beckon us away. Holding expectations of what we think the end result of our requests should be can subtly interrupt and begin to distort what may have started as a beautiful connection with God. If we approach God with demanding and unsurrendered attitudes, the resulting unmet expectations we've placed on Him can cause us to feel disillusioned.

Perhaps we have a beautiful routine of being vulnerable, sharing our needs with God and trusting Him to come through. We practice faith, and we feel we have grown in intimacy with God only to discover that the end result of what we've been praying for is not the result we hoped for. What then are we to conclude? That we were wrong to trust? That the affection, nurturing, and the faith we believe to be true is less than? Maybe we shouldn't have trusted in the first place!

Or are we to take the opposite approach, once again trusting God and surrendering to His plan? God's love runs so incredibly deep with His goodness and plans to use everything in our lives for His deep, beautiful, and grand purposes. His resources are unlimited, and His ability to give is tremendous, but He is not out to raise spoiled, entitled children. His plans for us include building in us the most beautiful character of tremendous value.

> *He is in charge of it all, has the final word on everything. At the center of all this,*
> *Christ rules the church.*

> *~ Eph. 1:22–23 (MSG)*

We belong to Him, and mixed with His perfect rule is uncompromised kindness and goodness. In this we can trust.

Model of Sincere Surrender

The Lord's ways come out of the beautiful design that God has put in place. They should never be taken lightly. Seek, look, search, and listen for Him, and you will find Him. He knows when our hearts are faint, when they are working in self-interest or when they doubt the very thing we search for. He knows when our hearts are genuine, stubborn, and fierce in our search to find Him. God loves a sincere, surrendered seeker who looks for Him with such intensity that nothing else matters.

In times when our ability to control and direct our own circumstances is gone, we become incredibly ripe to receive the most sacred of wisdom. God loves to see our genuine response and a sincere pouring out of our hearts: He always comes to meet us with love and truth.

Job lost everything that the world holds dear. He had it out with God: he gave his full, sincere, vulnerable response. Yet within his enormous loss, he gleaned sacred wisdom that can only come through incredible hardship. Purified from the trial, stripped from worldliness, and done arguing and pleading his case, Job submits to God's control. He surrenders.

In the following statements, Job shows an invaluable and beautiful trust.

- "I know that you can do anything, and no one can stop you" (Job 42:2, NLT).
- Regarding how he'd questioned God's wisdom, Job confesses, "I was talking about things I knew nothing about, things far too wonderful for me" (v. 3).
- Job seals his declared intimacy: "I had only heard about you before, but now I have seen you with my own eyes, I take back everything I said, and I sit in dust and ashes to show my repentance" (vv. 5–6).

What incredible responses; what genuine wisdom. How blessed we are to glean from Job's wisdom what beautiful surrender to the King of all kings can look like, from one who faced hardship through loss. May we, too, find the place of standing in surrender in the promised power, wonder, and intimacy with Triune God.

Jesus' Surrender

There is no better place to look than the life of our beloved Jesus for how to approach surrender. He held all potential to control everything, yet He laid His own life down by coming to earth to carry out the love-plan God had from the beginning. His greatest surrender came in His willingness to allow the perfect, face-to-face intimacy He had within the Triune Godhead to be interrupted as He took our sin on the cross. His famous words now guide each follower: "Not my will, but yours be done" (Luke 22:42, NIV). Reassured by the promises which come with obedience, we can come to the safe place of relinquishing control.

What allowed Jesus—who came in the flesh and who was tempted in every human way—to stay the course, even when it led to the cross (see Heb. 4:15)? He is the example of one who lived out the fullness of life in the flesh while maintaining all Kingdom identity, faith, and obedience, no matter the cost. His intimate, strong love-bond with His Father was His strength: in it, He trusted the love, the purpose, and the help of the Most High.

Just as Jesus was under perfect love, we, too, are under the same intimate hold of love. This love provides us the strength to align every action of ours in obedience. For as God loved Jesus, and Jesus loves us, "absolutely *nothing* can get between us and God's love because of the way that Jesus our Master has embraced us" (Rom. 8:39, MSG). The intimate grip of the perfected Trinity relationship that Jesus dwelled in gave Him the strength to live in trust and surrender. Laying His life down was centered on the intimate love and relational factor of the Trinity's perfect plan. It was so that we would, through Jesus' sacrifice, fully know His deep affection for us. This alone would bring us into an obedience like Jesus' to the call for purposeful love.

I am the good shepherd. The good shepherd lays down his life for the sheep.

~ *John 10:11 (NIV)*

Surrendering Our Hearts

What does it look like when we love God with all our heart and surrender it fully to Him? Our heart represents our personhood, or who we are at our core, and God wants this crucial part of us. How do we honor Him with this part of us and surrender to His beautiful control? Some direction comes from Proverbs: "Trust in the LORD with all your heart, And do not lean on your own understanding. In all your ways acknowledge Him, And He will make your paths straight" (Prov. 3:5–6, NASB). There is direction here not to lean on the world's high valuation of reason, intellect, and comprehension when we approach the mystery of God. The truth is He actually can't fit there, and He possibly won't fit there. He's too big, wondrous, and untamed. This should come to us as no surprise, as He is a relational God, moved by heart- virtues such as faith, love, and desire.

Heart and faith outplay mind and intelligence when it comes to God. As we navigate to find Him, understand Him, and trust Him, we need to not rely on our thoughts and intellect as much as we do our hearts and feelings, contrary to what we are taught in so many other areas of life. Secondly, as the scripture says, acknowledging Him in all our ways allows us to know just how big our God is, whom we trust and are surrendering to. In this place, we can be secure even in uncertainty.

There is a place of heart connection with God where our personhood meets with His personhood, where we simply enjoy being together and where we see our true position as beloved children of God, our holy, mighty Father. Here we do not seek the mind's intellect, direction, or decision-making; rather, we seek only God. Fixing our eyes on God, walking hand in hand, and not letting go makes the intimate embrace possible. It allows us to trust and surrender our hearts, no matter what we face.

Surrendering Our Minds

Our minds, created by God with complexity, intricacy, and possibility, are nothing short of incredible. When our beautiful, powerful minds are submitted and surrendered to God, they have amazing capacity and potential. No wonder God wants us to love Him with all our minds and surrender them accordingly.

Our minds, at times, contain army's worth of troops of competing processes God has entrusted to us to control. We are the boss of our brains; God trusts us to command this mighty army of our personal minds. Like it or not, the reality is that we are at war. Thankfully, we have divine weapons to fight with: "We demolish arguments and every pretension that sets itself up against the knowledge of God, and we take captive every thought to make it obedient to Christ" (2 Cor. 10:5, NIV). To love God effectively with our minds, we need to be aware of the powers which work against us, and we need to be alert to and knowledgeable of the schemes of our enemy. In this way, we are prepared. We can stand firm and not waver in the belief that God is good, He loves us, and He can be trusted.

It is our responsibility to protect our minds. Of course, this requires wisdom. Thankfully, we are promised success not by merit of our own hard work but by calling on God for His help. "If you need wisdom, ask our generous God, and he will give it to you. He will not rebuke you for asking" (James 1:5, NLT). What promises we have as beloved children of God! We have divine help to direct the powerful army of our minds. We are told we have the Spirit's words to explain spiritual truths and that we are blessed to have the mind of Christ. His intimate love holds our minds and empowers our battles for victory as we trust Him and surrender.

Surrendering Our Emotions

God created us in His image. We are incredible and wonderful beings with emotions, just as He, too, is an emotional being. What potential we hold to reflect God and His Kingdom well when we master surrendering and submitting this intrinsic part of our being. We know our emotions are powerful: they influence how we present ourselves, the people we interact with, our perspective, and productivity. They have an important role in how we experience intimacy with God, as they affect our minds, hearts, wills, and choices.

We need to be consciously aware of our emotions, as it is not healthy to suppress, ignore, or disregard them. The safest place to explore how we are doing emotionally is from within the intimate embrace of the Father. The Psalms tell us:

> *Look at him, give him your warmest smile. Never hide your feelings from him.*
>
> *~ Psalm 34:5 (MSG)*

Not that we could hide our feelings from Him! We can trust He is the One who cares for us most and will help us gain wisdom and proper perspective as we explore our emotions.

The Bible notes that we can be confused by emotions; they can be exploited; they can affect our health; they can cause fights; they can run away from us and even torment us. Thankfully, it also says our emotions can be managed. God, through Jesus, demonstrated how to live out emotions well. Jesus displayed the fruit of the Spirit even while He had unpleasant emotions and was always divinely rooted and controlled.

Scripture teaches not to let our emotions rule over us: they need to be submitted to the truth of God. Even though they are real, true, and affecting, this does not make emotions themselves the truth. We need the person, Truth, first, and then we need to submit our feelings to Him. God is full of emotion—of love, joy, affection, enthusiasm, and serenity. As we surrender and commit to truth, we will experience emotions that bring the fullness of life. When we live in intimate embrace with God, our emotions will reflect our beloved God's likeness in our character.

Surrendering Our Will

Along with surrendering the other areas of our being, we need to surrender our will and intentions. One could say our will is the direction we choose to take. Every choice moves us along our self-designed path. To whatever degree we are faced with choices (apart from divine intervention), we make a decision with each step. To what extent will we surrender this will of ours before our Father, asking for wisdom, help, and His direction? Within His intimate embrace, God has designed our lives to include immense freedom. In granting that freedom, He allows our hearts to respond to Him and to give Him ourselves. Will we choose to build His Kingdom or our own? Will we choose to trust what He says is truth, trust His love, and what He reveals of His character? Can we accept the love He lavishes on us? To what extent do we authentically, intimately, fiercely pursue Him?

It can be unnerving to discover our choices unveil the depth of our love for God. All our little moment to moment choices add up and make us who we are. They reflect whether we live for Christ or self. Ultimately, they reveal our hearts' capacity of love for Him. Thankfully, we are not alone in our venture to love Him well and make choices that build the path toward fully living in His love and building His Kingdom plans. On our own, each of us would be on the wrong path of selfish choice. But He promised a helper, the Holy Spirit, to guide, correct, and empower us to live and love Him well. On our own, we tend to be self-living, self-path making, and self-kingdom building.

Yet as the Holy Spirit reveals just how deep His love for us goes, as He teaches us all truths about Jesus, our hearts can't help but surrender to give our will and capacity for His purposes. We start to surrender the very direction of our life, its path, plan, and every little bit of our say in it—all of it—over to the One who has showered us with compelling love.

Embracing His Picture for Our Life

So, say we take up trusting the love, the salvation, and the invitation to relationship. We commit to living for the Kingdom of God rather than attempting to build our own. Why do we still struggle with the instinct to take back control? Even as we sincerely love God, we see this tendency in ourselves.

> *And Israel, who seemed so interested in reading and talking about what God was doing, missed it. How could they miss it? Because instead of trusting God, they took over. They were absorbed in what they themselves were doing.*
>
> ~ *Rom. 9:31–32 (MSG)*

Even in those of us with heavenly-minded focus, a struggle exists with the desire to take control. It's a struggle for self-importance, self-agenda, and independence. Yet God designed—whether it be concerning our salvation, our lives, our calling, or ourselves—that He wants the first seat in it all. God's intimacy runs that deep.

Truly, we should be flattered that He loves being involved with us to such an intimate degree. No self-projects, no going our own way, doing it on our own, or pursuing our own thing to any capacity, even if it's something we are doing for Him. He wants to be the center of all. He knows that is His proper position for all things to take place well. If our hearts step away from Him, we run the risk of living like "unshepherded Sheep, taking turns pretending to be Shepherd" (Psalm 14:3, MSG). He knows our weakness: we can become so "absorbed in [our] 'God projects'" that we might not even see Him "right in front of [us], like a huge rock in the middle of the road" (Rom. 9:32, MSG). For all is from Him, for Him and about Him, and He is the One who invites us in. He loves for us to join Him, allowing Him to lead, for there, we are in the place of love, intimate fellowship, and joy within the unity of His heart.

The goal in Kingdom-building is to lead others to the Father as we trust Him to set all things right. That goal requires us to surrender our selves to the wondrous truth: Jesus is our Master.

So, we embrace what He alone did and point others to Him.

Surrendering Our Body to Holy Spirit

We have become aware of so many wondrous complexities we as humans are made from, with such potential to lavish love on Him by surrendering more of ourselves. One more element of our lives surrounds all others, and when we surrender it, we find a key to unimaginable strength. What is it? Our physical bodies. They hold our hearts, minds, and will.

We are incredibly, intelligently, uniquely designed, with extreme detail and care. We are sealed with immense worth by the powerful truth that we are all created in His beautiful image. Through what Jesus accomplished on the cross, we are invited to new life, to be new beings, to a new beginning. The sin-patterned way of living is no longer our reality. All our disappointments in self, flesh, and sin are gone. For truly, wonderfully, we are a new creation, the old is gone, and the new has come (see 2 Cor. 5:17). If we doubt, we are given this truth by the picture of our old self dying on the cross with Him and our new self being raised up when we are baptized. But suppose there was still possibly any misunderstanding on the matter, on what our bodies actually are, any feeling that we are still less than worthy of love. In that case, we have the most amazing promise of all that changes everything. Because of what Jesus' did, we now, in our new selves, are actually inhabited in love by God Himself. Our bodies have become the temple, His place of dwelling. They are the containers, holders, and vessels of the very presence of God through the Holy Spirit. These bodies of ours, which sometimes feel like they fail us in sin, sickness, and weakness, are truly sacred vessels of the Holy One.

What value and worth He has given us as we surrender our bodies to Him! What gift could be greater than the gift of Him dwelling in us His beloved?

Surrendering Our Weakness to be Empowered

What does it mean when we hear that His power is made perfect in our weakness? It takes place around the time that we start living in our new life, with the old gone and the new that has come. Yet even in the new life, as a believer, there is this incredible frustration. We come to the point of understanding surrender, knowing how important it is, and the potential it has to bless our Lord with love. But at the same time, we encounter our incredible flesh weakness. We see how living surrendered to Him seems almost impossible. Yet it is at this moment, in this realization, that there is a turning point that holds great potential for truest strength. "I realize that I don't have what it takes. I can will it, but I can't do it. [...] The answer, thank God, is that Jesus Christ can and does" (Rom. 7:18;25, MSG).

With this honest confession, we find God immediately reciprocate intimate love gestured in the surrender. We are extended hope in the truth that it is not about our strength, power, or ability, not about severe, extended effort, but rather a genuine welcoming and implanting what the Spirit is showing us. Trusting, inviting, and allowing in the fullness of Christ's very Spirit living in us is the key. We are likely intentionally designed with weakness so that we can learn the delight of being able to look to the Holy Spirit alone for the help we need. We can operate then not in well-tamed flesh, but the fullness of Holy Spirit power. Perhaps as we find our frailty and weakness, He is able to get past our own human strength and effort and bless us with the true strength we were intended to rely on. The weaknesses that we have been so frustrated by serve as an amazing opportunity for us to begin operating in the Holy Spirit's power. Dwelling in that power, we know success is not our own. We find new life that exemplifies beautiful surrender as it joins in intimate, close living, in the divinely ordered step by step bond with Him.

Surrendering All to Our Sovereign God

God designed us with love in mind. He wants such a united existence with us that we do not live independently from Him in anything. He loves to hear our confessed deep need for Him, and He invites us into a relationship in which He sets us right and whole. He is our holy Master, perfect in goodness, worthy of trust and surrender. His understanding is far beyond ours, yet because of His love for our company, He invites us into His incredible plans and workings. "His purpose is not a hit-or-miss thing dependent on what we do or don't do, but a sure thing determined by his decision, flowing steadily from his initiative" (Rom. 9:11, MSG).

We don't like to admit it, but we have a tendency to try to keep little bits of our lives to ourselves. What harm, we think, could holding just a small piece of our own goals, plan, rights, or even struggles do? We will secretly battle to maintain a hold on the smallest piece of our selves. Yet, God's purpose is what's ultimate, His plans are determined, and He is fully sovereign. He allows no independent self-piece to be kept. His desire is for beautifully intertwined intimacy and our full abandonment in Him. Not holding anything back, may we become willing to lose, to surrender it all, to find the fullness of life our souls are looking for!

Among the challenges in my life, I have had the consuming struggle of living with chronic fatigue syndrome (CFS). It started over two decades ago. I have been tested for everything under the sun. Still, it remains. I am thankful I am still very functional. I know it could be worse, but it is a condition that affects me every day. I've asked for healing. I've prayed. I believe in God's healing. Over the years, I have been healed of many things.

I didn't realize it at first, but CFS isn't just fatigue. It causes all sorts of havoc on one's health - and perhaps that is why I've needed so many healing interventions. But the truth is, with misunderstanding over the years with the diagnosis itself and despite having a background in nursing, I refused the diagnosis until only very recently. I simply did not accept it. I hadn't fully surrendered this area of my life.

My family doctor gave me a new book about the condition. It showed the importance of accepting a CFS diagnosis, and it gave me a new, up-to-date understanding of the condition which helped me so much. In a sense, I am still surrendering this area of my life and asking for full healing.

The Lord is good! He has shown me that when this disease limits me, it draws me to Him for strength. When I don't have the energy to pursue all I want and need to rest, He meets me there. He is using this condition in my life. When I have pushed Him for healing, I have, in all honesty, received much healing. Where there hasn't been full healing, He has given me a promise: what remains is allowed to stay to benefit, not to harm me. In surrender, I have found a significant breakthrough in peace, hope, and understanding, making the situation more manageable.

It is funny how we hold onto little pieces of ourselves, thinking it will make us happy. We fear laying it all down, even though the promised prize of obedience is that of truest of connection. God's offer on His terms is flawless and unspoiled. Why then would we trade it for a foolish trinket from our little, self-preserving world?

When we finally surrender, let go, and give in to our unchangeable circumstances, we often find the breakthrough. As we finally place our chronic challenge, struggle, or condition in the hands of God rather than in our own control, we find strength. We gain perspective that someone so much greater is in control, no matter the outcome. It is there that the situation often alters, the problem is solved, or the challenge becomes manageable. Or, in the best of circumstances, the Almighty intervenes and complete victory is found.

The Outcomes of Surrender and Trust

What are we trusting God for as we surrender? The scriptures are laced with beautiful promises of many benefits lavished on us as we trust. When we stop questioning God and step into trust, it heals something in us. Deep down, we know without trust, there is an often-unspoken offense: we are putting the character of God into question. But the faith-walk of embracing Him fully in trust releases this doubt and places our hearts in a proper position of giving Him all the respect, honor, and love He deserves. As we embrace and trust what God has done for us, we find ourselves in the place of perfect, right standing with God. We are promised a divine love that never runs out.

Along with this, as we ask, we receive freedom, new life, wisdom, and royal identity. In all these blessings, we steer through our new life path, finding His promises to be true, and that trust leads us to straight paths. On this intimate, lifelong path of walking in faith, we find we are never alone, always in good company, loved incredibly well, and cared for in each step. It is a path of living in His incredible light and walking towards and in Kingdom living. Possibly, the most valuable gift we receive in surrender is purpose: the certainty that we are living for something and someone truly great. The relationship of love we enter gives us significance. We are living for something true and wonderful.

There's a fiercely loyal minority still—not many, perhaps, but probably more than you think. They're holding on, not because of what they think they're going to get out of it, but because they're convinced of God's grace and purpose in choosing them. If they were only thinking of their own immediate self-interest, they would have left long ago.

~ Rom. 11:5–6 (MSG)

As we surrender, we are trusting for freedom from ourselves so that we can embrace love as we are truly loved.

Place of Surrender, Place of Rest

The place of surrender can be the same place that we find the place of rest. Trusting our agendas, plans, hopes, and lives over to God are big steps toward developing intimacy. When we resolve to take a position of authentic surrender, we will find an incredible calmness in our very souls. Surrender with God is not a giving up or an admitting of defeat. Rather, it is an intimate trusting in the One who knows best, wants our best, and works for it. We believe that this surrender benefits the relationship, as it exemplifies a trust contrary to defensive, tight-fisted control.

In the absence of surrender, we find the image of one who vigorously resigns themselves to their own human plans or will. They are in the terrible place of resisting the Almighty who created them. However, we know deep in our hearts that if something is out of God's plan, no peace can come.

We can make our plans, but the LORD determines our steps.

~ Prov. 16:9 (NLT)

It is wrong to think we are ever truly in control. We are here for such a short time, given eternity, and we have no control over how long our stay will be.

Moment by moment, we are under the beautiful mercy of God, who gives us our very life and breath. We only fool ourselves when we try to do things our own way. How much better to bask in the beautiful embrace of the One who loves us and allow Him to lead us in His perfect way. What a blessing we can trust Him who always has our best interest at heart.

Truly, His ways are far beyond our ways, and when we believe, He will lead us to the exact place we ought to be. In this place of trust, we find deep rest in surrender. May we be counted among those who "trust in the LORD [and] find new strength.... They will run and not grow weary. They will walk and not faint" (Isa. 40:31, NLT).

A Surrendered Life

There is incredible freedom for us who live in intimacy with the Creator of this world. Our full being and life is a love gift from Him to us: "We've been given a brand-new life and have everything to live for, including a future in heaven—and the future starts now!" (1 Pet. 1:3–4, MSG). We have the joy of loving the Lord back by giving Him the very gift of ourselves. To commit our lives and selves back to Him, we surrender these elements over to His divine Holy Spirit's intervention and hold. We were initially brought into new life when we chose to trust Him and surrender our old life. In our surrender to His truth, love, and relationship offer, we are raised to full, new life. We die to the flesh and take up the cross of surrender, of death, but also of victory, Kingdom living, and wondrous new life.

Our surrender to the cross and death can be difficult, as it makes us quite vulnerable to the unknown. But God is gentle and patient as He leads us. He understands how difficult it is for us to let go of our selves. Yet He knows surrender is required if we are ever to live in complete intimacy. Jesus wants our full-hearted devotion: anything less than authentic surrender allows a subtle robbing of our intimate connection. The surrender of our life becomes a love offering. Our life was a gift to us in the first place. But He is trustworthy, and His love frees us from all fear. He beckons us to the fulfillment surrender provides.

So, we can take courage and boldly set out to give Him our all to encounter the depth of intimate love He promises. In all that He gives us, may we seek to give back to Him passionately, vigorously, and with surrender as our intimate love offering. He always remains the One whom we can fully trust with our lives and all we surrender.

Section 6:

ENCOUNTER THE
GREAT BIG LOVE
OF GOD

God-intimacy offers a safe, tranquil place. In His presence, we experience beautiful closeness, connection, and belonging in the midst of the chaotic world surrounding us. Under divine intimacy, enfolded in His utmost company, we enter into a lifelong friendship that offers both exhilarating adventure and calming familiarity. He desires us to embrace the reality of His care for us so fully that we take His hand and let Him lead our lives.

May we come to understand how highly He treasures us, and may we know well the value of this relationship of greatest worth. All else fails in comparison.

This is the kind of love we are talking about—not that we once upon a time loved God, but that he loved us and sent his Son as a sacrifice to clear away our sins and the damage they've done to our relationship with God.

~ 1 John 4:10 (MSG)

God Is Love

God is love. His mission is love. His identity is love. His purposes, pursuits, and everything He dedicates Himself to are enfolded in love. He is committed to us and continually perseveres in developing an intimate love relationship with us. Even before creation, His objective was to focus His love on us. Love makes up so much of God's disposition that it is His primary overflowing quality, and He is resolutely dedicated to it. It is why He had the perfect redemption plan from the beginning and why Jesus came in the flesh—*love*.

Love will be the principal object in our lives to face significant opposition from the enemy. Even though it is the greatest of truths, we will have a challenging time fully believing it. The depth of it is so extensive we will never be able to understand it fully. It is the biggest gift and blessing, and it is worth fighting for every breath just to be able to live in it. If we can grasp the significance that our Creator, Maker, King is called *Love* (see 1 John 4:8), if there is one solid resolution that will aid us in every ambition, battle, or situation, it is forever to know the truth of His love. In Jesus, nothing can move it, separate us from it, or undo it.

God's love is forever. It encompasses every moment and experience of our life. God is an intensely affectionate and watchful Father who holds complete control and omnipotence. His love and goodness work through every detail for each of us. Because of this nature, we, in His likeness, can also truly love. His sincere, intimate embrace trains our hearts and enables us to share in this most genuine of all love.

We Love Because He First Loved Us

As a parent who fathers a child created in his likeness to be like him, so our heavenly Father's desire is to duplicate His love in us. He teaches us daily, revealing His love. He secures us in His acceptance, reassures us in our belonging, affirms His affection, and solidifies our calling.

A sincere, deep, and full relationship is not likely to be built in a day. True intimacy and trust build over many experiences between people as we spend time together. It is also so with God. Indeed God designed the development of intimate relationships in such a way to best satisfy the divine desire for connection He has for us. His love is too big and great for us to take it in all at once. Over time together, we begin to take in all the capacity that our God has for us. It is in this place "we can grow up healthy in God only as he nourishes us" (Col. 2:19, MSG).

He does not want us to independently attempt to nourish ourselves and try to make it on our own: that is not love. Instead, He knows as we come with our needs, He meets us in those needs, He demonstrates His perfect love, and through that, we learn how to love. He is the perfect example when we allow Him to be. Providing, protecting, teaching, He always helps us with gentleness, patience, and never-giving-up perseverance.

So then, once we are well-loved, we have an incredible capacity to love. We can become ones who "love one another, for love comes from God. Everyone who loves has been born of God and knows God" (1 John 4:7, NIV). His love allows us to love Him *and* love others. He blesses us in our being with what He designed us to have: completion!

When we have settled in our bodies, minds, hearts, and deepest spirit that we are truly and fully loved, we find ourselves in the best of all places. That is the peaceful, exciting, satisfying moment of finding, living, and being in completion. Yet it all begins in the place that it was Him who loved us first.

Genuinely Loved by God

Knowledge, understanding, and wisdom are the beginning steps into entering the genuine love of God; however, none of those things can ever take the place of authentic experience. We can know the truth that God loves us, and we can understand its potential to impact the love we can give to others. We can even know that God's love is the key to our heart's desire, the greatest treasure of all gifts, and that it's what we were designed for. But if we don't slow down, bask in it, live in it, and seek it in increasing amounts as our very lifeline, we have not really experienced the fullness of His love.

It can seem contrary to what we have been taught of the Christian selfless, servant-based nature to seek to be loved. Yet God loves to lavish His love on us. It is who He is and what He does, for God is love. To believe it is noble or honorable to deny ourselves the pleasure of enjoying and basking in this love, is right where the enemy would delight to have us.

But it is God's pleasure to love us and bless us: He acts in love and love is the very nature of who He is. So rather than always coming to God with our concerns, worried prayers, requests, or even thanksgiving and praise, we should take time to come to Him simply to allow Him to love us. We enter into His presence to let Him do what He does perfectly. Our Father knows us more than we know ourselves. To grow, mature, and be made complete, we must spend time under His love.

To allow Him to love us requires only our time, the belief that He meets us there, and an openness to experience His way of what He wants to show us. To make His thoughts known to us, He may whisper to our hearts, make a personal promise through His Word, or give us a dream or vision. The possibilities of how He'll reveal His love are unpredictable and immeasurable. God is love. His methods for each of us may never be the same, but we can count on the faithfulness of His nature. If we come to be loved, He will meet us there with the deepest affection.

Today, I was reminded that when life feels busy, I need to find extra time to bask in the Lord's presence and have a real, genuine conversation with the Almighty. Some days, cares and responsibilities seem endless. What truly makes me feel alive is coming to Jesus. So I stopped, sat, and basked in His presence. What beautiful encouragement He had for me.

Jesus has the perfect lens to see everything, and He impressed His perspective on me. I had been seeing shortcomings rather than victories. He reminded me of all the good He sees in me. I was blessed with reassurance: even in chaos, He is there, always by my side and ready to help. I had been starting to feel a little overwhelmed and had been allowing less-than-worthy thoughts of stress, busyness, and frustrations to overtake me. But He told me to fix my mind on whatever is true, noble, right, pure, lovely, admirable, excellent, and praiseworthy (see Phil. 4:8).

How wonderful to bask in the Lord, to align my thinking, and remember whose great company I share. Just by spending some moments with Him, whose very nature is peace, my mood shifted to peacefulness. Promises came again. I know He sees me, and I am in the exact place He wants me to be. In those precious moments under the "fullness of love," I found the breath to keep going with the responsibilities of life.

Loves' Refuge

What promises we hold from the One who loves us! He is our refuge. He hides us in the cleft of a rock, wonderfully protecting us, allowing us to live in true freedom. The mighty Father is watchful, aware, and capable, and we are under His meticulous care.

> *So be content with who you are, and don't put on airs. God's strong hand is on you; he'll promote you at the right time. Live carefree before God; he is most careful with you.*

> ~ *1 Pet. 5:6–7 (MSG)*

We are blessed our Lord so dearly loves us that we are able to live in Him, carefree from trials and attacks, carefree from concerns and worries. We cannot protect ourselves, even if we are as watchful as possible and concern ourselves over every detail, even if we are cautious and steeped in lookout out for our self-concern. The Lord knows that in and of ourselves, we come from a place of powerlessness. Yet in Him who is able, we have a mighty shield. He holds all power and authority. His eyes see and know everything. He holds the full picture of all details in every situation. He is aware of and cares about us tenderly, far beyond what our self-protective instincts could ever provide us.

So, may we fall into His safe embrace and delight in the love we have from our Almighty Father. With God and His perfect love for us, we do not need to live concerned by the *what-ifs* of trials, for He promises greater good. What a place of favor and protection. Even in trials, we have promises of goodness. For when we face trouble, it "is a clear sign that God has decided to make you fit for the kingdom" (2 Thess. 1:5, MSG). Even in the middle of our struggles, He is working towards bigger and better purposes. Unseen, mysterious Kingdom work surrounds us in ways we may never comprehend, in our personal lives and in the big picture of the world scene. Our faith can grow stronger through adversity, and that is a valuable treasure of great worth. Through trials, God further develops us into the completion of what we are designed to be in Christ. During these times, if we focus on His direction, we can experience the tangible sense of resting in His refuge. Trials build our relationship with God. For in the place of hardship is the place of refuge. There we have Triune God's presence of divine, attentive counsel, real comfort, help, hope and personal tending over us.

Old Covenant: Love Hidden

What about this Old Covenant that binds—written in ink, on stone—one may ask, where was love in it? Why does God, who loves us so, make such rigid demands? The Old Testament seems to embody harshness, extreme discipline, and hard-and-fast rules. Yet, for those who believe and look for it, we find rich promise, hope, and determination laced throughout the books of the Old Testament. We see God, gentle, self-controlled, and purposeful: "Quiet as warmth that comes from the sun, silent as dew during harvest" (Isa. 18:4, MSG). In the midst of anarchy, chaos, and killing, there is an underlying root of love. It is a promise of love, even if it is saved for a later time. Love is always there; the heart desire is always the same; the plan always works towards hope.

In Isaiah 19:16–25, we read about God's seemingly merciless discipline of the Egyptians. Yet alongside the discipline of God, we encounter an image, or a vision of cities learning to speak the language of faith and promising their commitment and even worship to God. In the center pictures of hysteria where God's wrath has struck, God also listens to prayers, sends help, and promises a Savior who will bring safety and care. God even openly shows Himself (see Isa. 19:16–25). His tender, gentle, and compassionate nature is present. His purpose to draw hearts to seal relationships and to reveal Himself is unchangeable.

We must align ourselves with God's purposes and trust them even when we read about His severity in the Old Testament. We must hold to the goodness of God even during harsh, heavy discipline from Him. We must choose to surrender to Him when we can't fully see, know, or understand. We can trust in the One who heard the cries, the One whose heart is spoken of to have showed mercy, brought help and teaching to those who sought to know Him through the "language of faith" (Isa. 19:18, MSG). May our hearts be convinced; may we be unwavering in our belief in who exactly our Father is. Even under the Old Covenant, He laced every detail with intimate love. We find hope, a promise, a newness coming where the heaviness of law would end and the life-breath of the Messiah would set all things right and in their place.

New Covenant: Love Revealed

In the New Covenant, we find the fullness of God's perfected love-plan set in place from the beginning. The Old Covenant had the purpose of magnifying the ultimate lavishing of love that would come through the grace of the New Covenant. In it, we are blessed with incredible honor and favor. A season of good news, healing, freedom, and pardon was promised in Isaiah's time. The year of His grace was announced: it would bring "bouquets of roses instead of ashes, Messages of joy instead of news of doom, a praising heart instead of languid spirit" (Isa. 61:3, MSG). Love was there from the beginning. God's plan for redemption from our failed attempts to satisfy the law was always in place.

Yet the roses, joy, and praise would not have been so glorious if it was not for the ash, doom, and languid spirit. The love went so deep that it was said that this plan was not for paper or stone, as with the old covenant. Instead, God revealed: "I'm writing out the plan *in* them, carving it on the lining of their hearts. I'll be their God, they'll be my people" (Heb. 8:10, MSG).

In the open communication we have with God's Spirit, we are blessed to be spiritually awakened to the truths written upon our very hearts. The covenant satisfies all, remains in glory, and is unchangeable. Because of it, we stand righteous, forgiven, with our eyes opened, the veil removed, and Spirit-filled. The purpose in this plan was to satisfy God's desire to lavish love on us and make us completely and forever right with Him, by Jesus's pure gift. Additionally, He wanted to rename us "'Oaks of Righteousness' planted by GOD to display his glory" (Isa. 61:3, MSG).

By this generous, all-surpassing love, we are a display of His glory to all the world around us. While religion is about self-effort and tallying our good vs. our mistakes, our "religion" is really not one at all. It is a relationship in which God's sacrifice and love fully embrace us. We are His display, His fragrance, and His testimony to the world of His limitless love.

Our New Nature: A Hedge of Blessing

When we embrace being children of God, we become completely new in nature. Our new nature creates a hedge of blessing and influence around us, and it declares we are loved. The significant, life-altering change in us is possibly best symbolized through the ritual of baptism. As we go under the water, the old is gone. As we come up from its depths, we are lifted by the hands of Jesus with newly created natures that come with abundant blessings.

Let there be no confusion: we are no longer slaves working towards a new life. Now we are beloved heirs living fully in this fresh life. The old is gone, and the Holy Spirit of God takes residence in us. As new Christians, we aren't put on a mission to jump through the right hoops, work hard enough, or solve a mystery in order to receive the Holy Spirit: it is rather a priceless gift from Jesus to us.

It is the same regarding our immediate entrance into an abundance of the Triune's generous promises and blessings. We do not strive for our completely new nature, for our identity, to be forgiven, to live in freedom, power, authority, and capacity, but all these are freely given with the calling to live out from and for God. He wants us to be confident in this and to operate out of these truths. He does not set us out on a mission to find them.

Take, for instance, having the "mind of Christ" (1 Cor. 2:16). This is a rich blessing we receive. It is not something that we are out striving to attain as children of God. Christians can get trapped trying to acquire these inherent blessings through their own discipline and effort. Yet, they are not ours to earn. Through maturity, we can improve at allowing the mind of Christ to direct us, but the mind of Christ is irrevocably already ours.

So, we can rejoice, celebrate, and bask in the love He lavished on us when He brought us into new life. The changing power of His presence has already occurred. It is now our calling to live in it.

Welcomed with Love to Family

When we sign up as followers of Jesus, we are assigned a new birth, a new identity, a new family, and a new name. It takes a deep understanding of these to move into the completeness of our new, complex, and wonderful identity. Yet like a continual unwrapping of blessings and gifts, God delights in unveiling these mysterious offerings of new positions, abilities, and to expand our comprehension of how we belong to Him, and all that this means.

Suppose we step past the very personal, *God-and-us* type experiences. Then we find we have been joined into a beautiful family, community, and belonging with our title, *Christian*. Sealed in the name of Christ, in our new birth, we may not realize the full extent of our blessings as those whom He is free to lavish His love upon. We have not only stepped into association with a people and family going back to the beginning of the new covenant, but so much comes with that association.

We find we have entered into generations of promises, favor, wisdom, and establishment. New guidelines for healthy living and strong relationships, and godly advice and directions for our existence replace our past ways. We step into secure promises of unconditional love, protection, belonging, care, and strength. Forever-promises of victory, hope, and eternal heavenly dwelling with our Father are ours.

Blessed are we to unravel the wonder as we explore the heritage we have stepped into and the birthright we've been given from our mighty Father. How He loves to show us the fullness of all we've moved into. He will place beautiful new confidence in us that makes us excited to tell anyone that we are Christian. It is who we are—our identity, our association. We are identified as ones deeply loved. With our sealed invitation into being a member of Christ's very body, we are invited to the depths of intimacy (see 1 Cor. 12:27).

God Loved Us with Jesus

Consider some of the most famous words in scripture: "For God so loved the world that he gave his one and only Son" (John 3:16, NIV). These are often the first memory verse for children. They are engraved on our walls, in our books, copied down in our journals, and are repeated every Easter. Yet, they are so much more than words to memorize by routine. May the common never rob this verse from its incredible revelation.

The words of John 3:16 are a love declaration. It wasn't simply because God liked us, felt obligated toward us, or pitied us that He sent Jesus with the redemption plan. It was so much more—it was because His heart was full of *so* much love. The sacrifice that Jesus made on the cross was full of pain and sorrow. He experienced deep grief in taking on the weight of sin of the world for the sake of saving humanity. Though He lived in the perfected, incomparable, wondrous love of the Triune, He chose to sacrifice that heavenly great company for a time to come to earth for another love, in order to make all things right.

The Father's love for His created and beloved was and is that deep, that complicated, that concentrated and ever fixed. It's a paradox: giving His Son Jesus doesn't make sense. The gift is too big. The love He offers is so incredibly undeserved and can never be fully appreciated. It is, simply put, incomprehensible. With Jesus, we were given absolutely everything. The forgiveness, the salvation, the redemption, the freedom, the family welcome. He poured over us love letters, healing, newness, gifting, and victories. Yet all this doesn't compare with the statement that God was making in giving us Jesus. He was giving Himself to us; His life to us, for us. For a love price so high, the relationship is eternally bound. His declaration of love for us is irrevocable. The Father's affection is sealed and on display for all generations around the world to know until He returns.

Oh, how He loved us with Jesus. He showed us His signature mark of who He truly is and what He is up to and all about!

The Love Gift of Holy Spirit-Presence

In sending Jesus, God declared His love for us. In sending the Holy Spirit, He empowered us to live in that love. The Holy Spirit is an incredible and generous gift. The Father gave us Jesus, our Immanuel, to dwell with us. This would seemingly be the greatest of all gifts we could receive, except that Jesus said to the disciples, "It's better for you that I leave. If I don't leave, the Friend won't come. But if I go, I'll send him to you" (John 16:7, MSG).

The Trinity shares a mysterious, beautiful, intertwined identity. Yet each part of it is distinctively purposeful in how it uniquely works with its beloved mankind. The Trinity is the perfect example of what true intimacy is and how it can exist. Incredibly, they invite us into their bond—into a permanent, indwelling Presence. Like the blood that runs through our veins and arteries, His very being runs through each of our fibers. This indwelling unites us to God in a beautiful dance of togetherness.

The Holy Spirit gives us hope to understand the capacity of His love. As we, the beloved creation of God, join with the Holy Spirit of God, this merging of beings creates our new beings that hold such powerful, effective potential. For when we do not doubt, quench, or resist the lead of the Holy Spirit, every element of our life transforms. His presence embeds in us with permanency, promise, and a calling to excellence. The Holy Spirit will lead us through life from priority to priority when we ask Him to. As we follow, we will be set on the path of being used to manifest the reality of God to our world. Holy Spirit makes Jesus and the Father's love real to us in supernatural ways beyond human reasoning, in the same way that He came to us from the unseen world in an inexplicable way.

May our beloved Jesus "ignite the kingdom life within you, a fire within you, the Holy Spirit within you, [to change] you from the inside out" (Matt. 3:11–12, MSG).

The Love Gift of Holy Spirit-Promise

The love Jesus gave us through the extravagant gift of the Holy Spirit granted us an incredible promise. We have living in us the very One who will keep us aligned with our Father's best plans. The Holy Spirit guides us into all truth, teaches us, and reminds us of everything Jesus has already told us. He is the One who gets us back in place when we get off track. It's a promise of accountability and principle. It does not come with judgments to break us. The promise comes with a gentle conviction to lead us on the right path.

When we feel a heavy sense of disapproval over us, it is likely the enemy trying to entice us back on another path—condemnation. He makes us feel as though God has an overall displeasure in us, or that we face harsh judgment from God. Holy Spirit rather comes in love, with a gentle rebuke, reminding us we were called to better, and are empowered to do better.

As well, this truth of the Holy Spirit being the one who convicts the world of sin (see John 16:8), actually frees us. It shows us we do not need to point out others' shortcomings and try to fix them. We are freed up to love them instead.

Jesus referred to the Holy Spirit as our advocate—one who works on our behalf to promote, support, and uphold us and our causes. We were sealed with the promise of His presence when it was said the Holy Spirit will be with us forever (see John 14:16). Jesus was incredibly excited when He shared what this would entail:

> *There is so much more I want to tell you, but you can't bear it now. When the Spirit of truth comes, he will guide you into all truth. He will not speak on his own but*

will tell you what he has heard. He will tell you about the future. He will bring me glory by telling you whatever he receives from me.

~ John 16:12–14 (NLT)

We were lavished with love through the immense promises that came through the gift of the Holy Spirit. May we seek, embrace, and live in the luxury of the extravagant gift the Father has given us through Jesus, and in what He further blessed us with through the gift of the Holy Spirit.

The Love Gift of Holy Spirit-Power

What Jesus set into place on the cross as He reclaimed all power and authority here on earth is a secret the enemy would love to keep quiet (see Matt. 28:18). When He breathed and "they received the Holy Spirit" (John 20:22), His fullness, power, and authority dwelled in them as men and women of God, just as it also does with us today. On the cross, he brought about our forgiveness, redemption, and freedom. He also put into place the power for us to live in the divine relationship of undeniable love.

And God has given us his Spirit as proof that we live in him and he in us… All who declare that Jesus is the Son of God have God living in them, and they live in God.

~ 1 John 4:13–15 (NLT)

We have proof that testifies by Him living in us. With this, we have the same power that raised Jesus from the dead (see Rom. 8:9–11). We were told we would even do greater things than what we saw Jesus do (see John 14:12). Jesus gave us power and authority to reclaim this earth and His people by living in an undeniable, solid relationship with Him. To reach hearts, He will empower us to manifest His presence in whatever way required. Jesus sealed us with a calling and His gifts of love, presence, authority, and power.

With the promise of the Holy Spirit and power coming on the disciples, they were commissioned to be the witnesses to proclaim Jesus to the ends of the earth. This calling remains for each of us who live in the power of the Holy Spirit. In all our working and reaching, we are empowered from on high, in sealed relationship. God lives in us and enables us to be His very witnesses in excellence wherever we go. He loved us by giving us the incredible gift of the Holy Spirit to enable us to live out our calling and fully join the incredible Triune company.

Love Calls Us Sons and Daughters of Light

As beloved children, full of Holy Spirit, we live in the new covenant of grace, where God's presence dwells in us and equips us. When we reside in that place, excellent living is in store for us. The Holy Spirit in us gives us the power to reflect God Himself to the world.

> *For the Lord is the Spirit… So all of us who have had that veil removed can see and reflect the glory of the Lord. And the Lord—who is the Spirit—makes us more and more like him as we are changed into his glorious image.*
>
> *~ 2 Cor. 3:17–18 (NLT)*

This truth reflects the love of the Father in the highest capacity. It was love that reached out in sacrifice and reclaimed us. Love took on our burden of sin and set us free. Love called us a new creation under the new covenant. And now, to be clothed as beloved children in our mighty Father's likeness, stretches intimacy to a new level, to the deepest level.

He grants us such a call to nobility that He declares us to be those who glorify Him. To glorify God is an honor: it is to join Him in making Himself known. We glorify Him by reflecting Him more and more as He changes us into His likeness. This is nothing short of amazing! When all doubt of the love He gives is gone and we find ourselves confident to stand in the truth of who we really are, we can look into our Beloved's face and see just how true, personal, and intimate He is. There we become free and at peace, recognizing God's alive and very real presence, and we are transformed and filled with light and beauty as those in His likeness.

This is our call to deepest intimacy. This is our strength to live in excellence and be an example in how we live in love, faith, and purity (1 Tim. 4:12). We have the One with perfect love and knowledge living in us and inspiring us to reflect Him accurately and beautifully as sons and daughters of light (1 Thess. 5:5).

I enjoyed being part of my church's 1-1 discipleship program many years back. In the program, you are paired with a new Christian to help them learn the basics of the Christian faith. At the time, I was matched with an enthusiastic lady in her early 20s. One day she came to me and said, "I think I know why some Christians seem alive, on fire, and have incredibly changed lives, while other Christians don't." She went on to say it's because some of them have allowed the Holy Spirit to live in them, and some of them haven't.

I was both surprised by her honest, new-Christian assessment and challenged by her conclusion. At the time, I was in my late 20s, and though I believed in the Holy Spirit and knew it was Him I wanted living in me, I had to ask myself some tough questions. Was I truly seeking to understand, grow and live in the mysterious Holy Spirit? Had I fully embraced what Jesus said was the greatest gift, the Holy Spirit who would do amazing things in our lives? This was one of many events that encouraged me to delve deeper into Jesus' great love offer.

I believe the Holy Spirit is present from the beginning, from even before we accept Jesus - for it is Him who leads us into all truth. I also think when we look back on our spiritual life stories, we see Him integrated throughout our entire walk - maybe we just didn't recognize Him at the time.

I acknowledge there was so much more that I needed to understand to live more fully in Him. Even though I hoped I was one she saw as alive, on fire, and with a changed life, I knew there was so much more the Lord wanted me to step into to allow the Holy Spirit to move me to glorify and reflect God even more as a daughter of light.

Love's Call to Greatness

So just in case we forgot how amazing God says we are, this verse should help us believe in His call to excellence within His great presence and under His protection:

> But you are a chosen generation, a royal priesthood, a holy nation, His own special people, that you may proclaim the praises of Him who called you out of darkness into His marvelous light.

~1 Peter 2:9 (NKJV)

We are under divine love, and we are set apart by His love. Through Holy Spirit, we are joined intimately with our Lord, one in Spirit. Our dwelling with Him still extends further. We have direct access to the throne of grace through Jesus Christ. He has blessed us with the honor of being in His constant presence, but our existence in the spiritual realm conveys even more honor.

Just as we long to be in His physical presence, Jesus' love for us is so deep that He declares us in places that draw us into the depth of His amazing existence. Even here in the land of the living, we are declared "citizens of heaven" (Phil 3:20, NLT). We have been raised up and are seated with Christ. Love seals us in a place with Him, in His presence so alive and close, though our physical eyes and minds often cannot grasp it. We are blessed to be seated with Christ in heavenly places. He can't wait to be with us, just as we often feel we can't wait to be with Him.

We are "hidden with Christ in God" (Col. 3:3, NLT) because He wants us to feel completely safe. He also wants us to know our power in Him, that we are born of God, and the evil one cannot touch or harm us (1 John 5:18). We are sealed under the promise of love in our physical (seen) and spiritual (unseen) existence. This builds our confidence to go in excellence to live out our call to glorify Him. We are called to the greatest of company and the surrounding protection it offers. We can live secure in the promise of His constant and very real presence.

He Loves Us Through Personal Promises

God is extremely detailed and personal when it comes to us, His beloved. In our lives, growth, and spirituality, He is so very present, always aware, and always working. Scripture is filled with His promises over us—it declares our value, our deep worth, and the blessings He lavishes. Yet to experience the fullness of all God has for us, something must touch our hearts deeper than any other thing. This touch comes when we slow down and recognize just how God speaks individually to us.

He is always speaking, but it takes focus and attention to see how He speaks. Once we know how He speaks to us, He will likely give us personal words with promises particular and intimate, meant just for us. These promises always align with truth in scripture. They may come in a quiet meeting time with Jesus, through a prophetic word from another believer, in a vision from God, a dream, or from His delicate yet strong, still small voice. As His sheep, we will know the Shepherd has spoken.

Given this intimate God-gift, a bridge, a way into our hearts begins to form from the incredible realness of the love. Words from Him are a declaration over our identity, call, or promise. While the enemy is always up to his old schemes to steal, deceive and destroy (especially in this area), if we trust the voice of our Shepherd, His words have the power to change everything. His personal promises to us strengthen our deep, intimate foundation with Him. They are an irrevocable gift from the Father to us. Our hearts could not imagine giving them back as their worth is simply too valuable to our spirit. In the spiritual realm, His personal words to us seal the biblical promises we often try to seal in our hearts, but without Him, we often can't move those biblical promises past surface knowledge. His true promises that transform our reality are priceless, greater than any earthly gift given.

Place Full Attention on His Love

As we explore the love extended by Triune God, we may end up mesmerized by what we find. Desperate not to lose sight of the experience and determined to remain in the company of our Savior's love and transformation, we must call out and ask for help. For the path is brilliant, and He can lay it out smooth for us.

So, desire and ask, for He is delighted when our deep desire is to remain in this place of love. It is His heart that we not look in the mirror and walk away forgetting what we look like (see James 1:23–24). Instead, we are to hold the reality of who He is in front of us constantly, growing in understanding and maturity in who we are in Him. Like that of a vision that dominates our full attention, forever before us, may we find awareness of His Presence, might, beauty and light going before us. May our eyes be fixed with concentration on our Beloved as we focus on the reality of One who is excellent, virtuous, and all-powerful.

As the Holy Spirit lives in us, He brings our attention to Jesus in a way that can make us always aware of His presence. We are not alone in having this upright ambition. Indeed, we have the most powerful help from Our God, who provides everything we need to become all He desires. So, given the generous offer of *everything*, may we seek, knock, and ask: after all, we have His generous permission! He seals us in understanding the love and all He offers as we mature to stay and live in Him. "Pray that our God will make you fit for what he's called you to be, pray that he'll fill your good ideas and acts of faith with his own energy so that it all amounts to something" (2 Thess. 1:11–12, MSG).

There is always a choice to put Him before us. Will we give Him our full attention and allow His love to mesmerize our heart and captivate our full energy and effort? For the truth is amazing: we are under His seal of affection in His great big love.

Section 7:

OUR HEART-ATTEMPT
TO
LOVE HIM BACK

To authentically encounter love, we have to love. God's love is our perfect example, and we strive to love Him back. So, we must diligently guard our perception to truth about the One we love. We study, seek, and journey to understand our Beloved more and more. Our heart's desire is directed toward always becoming greater at loving Him well.

What an adventure, what a great purpose, to have a daily, moment-by-moment, careful aim to love God with our all. Jesus said that loving God is the greatest of commandments. So, may we take great joy in entering this sacred and extraordinary ambition, which reaches far beyond any other thing we will do in our lives. May we set out to love God as our number one priority.

> *Love the Lord your God with all your heart and with all your soul and with all your mind.*
>
> *~ Matt. 22:37 (NIV)*

Transforming Love

As we experience the immense love of God and the significance of His affection for us through the pledge of our acceptance, forgiveness, and belonging, something powerful happens in our hearts. Our souls encounter something so profound that it transforms the core of our being. "God's love is meteoric, his loyalty astronomic, His purpose titanic, his verdicts oceanic. Yet in his largeness nothing gets lost" (Psalm 36:5–6, MSG). In encountering God, we come face-to-face with the most prevailing and influential promoter of lasting change—love. Without it, we have nothing. With it, we have everything. Love opens endless possibilities.

It is impossible for anyone to buy, earn, warrant, or achieve this love by any human means. It is simply a gift, through and through. When we feel we are at our best, we may believe we receive love as though we somewhat deserve it. At other times, perhaps due to our personal sin battles, we may feel like we cannot secure love. Yet, we gain it by nothing less than trusting in Love's giving. He wins over our hearts by His love. When we really see it, believe it, and accept it as a gift, it can do nothing less than totally transform our hearts and beings.

One cannot take in His love and remain the same. We couldn't possibly bask in His affectionate offer and then immediately turn from the experience and resort to foolish self-ways. No matter how it tempts, empty sin will never fill us. While we turn to selfish ways and iniquities to try to fill our needs, only true love can fill us.

So, once we've tasted this goodness, it is as though our heart has only one option in response. That response is our attempt to love Him back! Our attempts may be delicate, and they may often fail, yet they are treasured by our Father. We are transformed by His love. We want to obey with every step and ultimately work towards living to glorify our beautiful God.

Proper Perception

To authentically love someone well, we must first know and see them as they sincerely are. For us to trust someone else and receive their love, we must aim to know their true nature. The thoughts we allow ourselves to form about God profoundly shape our lives. Without a doubt, those thoughts represent the most significant beliefs we hold. We need a correct perception of God's nature and character to build a close and intimate relationship.

May our hearts celebrate just how big our God and His love is! Our world has constant stress, hardship, and chaos, yet our God is never uncertain, strained, tense, or worried. He is also never un-compassionate nor unconcerned by our trials and hardships. The ultimate work on the cross sealed the ransom, redemption, and reconciliation and provided all that was needed for our salvation. God is filled with complete peace. Jesus said, "It is finished" (John 19:30). In other words, the battle has been won. We do not find God under pressure, working hard to complete something: the work is complete. He is confident: the salvation He has provided is sealed.

So, may we come into the presence of the One who is genuinely joyous and be filled with His joy. We can approach Him with confidence, and as He is so very peaceful, we are transformed by His peace. Our Lord is loving, gentle, and kind in disposition. So pure in His goodness and admirable in His character, we will find no other company compares to our Lord's. God's nature draws us into intimate connection with Him by the sheer, immense affection He has for us. It compels us to authentically reciprocate affection and to have tremendous regard for Him. His incredible love allows us to pour our love back to Him.

May our hearts be so sealed in the proper perception of our God and His love that our lives would be lifted up as a treasured gift to Him. Let us focus all our affections on a full-hearted effort to genuinely, increasingly love Him back.

To Love Him by Glorifying Him

Glorifying God can be described as the attempt to bring favorable attention, recognition, and acquaintance to Him whom we so delightfully call *friend*. We love Jesus and it is our desire to see others look towards God with admiration and come to the same place we have found. Often, our attempts, made in human weakness, feel feeble; other times, we feel fully empowered by the Holy Spirit. Because our hearts have been undeservingly honored by our King with His love, we are determined to honor Him who is so solemnly deserving. We attempt to represent Him in a commendable way and in such a manner that our pursuits, behaviors, and doings would bring Him honor. Under God's love, our transformation brings an intense desire to make sure we live in such a manner that our actions accurately reflect the love we have experienced. We want to nurture great respect for His righteous reputation. Our heart's desire is to obey, surrender, even sacrifice—all with hopes to correctly represent our God!

Because we know Him, we have experienced His goodness. We want now to make Him known, so others will see and encounter His excellence and splendor. Will there be times we fail? Of course, and yet He in His deep love will use even these situations. He will extend His magnificent love to help us live in grace, beautifully exemplifying yet again His kind nature.

This transforming factor of being loved first cannot leave us stagnant. Perhaps we haven't even realized our deep desire to make Him known, familiar, and honored to all. Yet, our hearts' attempts to reciprocate His love will often exemplify Him to others. We have been transformed with pure hearts and a focused desire to draw people to His beautiful name, that they would experience His love, and ultimately set their hearts' goal on existing in the richness of living for His glory.

Invite Him Into Everything

Hunger for more of God is a gift from His hand. "But all who are hunting for you—oh, let them sing and be happy" (Psalm 40:16, MSG). To desperately want more of God leads us into a place of growth where we continually ask for further revealing and more of His presence. Desire is God's design. He made us to want, and He wants us to seek and ask. For as we want and ask, we are invited in to accept the surplus of His riches and to enjoy His capacity to give of Himself.

Our God loves to be loved. What is it that we really desire, want, and ask for, if not for the realness of His presence? Divine encounter is our heart's truest wish, and it is our Maker's designed desire for us that we would want Him, seek Him, choose Him, and love Him.

Our love for God is solid when we come to the place of sincerely desiring to see Him in every area of our lives. We show true love when we ask for a full-out invasion on each encounter, relationship, and conversation—down to every last daily task. Like that of a close companion you don't want to part from, we are pulled towards spending time with our God, delighting in His presence, so much so that parting from His company is something we don't want. So, we plead for His longstanding, permanent, no-conditions-apply continual presence. How our Lord loves this desire in us as He desires the very same intimacy.

As we want to be in His presence, to represent Him, and to be great for Him, we open the door for Him to accomplish Kingdom work through us. We are told that He stands at the door and knocks. May we ask Him into our hearts and the fullness and capacity of our everything. Let's invite Him in— He cannot resist what is natural to Him, for He is so deeply relational. His passion, love, and truth are all that keep us together (see Psalm 40:11, MSG).

Accept the Gift

As we ask for more of God on our authentic love quest, He has a great plan to satisfy our request and position us to be fully equipped with all that we need. To have the genuine presence of God live through us, we must love Him with passion and invite Him into our every moment. Just as we needed to accept His sacrificial gift of salvation to enter His love, we need to accept another gift.

For us to fully love Him, accepting this additional gift is essential. This gift brings us to a deeper level of intimacy: the gift is the promise of His indwelling Holy Spirit. We may not fully understand His gift, yet we know having Holy Spirit living in us was Jesus' plan and promise. We may have already received the Holy Spirit at conversion or baptism, or perhaps we feel like we lack His Spirit. Either way, we have these words that move us to ask for it: "How much more will your Father in heaven give the Holy Spirit to those who ask him!" (Luke 11:13, NIV).

As I confessed earlier, I have not always been the best at figuring out the Holy Spirit. I have genuinely wanted to grow in comprehending and operating in all God's offer. It has become a passion of mine to try to unravel all that this indwelling, empowering gift of His very own Presence is. I still feel like I have so much more to understand. However, I have learned a few things. First, what Jesus offers with this gift is truly incredible, and I want to seek it with utmost seriousness. Second, it will be my joy to unravel the mystery of the Holy Spirit all my days on earth. He is that big and wonderful. Throughout my journey, the words in Luke 11:13 have given me peace: I can rest assured that the Father who conceived me in love will give the Holy Spirit to those who ask Him. In all reality, it is the Father's joy to give us this great gift. We have only to sincerely want and request it.

This exciting wisdom of having the Holy Spirit live in us is key to moving all mountains in our lives, for His presence actually dwells in us. The power, truth, authority, and victory of the very Spirit of God operates through us. His nature can be seen in us as our lives produce the fruits of the Spirit, which are a testimony to the world around us. We love God when we accept Jesus' gift of the Holy Spirit, when we believe and try to understand what it means to have Holy Spirit live in us. If we do not fully embrace the gift of the indwelling Spirit, we will always feel like we are missing something in our attempt to fully love God.

As we cling to this promised One and seek to grow in understanding of what it means to have God in us, we journey along a revelation path of potential in all areas of our lives. We will find a place in our flesh unreachable without Him. For it is in having the Holy One, in all His divinity, indwelling us, in our human strength and ability, which transforms us into living in His Spirit of "power, and of love, and of a sound mind" (2 Tim. 1:7, KJV).

Believe in the Impossible

In obedience, when we deliberately step into a place of doing something for God that is otherwise evidently impossible, we are beautifully positioned to rely on our intimacy with God to be what leads us through the challenge. In this place, we are alert, knowing we must entirely rely on our Almighty. When we take risks for Kingdom work, we have a unique opportunity to practice absolute dependence on God. Perhaps this dependence can come in as simple a form as believing and walking in a new truth He is teaching us about our identity—really believing we are accepted, forgiven, and have strength. While this can seem simple enough to some, at times it can seem impossible on our own. The walk of dependency facilitates continual contact and interaction with our First Love, which further establishes us and deepens us in the relationship.

God wants us to step into the place where we know that the incredible strides we need to take will require us to rely on Him for every step. He knows that this will be the same place where He can bless us with the joy of genuinely depending on Him and experiencing togetherness with Him in working towards the seemingly unconquerable. In bigger moments of life, maybe God is calling us to seek out reconciliation with someone we were estranged from. Maybe God is leading us to join a ministry that could use our gifts and talents but is outside of our comfort zone. Or in other season, maybe He is calling us on a mission across the world.

The dwelling place of the impossible clearly points out the limits of our attempts to succeed independently. God wants us to see that progress in completing challenging advances which come through togetherness and reliance on Him. For some this could look like God moving us to pray for a stranger, witness to a friend or even intercede for someone's healing.

We can step out in bold faith to do great things with God. Each event contains the same purpose: to develop our beautiful, genuine faith relationship with God. "This is the life of the Spirit he invited you to through the Message we delivered, in which you get in on the glory of our Master, Jesus Christ" (2 Thess. 2:14, MSG).

What a place of honor we are given when we are invited into the impossible to live for the glory of the One we love, desiring to make Him known. Again, to do this successfully requires a close, intimate connection with Him. We can be confident the impossible is possible with Him because Jesus tells us: "You will receive power when the Holy Spirit comes on you; and you will be my witnesses" (Acts 1:8, NIV).

May we be agents of faith who moment by moment find our purpose in seeking to live in the Holy Spirit who lives in us. We love God well when we seek to accomplish the impossible, as the opportunity to fully depend on Him intertwines us into His will and purpose.

Accept His Offerings

Accepting gifts from the One who loves us is as important as our efforts to give gifts to our Beloved. Embracing His promises is essential to being loved, as those promises allow us to fully love. "We who have run for our very lives to God have every reason to grab the promised hope with both hands and never let go. It's an unbreakable spiritual lifeline, reaching past all appearances right to the very presence of God" (Heb. 6:18–19, MSG). We are encouraged to fight hard to embody the promises, which are like a door into the intimate company of the Lord. For it takes the proximate quality of trust to believe words given, and we can only trust one whom we know and love. So, we show love for God well when we do not rely on our hearts and emotions. They are fickle. We show our love when we refuse to allow our minds or convictions to be tossed about (see James 1:6).

May we fight to find a steady place in our spirit of loving God well by believing the truths He placed in us at the time of salvation. We have received such incredible promises of eternal hope, of the supernatural working of God through us with goodness, power, favor, and truth pouring out. May we now go and live in those promises. God's promises are of unsurpassable high value, and so we should treasure them accordingly. "God wanted to guarantee his promises, he gave his word, a rock-solid guarantee —God can't break his word. And because his word cannot change, the promise is likewise unchangeable" (Heb. 6:17, MSG).

How incredible that we are securely loved in carefully kept promises. What permission the commitments allow us to know we are safe in this love, which opens wide the capacity of our devotion to growing for the Father. As we stand in this goodness, we love better, and He is more perfectly placed in the deserving stance of the highest position of all our affections.

Quality Time

What delight we bring our Father's heart when we seek quality time with Him and enter the sacred place merely to enjoy His company. It's a sacred position to simply be still and present with Him and to seek and find the holy encounter to know our Lord (see Psalm 46:10–11). When we set time aside purely to enter His presence, we love God well. We can read, study and even intercede and never genuinely experience the One who desires profound camaraderie with us. Intimacy takes spending time without any itinerary apart from a sincere desire to build our divine friendship. In those times, we find ourselves in a dwelling place like no other.

Perhaps it will entail honoring Him by rejoicing in His pure goodness. In other instances, we will find ourselves overwhelmed with thanksgiving, and we will offer detailed, specific gratitude over the extreme care He has intervened with for us. Sometimes it will be us lifting thankful hearts over the journey He has invited us to. Each event has in common that it is a simple, yet profound time spent with God.

Our hearts were designed to be with God and filled by His Holy Spirit, giving Him space for this undivided attention. To connect with Him in authentic silence allows Him to bring our hearts into His plan and into our role in joining Him effectively in Kingdom work. He will never show us too far down the journey, for He longs for us to return very soon to spend more time with Him and have Him then reveal more.

When intimate love is in place, and we are comfortable within the trust relationship, we naturally place our needs before Him, believing He will intercede and intervene. We will hear His whispers of truth and promises for help, for Jesus made it all possible. It is Him who invites us to the place where He reveals His heart that moves us into a life that pleases Him, simply because we come.

Give Him Gifts, Talents, Time, and Possessions

As God's beloved children, we have a unique opportunity to love Him well, as we seek to live daily as agents who promote the faith. Surrendering all we have in our time, talents, and possession puts us in ready gear to live for His glory alone. God chose us to purposefully lead us in a particular direction, to get out the accurate word on our amazing Savior. Under the guidance of the Holy Spirit living in us and through us, we have a moment-by-moment purpose. In every step forward, in each problematic situation, in our encounters with others, in interruptions—in each occurrence, we are positioned for an opportunity to give God glory. How we live out our daily tasks, relationships, faith, and prayer life, each circumstance is another opportunity to live for His Kingdom's cause and grand purpose.

> *I have better things in mind for you—salvation things! God doesn't miss anything. He knows perfectly well all the love you've shown him by helping needy Christians, and that you keep at it.*
>
> ~ *Heb. 6:9–10 (MSG)*

His plan for us to love His people and work towards drawing His loved ones home to His heart will be the plan as long as we are on earth. Recognizing everything He gives us and gifts us with is, in turn, an opening to work towards drawing home His lost sheep with love. Whatever He has equipped us with has the potential to bless someone else, to appeal to their hearts for God. Each gift, talent, portion of our time, or anything He has given us ownership of represents an opportunity to make God and His love recognizable. When we live so that all we have is most truly the Lord's, we can steward with faithfulness all He entrusts.

There are many ways we can love God well. Casting all we have before Him as a sacrificial offering, we glorify and adore Him through our life's stories, shining out love, light, and life in His name.

Purity, Integrity, and Sincerity

Even though we know that we bless God's heart when we give of ourselves and our lives, we also have these words to measure: "doing something for you, bringing something to you—that's not what you're after. Being religious, acting pious—that's not what you're asking for" (Psalm 40:6, MSG). What is it that our Lord is after?

Thankfully we have scripture that gives a glimpse of what it is that makes His heart feel loved. One of God's greatest treasures is when we live authentically with Him and take joy in doing His will. No pretending, putting on airs, seeking to look important—it is in our being with God for the genuine and simple love of His company that draws His heart. "The purpose of my instruction is that all believers would be filled with love that comes from a pure heart, a clear conscience, and genuine faith" (1 Tim. 1:5, NLT).

Living authentically, in focused love for God and others, sets us apart for holiness and integrity. This is what the Lord is after. *Acting* as people who love through service done for recognition, image, or reward, does not impress God.

The Lord is after men and women with genuine character who reflect His nature and love in day-to-day life. We will all likely face seasons where our capacity will be limited, perhaps through aging or illness. Our visible, measurable acts of service may be restricted during these times. However, in seasons when observable good deeds are not possible, God values something above these that cannot be taken away. If we have a good, pure, and honest character, this is a great pleasure to God—more than any act of service. Speaking of His faithfulness, living in thankfulness, devoting ourselves to prayer, and reflecting on blessings and lessons as ones full of joy honors Him greatly. This is true even on our deathbed, when we have no obvious service left to give. Yet we must remain true to the instruction that comes from staying in His word regularly. In reading and reflecting on scripture, we find the encouragement, promise, and affection, of our God. His Word strengthens us to be all we can be and to love Him well in action and character.

Through reading the love letter He has written about us, may we allow the words to enter our lives and become our very being, and may we come to the party He's throwing for us (see Psalm 40:7–8, MSG). We are invited to live beautifully before our God, and to authentically, honestly, and purely trust in the celebration of His love over us. In every season of life, may we embrace always living with an upright character, that our God would be most sincerely lavished in our love.

Obey His Command

Our hearts want to give God our all, to reciprocate the love He has so generously poured out on us. When we are seeking to love God more, may we not forget Jesus' simple instructions on how to love Him. Jesus replied, "Anyone who loves me will obey my teaching. My Father will love them, and we will come to them and make our home with them" (John 14:23, NIV). What a promise: as we seek to honor God in obedience and demonstrate our commitment, love circulates between us, the followers, and our Maker. As Triune God extends us the treasured gift of intimate love, may we demonstrate our heart of love by stepping out in every effort to live in obedience. Our dwelling will then be such that the Trinity would call our presence the delightful title of *home*. It is here with Triune God's indwelling that makes us able to do the impossible and live a victorious life of obedience. In our flesh, we are weak and tend to fail, but with our Lord and His presence, we can do the impossible. In the company of God, we are positioned to obey.

> So now Israel, what do you think GOD expects from you? Just this: Live in his presence in holy reverence, follow the road he sets out for you, love him, serve GOD, your God, with everything you have in you, obey the commandments and regulations of GOD that I'm commanding you today—live a good life.

> ~ Deut. 10:12–13 (MSG)

What a beautiful display of unity with our beloved God when we live with a devoted effort to honor Him in all things. In our obedience, God makes our dwelling His home, and we live in His presence. Faithful in His love, He has set a path for us, allowing us to truly live in His commands. In the place of standing in agreement with His will, we proclaim and seek His glory alone—this is a picture of success in loving our God.

Love Him Well: Examine Your Heart

In our journey to love God well, we find a starting point when Jesus said it was of utmost importance and the highest command to love God with all our hearts. What an incredible gift to give to our Lord! However, the question stands: what exactly does giving Him our hearts look like? If our heart is essentially our personhood, giving Him our hearts means offering our very selves. Before we can do that, we likely need to begin with an honest assessment in which we examine our hearts to better understand our motives and identify our top priorities. Then we will discover what we are living for.

As we become increasingly aware of the incredible love the Triune God lavishes on us, it's important to ask the question: are we genuinely trying to love Him back by living full-out for Him? Our culture and world present convincing alternatives to living for God, such as material possessions, pleasure, power, and prestige. Other seemingly more virtuous ambitions also beckon: living for enjoying the moment, trying our best, or being strong in ourselves. Yet, these are all imposters that wholly fail us in the end when we compare them to full-out, honest, heart-full living for God.

Ironically, they are all ambitions in opposition to our actual call, which is to a dependent, intertwined, loving relationship with and for God. We are called to operate in the Holy Spirit and find our strength in Christ. When we pass on from this life to the next, the only thing that will count is whether or not we entered a solid relationship with our God. So, let's ask ourselves: is loving Him well, as He has loved us well, what we value in our hearts beyond everything else? Anything less will leave us with deep regret.

May we purify ourselves and come to a place where we live in the beauty of giving Him the fullness of our hearts. May we fix our eyes boldly on Him and live poised with the purpose of following our first love, our treasure. Holding nothing back, may we lavish God with our love by living out the all-consuming desire to honestly give Him our whole heart.

When I was in my late teens, our pastor handed out accountability cards in the church bulletin. These were the directions: find a friend in the weeks to come and ask each other these questions. The questions were like these: Am I spending time with God? Have I had quality time with my family and friends? Is there any unconfessed sin in my life?

I love authentic conversation and was blessed to have two friends whom I met with separately, and we delved into these ten questions. They transformed our conversations, our friendships, and our relationships with God. Over time, our accountability questions transformed. When someone regularly asks you particular questions, you work towards creating the answers you want. You get better, and you find victory. The accountability allows you to move on and work at improving new areas that need attention in your life.

Did I have battles I felt like I could never share? For sure. Sometimes, even after sharing over 20 years of accountability with these same ladies (who certainly have become my best of friends), I still have things to confess and ask for accountability that I don't want to share. However, it's those same things I know I need to share.

The enemy's greatest tool is to isolate us and have us keep secrets. He uses that against us. As I take courage and share, or they do and confess, more often than not, our response is, "Yes, I too have that same struggle." We talk about even the hardest struggles we face with vulnerability and truthfulness, and we find freedom. Taking seriously the call to examine our hearts, I believe, has helped us personally in so many ways. However, I also think it has blessed us to love God well, as we actively seek to live lives that honor Him.

Love Him Well: Our Minds Set on Truth

As we read God's word, take time to be silent, and meditate on truth, our minds change. Seeking God's perception empowers the transformation of our lives. "I want you woven into a tapestry of love, in touch with everything there is to know of God. Then you will have minds confident and at rest, focused on Christ, God's great mystery" (Col. 2:2–4, MSG). For in this place where we find the wondrous truths about Jesus, we are consumed in our deepest thoughts and our very being, yet in great rest. We need to resolve to be stable in all God's truths, unshakable by philosophies, popular ideas, and false teachings that may come our way. We must remember that our sincerity will be tested, and our faithfulness to our first love will be measured. While we may worry we hurt or disappoint others, at times, to stay faithful to our known truths, in staying faithful, we know we have placed God in the number one spot, above any other person.

Our minds need to be stable in the truth that first, God loves us, and second, He is trustworthy. For it is here that we enter having the "mind of Christ." Those fundamental truths need to sink deep and be unshakable in our being, despite opposition that seeks to destroy them. When these two truths are decisively sealed and guarded in our minds, we will see everything else through the pure, clear lens of His goodness working in every area of our lives.

It blesses us to see all things through the mind of Jesus, to hold His perspective and set out in effort to align each of our thoughts with His. When we do, we gain truth in our minds over our calling, life, relationships, and work. The mind of Christ infiltrates every inch of our lives as we obey and give it permission. Committing our mind to His and joining in His thinking loves our Lord well.

Our Souls: A Fragrant Love Offering

From the beginning, our souls were designed with love as a prominent part. Mysterious, splendid, and eternal, our souls were created to belong to God. All souls are His (see Ezek. 18:4). His breath (such intimate giving of Himself!) breathed our very beings into being. May we love God well by lifting the entirety of our being to live for Him alone. The love offering given to us, we give back to Him. May we offer our souls sincerely to the Shepherd of all souls as a thanksgiving offering.

When we allow our personhood, will, emotions, thinking, and being to operate for our King, we become a fragrant love offering for the Kingdom. Therefore, in joining with the One who loves us so, who placed His very breath in us, may we hold nothing back, but step in fully. He gives us no permission to shrink back in any way from this high calling upon our lives and from all He has called us to be. We do not need to fear the idea of adopting His calling on our soul as something prideful or crazy. Instead, with all our heart, mind, and being, we step fully into what God has called us to be.

We yield our soul to Him, for we are the temple of the living and holy God. We are His light, beautifully holding His glory and authority for His Kingdom purpose. We will take up all tools, devices, skills, gifts, and abilities He offers to be all He calls us to be. We will take our rightful place as His children and occupy the space and positions of influence given to us, to provoke change and transform hearts.

Loving God with our souls involves actively believing our personhood is incredibly valuable to Him. It requires us to believe in our God-given potential, promises, and the empowerment He gives us. In all of this, we will love God sufficiently by offering this essential, intricate, genuine, and powerful, unseen part of our very selves, our very souls.

Tests Refine Our Love

There are times our love will be tested to ensure our commitment is genuine, authentic, and pure. All valuable things face refining, and our love will, too. Rather than see refining times through a lens of concern, we can see them as times of great opportunity. Through adversity, what we treasure can grow and be reinforced. Such times provide us the potential to love God with all our strength. As we take on our identity as the King's faithful warriors, through the testing, we enter into a place of increasingly intensified love.

The nature of testing we encounter can vary in intensity: it may be unanswered prayer, feeling distance in fellowship, a sense of silence from God, or even hearing incorrectly from the One we commune with so intimately. From the struggle comes the opportunity to grow in wisdom.

"When troubles of any kind come your way, consider it an opportunity for great joy. For you know that when your faith is tested, your endurance has a chance to grow" (James 1:2–3 NLT). These uncertain places can serve to reinforce trust in what we know to be solid certainties. We fortify our faith by surrendering uncertainty and relying on promises.

If we anchor ourselves on all we know of the One we love, we demonstrate our trust in His nature. While we are tested, we can look back and remember past answers to prayer, the closeness we felt, and the clear speaking of God. Loving God with all our strength requires us to always protect, trust, hope, and persevere (see 1 Cor. 13:7, NIV). In-depth love forms as we trust God and endure, even through the refining. With all our might and strength, we fight through times of testing and hold on to His truth.

Once we pass through a few hurdles, we will begin to recognize and embrace the opportunities they bring. "When your endurance is fully developed, you will be perfect and complete, needing nothing" (James 1:4, NLT).

Fight for the One We Love

As children of God, we will be called out by our Father to fight battles so may we be found faithful as His mighty warriors. We are soldiers in the fight for light against the darkness. Through courage and boldness, we can demonstrate committed intimacy. We have been loved well, taught well, trained up, and are equipped by our Master with all we need. Now we have the opportunity to love Him well by full-out living in Him, with Him, and for Him as part of His army.

Given the unmatchable goodness of the Holy Spirit's dwelling in us, we have incredible power and authority. Our big God is by our side, and He is always victorious. "His power extends over everything" (Col. 2:10, MSG). Living, dwelling, occupying continually in His glorious presence, courageously believing in His all extending power is loving God well. As beloved children, we must live in unstoppable faith for the Kingdom of God.

Jesus fought for truth, righteousness, and the oppressed. He fought sickness, demons, and spiritual poverty with fierceness, unrelenting perseverance, and confidence. What opportunity we have with Him as our example! With mighty God by our side, promising us His will and His power, victory and authority are ours daily, and we can fight for goodness in every action and encounter. As we listen to our Master and His commands and are attentive to the Mighty Warrior's instructions, we have the opportunity to love Him by fighting well for Him.

Then we can say we have indeed embraced Christ Jesus, the Master. We can know who we are when we are deeply rooted in Him. When we know our way around the faith, we can live full-out in Him. May we do what we've been taught. "School's out;" so let us "quit studying the subject and start living it!" (see Col. 2:6–7, MSG).

Center of Our Affection

We love the Lord well when we choose to make Him the object of our total affection. How He delights in it when we have Him as our first thought of the day, when He is our pursuit, when we spend time with and talk to Him before we go to sleep. When we diligently focus on God and His call on us, it is a delight to remain on His set path. Proverbs directs:

> *Keep vigilant watch over your heart;*
> * that's where life starts…*
> *Keep your eyes straight ahead;*
> * ignore all sideshow distractions.*
> *Watch your step,*
> * and the road will stretch out smooth before you.*

> ~ *Prov. 4:23;25–26 (MSG)*

We are called to full attention, to a single-mindedness for God. To have that mindset, we must keep on task and disregard the countless, pointless things that compete for our attention.

Thankfully, we are not alone but hold a promise of help. The Holy Spirit reminds us about Jesus, convicts us when we are off task, and corrects us when we get caught up in worry, lies, gossip, and other diversions that distract us away from our focal point. We can walk the smooth road of peace stretched out before us. If we stand in agreement with His call and purposes, we can dwell in His presence with the ease He provides.

You're blessed when you stay on course,
walking steadily on the road revealed by GOD.
You're blessed when you follow his directions,
doing your best to find him.

~ Psalm 119:1–2 (MSG)

We love God well when we stay the course. On His straight path, we walk in intimacy, hand-in-hand. We find Him there on the road He calls us to and that He beautifully shares in community with us.

May we remain in the wonder of intentionally focused love. May we live in and under the peace that He has provided. In a life committed to the One who holds all our affection, let us faithfully walk the path He calls us to.

Love God: Working for Reconciliation of His Sheep

If we discover just the tip of the iceberg of the reality of the love of God, we find something incredible. He delights when we see that even when we were far from Him, His heart always ached for us to be near. He took extraordinary lengths through the sacrifice of the cross to restore humanity's broken relationship with Him, to bring it back to the place of intimacy, trust, love, and closeness. When we became Christian, we allowed our lives to be restored through Jesus to the One who loves us deeply. As we accept the gift of restoration, we become increasingly aware of the heartbreaking situation that has been undone. God's beloved are reinstated as His proper children. Ever since the relationship was broken with His created children, He has been longing, waiting, desperately hoping for it to be restored. For although the original bond was broken, His heart of love for each person never stopped. As with the father of the prodigal son, our Father's love is unwavering, and He waits for relationship restoration with each lost child, every one of His created people.

Once we are reconciled and personally know the love of the Father, we feel His heartbreak over our previous state of separation. As a natural outcome, we will want to do whatever it takes to help restore as many others as possible to our Father's heart. His desire is not in question. Scripture says God's will is that no one should perish (2 Pet. 3:9).

We love God well when, like Peter, we love His sheep and take care of His lambs by doing whatever He calls us to in order to facilitate reconciliation. We bless our Father with love when we seek to be His hands, feet, and heart, to make visible in this world His powerful, enduring love.

To love Him well, may we go and love, just as He loved us.

Determined to Follow

The image of our loving, heavenly Father in all His glory, calling us the object of His affection, the longing of His heart, is beyond understanding. To experience the power of His ways that transform our self-willed life to a God-pleasing life is incredible. He changes us! We come to the place of loving Him so much that His heart for people becomes ours. Our hearts' ambition becomes so passionately focused on doing whatever we can to make Him understood and accessible to every person. We pray that they, too, would experience His love by whatever means possible, and that they would find Jesus' offer for life.

Yet before we can help others see how to live in this fullness, we first need to discover the secret to truly living in it ourselves among the typical pressures of daily life. There is no exact formula. However, abiding daily in our God, asking for help, and seeking to live fully in the Holy Spirit is an excellent place to start!

> *Morning by morning he wakens me and opens my understanding to his will.*
>
> ~ *Isa. 50:4 (NLT)*

Our God will meet us; will we meet Him? Our God will direct us to His desire for us. Will we seek it? He speaks; will we listen? God will help and make clear what He asks. He will show us our role in the body to help restore hearts to Himself. He is relationship-oriented, always. He promises if we meet, and seek, and listen, He will help.

Will it be hard? Of course—but God delights in doing the impossible. When we face the impossible, we realize our need to depend on Him, and that realization fuels our constant need to connect. It will require us to set our "face like a stone, determined to do his will" (Isa. 50:7, NLT). We love

God well when we fully abide in Him, continually pursuing life within the reconciliation that is in the Father's heart and His perfect will.

Fear God

Our God is mighty and mysterious. It may sound contradictory, but to love God is to fear Him. It is not a fear of evil intent or harmful motives, for God can do nothing evil. He is always good. The fear of the Lord is one of reverent respect for His immensity, superiority, importance, and significance. This fear acknowledges we are loved with the same love He loved Jesus with, and we make ourselves at home in that love as we keep His commands (see John 15:9–10). We love Him well by remaining in His extended love. Remaining in His love requires our obedience. When we fear God, we authentically consider His significance as the distinct Creator of our world and our very selves. In that fear, we recognize the enormity that His reality is greater than all we see on this earth. His vastness and magnitude go well beyond our understanding of time, space, and reason. This *fear* acknowledges the fame, excellence, and impressiveness of the One who is entirely holy, righteous, and rules our world.

So, in weighing His prominent existence and commands, we choose to honor Him alone, above any other thing. We strive to live excellently for Him, accepting that He is a beautiful, incredible mystery whom we cannot put in a box and who deserves our highest esteem and trust. This motivates our hearts to live under the noble principle of His commands, upright, holy, and set apart in character.

When our devotion is challenged, our reason put to the test, or a choice set before us, will we seek the favor of God or man? May we choose well whom we fear!

> *Don't be bluffed into silence by the threats of bullies. There's nothing they can do to your soul, your core being. Save your fear for God, who holds your entire life—body and soul—in his hands.*

> ~ Matt. 10:28 (MSG)

To experience intimacy with God, we must fully acknowledge who He is and respect Him well, set our hearts on loving Him well by living in the extreme, devoted, honorable, and beautiful fear of our Lord.

Trust God in Out of the Ordinary Experiences

Over the years with God, we may grow deep in our knowledge about Him. We may get good at following His commands, understanding His ways, and adapting our lifestyles to align with His standards. Yet, He will often beckon us into unfamiliar terrain, stretching our understanding, trust, and dependency. Perhaps this is why He takes pleasure in moving us to new levels of trust and voiding our carefully-kept, safe-God boxes. As we enter new territories and are obligated to trust Him more, He sees the opportunity for us to be blessed and grow.

Fearing God means doing His will, beyond that of the world. We must ask ourselves: are we loyal to the point of being willing to risk feeling rejected by others in order to follow Him? If we feel God pushing us into new supernatural experiences beyond those our fellow believers experience, it can be that He wants to form something new in us. Will we choose Him and what He wants to reveal to us, even if it is controversial in our very church and circle of believing friends?

> Trust GOD from the bottom of your heart;
>   don't try to figure out everything on your own.
> Listen for GOD's voice in everything you do, everywhere you go;
>   he's the one who will keep you on track.
> Don't assume that you know it all.
>   Run to GOD!

~ *Prov. 3:5–7 (MSG)*

His heart's desire is that we would run with passion and abandonment, relinquishing all else. This is why, at times, He will give experiences between Himself and us that no one else can enter. They may come as supernatural signs or wonders, a healing, a prophetic word, moments of speaking in tongues, or an open-eyed experience of an angel or God Himself. He loves to give us these experiences to build deeper trust and love.

May we love God well by entering the unknown and the out-of-the-ordinary experiences with our hearts open to the reality and presence of all He is and all He offers.

Live in His Shelter

> *Those who live in the shelter of the Most High will find rest in the shadow of the Almighty.*
>
> ~ *Psalm 91:1 (NLT)*

We love God well when we find this place of living in Him, with Him, under His care, and in close intimacy. It is a place of the most profound rest. When there is nothing else that could help, satisfy, protect, or be sufficient to meet the need at hand, we can enter His shelter. In Him alone, we receive the most effective and gentle care. In His shelter, we have no fear because we are under the protection of the all-victorious commander of Heaven's Army.

In the shadow of the Almighty, we are taught, mentored, and ultimately clothed in His likeness. It's like when we first found salvation and put down all our self-efforts and hard-working performances to simply be with God. It is a place of maturity where "the basic foundational truths are in place: [where you turn] your back on 'salvation by self-help' and [turn] in trust toward God" (Heb. 6:1, MSG).

We may initially be prompted to live in the secret, sacred place of His shelter in a time of deep trial, perhaps out of necessity. Even though hardship may bring us to experience His shelter, once the storm has passed, we can find it challenging to remain living in the shadow of the Almighty. Yet to do so loves God well. He wants to be in close, beautiful, intimate proximity with His beloved children: in His shadow, He can tend to needs, care for, protect and love on them so well. There, our confidence and identity grow in His unshakable faithfulness and love.

May we, like Jesus, rest in the sacred dwelling place of the Father's shadow, knowing that we are not abandoned. He blesses us in His shelter, He gives us unshakable assurance, and provides peace no matter what troubles come our way (see John 16:33, MSG).

He Makes Our Love Lovely

Understanding how deeply we are loved compels us to want to deeply love God and please Him. We already know much of what God-pleasing living can look like. We can seek to live a holy life by pursuing unity and peace, speaking well to others, and practicing faith. These are an excellent place to start.

Yet, we can often feel like we fail the tall order of faithfully loving God and others. It is a noble pursuit to strive to always love God in increasing amounts. However, our hearts need to find rest in the fact that it is Him who makes our love lovely. The enemy would love us to be stuck in the lie of always feeling that we are insufficient. Scripture reassures us, though, of what God can do in us.

> *May [God] equip you with all you need*
> *   for doing his will.*
> *May he produce in you,*
> *   through the power of Jesus Christ,*
> *every good thing that is pleasing to him.*

> *~ Heb. 13:21 (NLT)*

Our love for God may not currently be perfect, but we need to trust that He is at work in us and will bring it into completion and that we, as His beloved, will increasingly grow to a place of loving Him well. Jesus had confidence in His identity and nature; He held solid trust, knowing that He was deeply loved by the Father. Now it is His intense desire that, as His followers, we too enter into that assured position.

Oddly, to love others well, we need to believe that we are truly lovely. Often when we find ourselves criticizing others, it is in those same moments when we do not feel strong in our own identity. It takes firmly believing that we are exactly who our Father tells us we are and that He is continuously working in us to love Him and please Him.

So, may we stand in our unshakable identity, mature in who we are. May we trust that what He says is true. Though flawed, we are deeply, wonderfully loved. We are full of potential, and we are God's work that will find completion. If ever we question whether our love is enough, we can rest assured that all power comes from the victorious work of Jesus Christ that works in us.

No Matter the Cost, Fight for Depths with God

God loves it when we want more of Him—when we won't rest or be satisfied with anything less than His fullness. What joy the Father has given us, that He is a beautiful, exciting mystery. He is the greatest treasure and offers the highest delight of adventure, and each of us is incredibly blessed to be invited to unravel His mystery. If life is all about relationship, then the journey of exploring deeper the One we adore is what life is all about. He wants intimacy, our sincere seeking, our love, and a fight in us to find depth in this relationship, whatever the cost.

Does He test our affections? Possibly. Perhaps He refines our desires, strengthens our resolve, analyzes our motives? He is God Almighty, after all. With the highest standard of love, mercy, patience, and justice, He sees us for everything we are. He loves us deeply, and He is captivated by pure hearts that are totally committed, growing, and pursuing Him with determination to know Him better.

To reach greater depth, one can wrestle God for the simple pleasure of having even more of Him, even if a cost is attached. After Jacob wrestled "a man" who threw his hip out of joint, he was told: "Your name will no longer be Jacob... From now on you will be called Israel, because you have fought with God and with men and have won" (Gen 32:24;28, NLT). After this incident, Jacob said, "I saw God face-to-face and lived to tell the story!" (v. 30, MSG).

We love our God well if we are willing to go to the length of seeking the intimacy of God's hand on our flesh, knowing the potential of personal cost connected to that contact. How He loves the commitment in us when we show that nothing, no one, no idea, no direction, and no reward can possibly hold more value in our hearts than God.

To strive, trial, labor, and fight for the deepness, closeness, and realness of more of His presence? This is love at its best. This is fighting to make clear where and with whom our loyalty lies. It pours out affection on the

One we want to love well. It seeks a new name, shows the resolve, accepts the cost, and rests in the deepest of joy from experiencing the encounter worth more than all else.

He Always Has More Goodness for Us

We love the Lord well when we pursue Him in faith, believing, trusting, and expecting that we will find even more of Him and His goodness. The Lord loves exponentially. He reveals more and more of Himself and loves when we seek after His revealing. The relationship He offers is unexplainable in its depth and length. But with steadfast disclosure, bit by bit, He reveals all possibilities that exist within the fullness of His goodness. If we feel as though our hearts have plateaued in the love we experience in Him, we can rest assured: He *always* has more to reveal. From within the intimacy we have valued, chased, fought for, and embraced, our Almighty whispers to us: *I will take you even further still.*

We have only scraped the surface of all His offering of love and relationship with us, for He is limitless! How it delights Him to show us new layers of the exceeding beauty that He offers, into which we have the honor to journey. Increased intensity of His presence, profound grace, and an even brighter shining of His realness entering the layers of our lives: all are part of His offering. He equips us to be light to the world, as He calls.

Where we have gone through joyous moments of mountaintop experiences with God in the past, believing we have only to journey down now, God calls us to a still higher distance. So, may we seek after the immeasurable, infinite goodness of God with continual endurance for more intimacy. May this foundational faith penetrate every fiber of our being, with increased godliness in us each step. If we maintain our being in proximity with a perspective of His continual goodness, this truly loves our God well, for His heart's desire is for us to walk on the designed path to completion. "How great is Your goodness, Which You have laid up for those who fear You, Which You have prepared for those who trust in You" (Psalm 31:19, NKJV).

Our Lives as Thanksgiving

With all the love, goodness, and blessing the Lord pours out onto us, it is natural for us to want to give Him something in return. We can study to know what it is that loves our Lord well. What favor that He has taken care of everything we need, that Jesus bought our freedom, forgiveness, and salvation on the cross, that there is nothing more that we need to do. To try to be good or work to earn any of this would be pointless and fruitless. Yet still, living a good life of devotion as a genuine thanksgiving offering with the pure intention to simply love God well is admirable. We were highly honored to receive the wondrous love offering of the Father, and He satisfies us by equipping us with the gift we can offer up to Him in return—our very lives. Truly nothing else would suffice.

So, with the purest intention and most in-depth love, we lift our lives to Him with gratitude, and we praise the One who gave us breath, taught us, and sacrificed His life for us. This gift and offering will remain pure, for we resolve that we do none of it in attempts to gain the acceptance He has already lavished on us. We do it as a way to show honor to the One who gives us life.

How fortunate we have His strength, equipping, and promise of help to live an honorable life that can please Him, for He sees us in the perfection of Jesus, as we live in Him. Our invitation was clear to "accept God's kingdom in the simplicity of a child" (Mark 10:15, MSG). How precious when we stand in simple trust in this love offering from the Father and accept it as His child.

When we offer ourselves up for His Kingdom, His heart is touched, and we love Him well. And so we strive to live honorably as a thanksgiving offering. Our Father adores this, and this loves Him well, for it acknowledges He is the source of all our affections.

Section 8:

LOVING OTHERS—
GOD'S
TREASURED PEOPLE

In a truly intimate relationship, there will always be a shared goal and direction. In genuine love, we join in God's pursuit of love and kingdom purpose. As we stand firm in the deep love offer He extends, we are securely positioned and powerfully enabled to live out His authentic love for all others.

Love your neighbor as yourself.

~ Matt. 22:39 (NIV)

This is my prayer: that your love will flourish and that you will not only love much but well. Learn to love appropriately… so that your love is sincere and intelligent.

~ Phil. 1:9,10 (MSG)

Invited to Join in His Love

God is love. As His beloved children, clothed in His likeness, He gives us great purpose when He invites us to love others. The practice of love is ingrained in our spiritual nature in God. It is the measure of our every action; it is what gives life and grants us the favor of living in glory. We are here to make our beautiful Jesus known by living out love "on earth, as it is in heaven." We are ambassadors sent to love people, His created beings, in ways that make His name, His presence, and His Kingdom ways known.

Unfortunately, the opportunity to love others practically often presents itself in complex ways. Life comes with intense demands, and we can be lulled into believing that simply doing good deeds means we are acting out of love. Busyness and constant "doing" leave little room to reflect on what it means to love authentically. When we genuinely care about others and see them as beloved people created by God, we take a powerful step forward to loving others well. As we seek to live humbly, honestly and empathetically, we represent the divine love we received and now want to give. Perhaps the secret lies in striving in to live like Jesus in the art of truly being present with those in our immediate presence. As Jesus on earth did so well, may we give whomever we are interacting with our attention. That confirms their value and can produce powerful, life-changing love.

It was a powerful revelation that I truly needed. I have often felt like there were so many lovely people in my life, and I wasn't quite sure how to balance it all. I want to be light, I want to love well, I want to pour out. But the needs are so many and the people, too. Then one day, while I was studying the life of Jesus, the Lord gave me a revelation. He had way more people to see, needs to meet, and requests made of Him than I could ever imagine. Yet He was not stressed, burdened, or wearied by them. Instead, Jesus was so incredibly poised and attentive to whoever the person in His immediate presence was. He loved well the person right before Him.

So, although imperfectly, I have tried to implement this focus in my life. This secret brings a balance into loving others that lifts off stress. Like Jesus, I will respond to the one person in my immediate presence. I give them my full attention. Whether it be my child, a friend or family member, a neighbor or stranger, whoever is right in front of me, they are my priority focus. This is my goal, to love others well. Like Jesus on earth did so well, may we give whomever we are interacting with our attention.

The Holy Spirit in us makes it possible for us to show authentic love for others. As we increasingly come under the influence of the fruits of the Spirit, love will grow in us and spill out of us. In this place, we have the Kingdom and are equipped to love in beautiful and visible ways.

The Kingdom of God is "righteousness, peace, and joy in the Holy Spirit" (Rom. 14:17, NIV). Dwelling in this place of assured righteousness leaves a mark of peace on us. As ones who are loved and able to love, our lives will magnify Him. Living in the joy of the Holy Spirit enables us to exemplify the love we experience through our intimacy with the Godhead. Our testimony extends the invitation to others to come into this place to experience authentic love.

Such invitation God opens to us, to love others by portraying His very nature, being, and fragrance in all our interactions!

Jesus: The Greatest Teacher of Love

With every calling He gives us, God extends multiple provisions to fulfill that calling. The call to love is no short task: our Lord knew that from the start. Humanity's great need for "Immanuel, God with us" includes our need for the divine in the flesh to exemplify perfect intimacy and love. Jesus's model of loving others is essential for us so that we can go and love well.

> *The one who keeps God's word is the person in whom we see God's mature love. This is the only way to be sure we're in God. Anyone who claims to be intimate with God ought to live the same kind of life Jesus lived.*
>
> *1 John 2:5–6 (MSG)*

Intimacy is God's heart's desire for us. We are intimate when we are living in Him and like Him. With entwined hearts, Him in us and us in Him, we live in the Word that was Jesus, and we are made mature in love.

Jesus was the perfect model of love. When we feel inadequate or need direction in how to love, countless biblical stories depict how God lived out love. The list of love examples is endless: reaching out to the stranger, the hurting, the seeking, the denying. His interaction with all sorts of people gives us direction regarding how we can reach out in love to those closest to us, those who fiercely oppose us, and everyone in between.

If we look back at our own experiences—at our unbelief and questioning before we knew Jesus as Lord—we know Triune God continued to reach out to us with patience and love. When we battle sins of complaining, pride or whatever our personal struggles, we see God tenderly, gently, and firmly loves us in all circumstances. Like in Peter's denial, or Paul's persecution of the church, or the woman at the well's past, Jesus' response of tenderness, kindness, and goodness towards them gives us direction for our own actions toward others. We, too, should go out clothed in His likeness, extending love as He has to us. Jesus loves our attempts to fully love as He loves. However, when we fall short, He gives us a beautiful promise. One day, when He is openly revealed, we will be like Him and fully love (see 1 John 3:2).

Make God Known to Others by Love

Jesus washed the disciple's feet. The story draws a picture of brotherly love, and it foretold how He would cleanse us of our sin. The humble act of washing others' feet demonstrates a directed, tender, attentive love. It provides a model of meek, personalized, purposeful love. It should be no surprise that as John 13 begins with this practical act of love and service from Jesus to His disciples, the chapter ends with a new commandment to love.

> *Love one another. In the same way I loved you, you love one another. This is how everyone will recognize that you are my disciples—when they see the love you have for each other.*
>
> *~ John 13:34–35 (MSG)*

There are no shortcuts to the process of developing a loving heart. To genuinely, effectively love others, we must first spend time being loved by Jesus. His tender, caring, directed affection must come first.

Jesus unfolds a circular mystery in this chapter. After He washes the disciples' feet, but before He gives the new commandment, He explains a bit about Himself, the Father, and their relationship:

> *Now the Son of Man is seen for who he is, and God seen for who he is in him. The moment God is seen in him, God's glory will be on display. In glorifying him, he himself is glorified—glory all around!*
>
> *~ John 13:31–32 (MSG)*

In the same way, we love God by bringing Him glory. We can display God's nature through our actions, just as Jesus did. We can glorify Him and make Him recognizable to the world.

What greater way to do this than by first spending time with the Father? When we are filled with His love, we can pour it out and love one another. God magnified Himself through Jesus' acts of love, and He will do the same through us. Through acts of love, we can glorify our Most High God as Jesus did.

He gives us the perfect recipe for how to love one another: by being loved by Him first, we can be so filled up that the natural result is to overpour the love we've received onto others.

Love Opens the Door to Living in God's Reality

Holy Spirit opens us to all-new levels of love that produce an atmosphere of profound receiving and giving. Through living in the Spirit, we can truly love others.

> *My dear children, let's not just talk about love; let's practice real love. This is the only way we'll know we're living truly, living in God's reality.*

> ~ *1 John 3:18–19 (MSG)*

What promise we receive in the act of practicing love's offer of the deepest intimacy in "God's reality"! Is this not what our hearts are longing for? More of God, more of His manifest presence, more face-to-face encounters, more intimate reality. In living in Him, we find the fullness of life He offers, and we are positioned exactly where we have always wanted to be.

Perfecting our love is not required: we grow into perfection. Practicing love is required. We should strive towards the goal of making love part of our moment-to-moment thinking and our entire way of life. In the position of practicing love in every circumstance, we come to see the opportunities to live out this calling that glorifies the Father and transforms our lives.

On our own, this is impossible. But with Jesus' gift of the Holy Spirit, we are more than able to live the transformed life because we are in His presence, His reality. In His presence, in the company of the One who loves the best, aware of the unseen Kingdom around us which more real than what we can physically see, we know we are in love. Love is no longer merely a concept, a feeling, or our best attempt for action, but a way of life we experience in the amazing, intimate presence of the Godhead.

As we go out, we are empowered to live out love with others. Our intimate circle with Father, Jesus, and Holy Spirit provides us such an experience of love that we can do no less than invite others to know Triune God personally themselves and come into the reality of that love. By living the transformed life through the power of the Holy Spirit, we demonstrate there is way to live apart from the world. In practicing the incredible love of inviting someone to know Jesus as Savior and Lord of their life, we most certainly love them well. We invite them into the amazing reality of God's presence to encounter and receive fulness of life.

How to Love Others: Abide in God

God simply and fully loves our company. To genuinely love others the way He desires us to apart from God's company is not only impossible, it is not what He wants. He wants us so close to Him, so joined with Him, so fully abiding in Him, that loving others as He does becomes what naturally flows out of our lives. Together with Him, we will love others, for apart from Him, we can do nothing. We can go through motions to serve others and do things that seem loving, but He wants more. He wants a deep, intimate joining of hearts with Him in all things because that will cause an outpouring of genuine love for others.

> *Abide in Me, and I in you… By this my Father is glorified, that you bear much fruit.*
>
> ~ *John 15:4,8 (NKJV)*

Sometimes we get so focused on bearing fruit that we miss the joyful journey He has for us. The Psalmist encourages us: "Keep company with GOD, get in on the best" (Psalm 37:4, MSG). He has much to offer us in the call to love one another. The reality is that joining with Him is required, for that union allows us to be filled to overflowing with the Holy Spirit. Then, we live out the fruits that the Spirit produces. As naturally as breathing brings oxygen to every part of our body without conscious effort, abiding in God transforms our very nature such that we become love as He is love.

There is no love apart from God—not true, sincere, unconditional love. Knowing that loving others was impossible without Him, God gave the tallest of commands. He wants us to be dependent on an authentic joining of hearts with Him so we can accomplish what He requires. Love from God must come first, love for God next, and then the natural outpouring of our hearts is in love for humanity. As we know God and love God, we know His great, big, deep heart-love for humanity.

As we abide in Him, our inclination to join Him in whatever capacity He leads increases. "The reality test on whether or not we love God's children is this: Do we love God? Do we keep his commands?" (1 John 5:2, MSG).

When we are in the place that we love God and keep His commands, then loving others comes naturally through the practice of uncomplicated, practical daily actions. Our love comes as an effortless rhythm, like a heartbeat.

Loving the Complex Person in His Strength

It seems so simple and yet so difficult to love. In our humanity, loving people with ease can be challenging. From temporary encounters with random, problematic people who treat us unkindly, to those we encounter more frequently, all the way to those closest to us whom we adore but at times upset us, each can present challenges. Thankfully, in order to navigate difficult interactions and relationships, we can learn to respond in love through Holy Spirit living in us.

Even though "to love others" is one of the greatest of all callings on our lives from God, He understands the challenges we face to succeed at this call to love. The reality is that sin causes opposition to love. Selfishness, anger, unkindness and many other behaviors place challenges to loving easily. But in God's omniscience and omnipotence, He knows how to steer us through challenges.

We all have difficult people in our lives. However, what makes it most strenuous is that at times we cannot escape a challenging person, because it happens to be our very selves. At some point, in some way, each of us have likely been the difficult person to someone and certainly to ourselves. Unfortunately, we have not yet fully reached the beautiful perfection of His likeness that He promised we will someday hold. Thankfully, He gives direction on how to live the peaceful life within ourselves and with others.

In the company of Jesus, who is the most encouraging, gracious, compassionate, and gentle of all, we find strength and ability to show love to others. We can always rest in the promise of help from Jesus, no matter our circumstance, no matter our person. He extends the wisdom from heaven down on us. For "when people's lives please the LORD, even their enemies are at peace with them" (Prov. 16:7, NLT). By His love operating through us, we can truly love those He so dearly loves in all their complexities. We are promised patience, perseverance and even the Lord's perspective on every person. People's actions should not always be accepted, especially if they are harmful to us, but in the Lord's strength it is possible for us to have a supernatural love for them. We can reject the unhealthy behavior, but still love the person. For those who have truly harmed us deeply, we know that the Lord is just, fair and sees all. No trauma we experience goes unseen or unnoticed but is held and weighed by the Lord.

Time in God's company heals us from hardships, insults and hurt so we can successfully face challenges regarding our ability to love others. Surely when we know the Holy Spirit's action and presence, God imparts us this supernatural ability to love. There, with Jesus by our side, we are empowered to love those who otherwise seem unlovable.

Feed My Sheep: To Love Others Is to Love God

A powerful conversation occurred between Peter and Jesus (see John 21:15–17). It's a great guide for us to better explore what it means to "love one another." Their dialogue revealed that the act of loving others is an extension of our love for God. Jesus didn't leave a chance for confusion on the point. He didn't present it in passing just once but distinguished the point by making it three times. He asks Peter, "do you love me? … do you love me? … do you love me?" (John 21:15,16,17, NIV). If you do, He told Peter, "feed my sheep." The implication is that Peter needed to show his love through his actions. Jesus was telling Peter to show tenderness towards His people's needs and actively care for them. Perhaps Jesus asked the question three times so that Peter could not merely provide a quick, passive answer. Instead, Peter had to pay attention and intentionally assess his heart.

As we evaluate our heart's level of passion and consider what value God places on loving others through intentional acts, it is undeniable that for God, loving others is of no small importance. Its worth to God is so significant that He said loving others is how we show our love and appreciation for our Savior. We are truly blessed when we have a humble, tender-hearted love towards people. The reward of living a life of authentic love is threefold: we bless God, others, and ourselves.

God was fully aware of the challenges we would face in living in relationship with others, even those who are difficult. He wants us to know they are significant and valuable to Him. Even though forming relationships can be demanding and costly, He desperately wants us to resolve to live lives of love with one another. In that place, deeper intimacy with our God continues to build itself, ever stronger and ever firmer.

People are a source of joy: it is a blessing to love, care for, and encourage them. However, if we ever feel weary in loving others, may we take heart that when we are faithful in it, we bless God. It satisfies something deep within Him and within us when we answer the call to feed His lambs and feed His sheep.

Evaluating Ourselves for Sincere Love

So, since loving one another is so highly important to God, how can we ask ourselves the tough question that Jesus asked Peter? How can we ask it again and again until its real value sinks deep and penetrates our soul? How do we evaluate our heart honestly: "Do I truly love him?"

As Christians, we are taught early to love God and love one another. The idea can become ordinary and routine, leaving it with little effect. It may appear to others, even to ourselves, that we are serving and therefore loving others. We do, we give, we share our homes, talents, time, and finances. Yet a motive other than the intimate desire to bless the One we love most by loving others can underlie our actions. An inner need to build a "Christian" image for appearances' sake may be something only we can know. Still, it will testify to our spirit that we have missed the mark.

We need to test our hearts and work to remove all self-living and pride that gets in the way of genuine love, for these will block us from faithful service for His Kingdom. On the flip side, there are authentic moments when we are filled with God's love and are secure in His intimate embrace. In those moments, it is as if we are so incredibly filled up with love that we have no choice but to pour out steadfast love to others. When we are yielded to the Spirit of love, the idea of loving others comes effortlessly.

The idea of being able to live a Christian life apart from humility and sincere love for others is so far off base, it cannot exist. To replace it, if it sneaks in, we must take the time to again allow genuine, beautiful love from our Savior to engulf us. Once we accept love from God, the refining purity of love for others becomes extraordinary in us. It is there that we can "in humility value others above [ourselves]" (Phil. 2:3, NIV), in a supernatural, filled-up-in-the-love-of-God way.

Practical Love: We Can't Be All Things to All People

I became very good at being a burden carrier. God had made my heart big to care for the people around me genuinely - maybe too big. As I've studied my personality type over the years, I understand this tendency I have better. To be loving is good, but there is an unhealthy place where we can find ourselves trying to be all things to all people. One could say it's out of love, but one can also flip it and say I didn't trust God to be present, real, and active in others' lives. I took on the roles of showing compassion, being good company, a listener, an advocate, a provider, and a counselor to many different people. That is not a realistic position for a single person. Over time, I have improved at remembering my human limitations, though the Lord still has to remind me. I work at trusting that He loves the people I care about more than I can imagine and more than I do. God alone can be all things to all people. My yoke with Him is easy, and His burden is light because He carries the weight of all burdens. In my efforts to love others, I find "peace settles" down well when I see the small role I am to play and I do it, and I allow God to be God in all the big ways to care for those around me.

Loving others well requires dedicated intentionality and limitations. It is a powerful and lovely position to find ourselves so loved by God that we have no choice but to pour out love for others. In this place, we find rest when we join with His very heart. However, the reality is each of us have limits to our time, energy, ability, and resources—even with the best intentions of loving others. How then do we stay in this resting place, and not "become weary in doing good" (Gal. 6:9, NIV)? Because the place of living in love for others is divinely designed, in it, we will face opposition from the one who wants to destroy it. The warning against weariness is given because of the enemy's potential to twist and confuse the virtues of doing good.

Christians dedicated to the call to love and serve others commonly face exhaustion and weariness. The burden becomes too big; the responsibility, too heavy. Could it be that we take on burdens God has not asked us to? Are we trying to become all things to all people? Or even naively but mistakenly trying to play "savior," when that is Christ's role alone?

Thankfully, God provides wisdom for us to find our individual responsibilities. Our first priority is always our relationship with God, not service. Second, we must tend to our own needs to ensure we are in a healthy place to love. Jesus taught:

> *You're blessed when you get your inside world—your mind and heart—put right. Then you can see God in the outside world*

> *~ Matt. 5:8 (MSG)*

Once you can see God in the outside world, you are ready to love those around you. The next priority rests with our families. God sets a high standard to provide for them and a rebuke if we don't (1 Tim. 5:8).

God creates us with a capacity to reach out in love to all around us, yet He is intentional and specific with how He calls us to love them. Balance in all this is experienced when we know we are following through with His specific asking over us. Which, oddly, we will be surprised with how little He actually asks and how much we initiate on our own. Peace settles on us when we place our cares for our loved ones on God. These cares include our loved ones' salvation, their direction in life, and their walk with the Lord. Each must be laid at the Savior's feet well enough that we feel the burden lift from our own shoulders. We find contentment when we tend to our relationship, our close loved ones and possibly others with a balance that doesn't feel rushed or overwhelming. We can rest knowing His love for others is far more profound than our love for them. He will equip us with mighty strength and spirit when we focus on the precise, detailed particulars of His calling on us to love others.

Loving Others by Remaining True to Our Gifts

When we seek guidance regarding how God intentionally wants to use us to love one another through our gifts, beautiful intimacy with Him follows. When we become followers of Christ, He promises a gift from the hand of God, just for us. God wants to use that gift for His glory and recognition. If we steward it well, it perfectly fulfills His plan to love other people through us and build His Kingdom.

However, in the battleground of kingdoms, we will face attack. The enemy of God seeks to distract, confuse, and keep us from being used in our gifted areas. Knowing this, we can be on guard against the influences of those (including well-intentioned Christ-followers) who would suggest where *they* feel we ought to be used. We should also be aware of becoming enamored with false callings that might look popular or important—even within Christian culture. We are wise to seek discernment which doesn't allow these enticements to influence where we pour out love.

We need to guard against falling prey to the chameleon effect, which influences us to mold ourselves into the models we have seen in believers around us. God has a unique call on our lives, which He places at the core of our beings. Because "many parts form one body" (1 Cor. 12:12, NIV), each of us and the part we play is beautifully unique. Our individual part is hand-picked by God, and it holds purpose and significance in His big-picture plan.

So, may we step in, fully believing that He has a wonderful gift He will reveal clearly to us. He intentionally plans to use us in the Kingdom within our gifting to love others effectively. May we seek clarification on the details until the draw to a particular call to love is so strong we can settle on nothing else, and we are compelled to act in the gift God has placed on us.

We are Empowered to Love

The far-stretching, challenging, beautiful call to love can seem so big. It can present itself as something beyond the reach of human effort or capability. Fleshly thoughts provoke us to follow our own ways, hold back generosity, and promote ourselves. The task of pouring out our lives for love can seem unattainable. Thankfully, God never calls us to love on our own or in our strength. Instead, the secret lies in the gift He gave us: it empowers us to love deeply, authentically, and entirely to lengths we could never imagine.

It all starts in the knowing—believing we are who He says we are and that He equips us with all we need. Trusting His very Spirit in us is a gift from Him that confirms we are living as He desires us to. Just as the mystery that it is "not that we loved God, but that he loved us" (1 John 4:10, NIV), so it is not that we must strive hard enough to abide in His Spirit to love others. Rather, He has already given us life from His life and His very own Spirit to enable us to love.

We must walk confidently in the belief that His Spirit, which He promised as a gift from Jesus, fully lives in us. The Spirit is in us; therefore, we are already producing fruit! We can know and live in the truth that God's Holy Spirit, His very love nature, actively lives and powerfully moves through us. It is a sure gift that His Holy Spirit lives in us. There is no room for unbelief in the matter. Doubting will only interrupt all manner of effectively living in the Lord.

It is in knowing, believing, and trusting that we can truly love. The call is a high-bar challenge, but by His Holy Spirit, He has empowered us to live fiercely, effectively, deeply, and tenderly all at once. We can live out His call on our lives to reach the hearts of people and testify to the wonder of Jesus and His profound outpouring of affection for humanity.

Call Out for the Holy Spirit Who Enables Us to Love

The Holy Spirit empowers us to love, so may we cry out, call out, and accept nothing less than fullness in our desire for love to be poured out over us. Too often, our desire is so small, our expectations far less than what they could be. The One who produces the fruits of the powerful traits which allow us to love, waits for us to ask for help. When we ask, we show the desire of our heart to join with His heart. This is The Father's desire, which is why He has already given the gift of the Holy Spirit to all believers in Jesus. However, receiving the gift of the Holy Spirit often lies in our ability to know and believe the truth of the gift's offering. Once we find ourselves in the position of understanding the offer the Father is extending to us, we become filled with all that we need to know we are loved and to love.

Empowered by the Holy Spirit, we can live out the virtues of "love, joy, peace, patience, kindness, goodness, faithfulness, gentleness, and self-control" (Gal. 5:22–23, NLT). What an expression of love to live these out daily with one another! Jesus shows us we cannot effectively love others without His Holy Spirit. He does not want us to set out in our own strength. His love is so deep that He wants us joined with Him, living in Him, and that connection is what allows us to love others effectively. Abiding with us—us living in Him and Him in us—is His desire. We will be powerless in our attempts to fulfill His will for us to love when we try to do it without Him.

What substantial equipping He provides in ability, intimacy, and Kingdom workings. So, may we genuinely call out for more of the Holy Spirit and all the offerings Jesus extends to us. As we grow, we find joy in joining with the nature of God as He loves others through us. Such intimacy He invites us into! What an honor it is to participate in God's deep labors in people's lives. The most lasting work of building the Kingdom of heaven on earth comes in aligning our will with His. As we accept His rich provision through the Holy Spirit and continually call out for more, He blesses us with the ability to love one another.

Seeing Others as Loved and Valued by God

Loving people becomes easier when we remember the intense, deep value each person holds to God. To have set in our hearts that people bring God tremendous joy solidifies in our minds that they are valuable, that they are His prized possessions. Every one of us is extremely important, simply because we were created in the image of God.

While all of us fail, sin, and are flawed, God sees things differently because of Christ. From Hebrews, we know that "by that one offering he forever made perfect those who are being made holy" (Heb. 10:14, NLT). If we understand that God sees Christ in us, that each person holds His beautiful, wonderful perfection, who are we to see people in any other light?

To believe the potential that every person has to know Christ transforms our perspective. We begin to see the incredible significance in every person. An individual may seem lost in failures, broken, or far from God, but only God knows their real heart. God sees the possibility in each person of all that they can be in Christ. There is a calling for all to come to God, live out their unique capacity, and use their God-given gifts for His glory. God delights over people in all their different, unique ways.

May our Father teach our souls to see ourselves and others in the truth that we as His creation hold tremendous value beyond our understanding. By the Holy Spirit, may we ask and allow Him to transform our perspective entirely. He will build it strong in the knowledge that each person holds intrinsic, beautiful, amazing value in Christ. That delights the heart of our Father. So, we ask Triune God, as people come into our lives, show us Your heart for each one, alter our vision to see them as You do.

Love That Receives and Gives

It should not be surprising that understanding our incredible worth is a prerequisite to believing in others' worth. Who would have known that having a solid foundation in our identity would be one of the most powerful ways that we can begin to love one another? To learn well that we are loved is to know God well—His heart, His nature, and His care. Understanding our identity as deeply beloved sons and daughters of the King of kings grounds us in freedom and fullness of life, and it opens us up to love others with great capacity. After an honest assessment of our strengths and weaknesses, we must find the place where we are accepted and able to receive love. It might take a lot of work, but when we can conclude that we are loveable, not because of us, but because of Him, we will see others around us, in all their complexities, as deeply loveable as well.

On the flip side, if we find ourselves in the undesirable place of criticizing others, we have likely stepped away from the truth of our own identity. Perceiving others in a negative light almost always follows stepping away from seeing ourselves as God does. To again be empowered to see the best in others and love them, we need to go back to Godhead-company.

Father, Son, and Holy Spirit are full of kindness, grace, tenderness, and love. From there, we need to ask how They see us and allow truth to rule.

What a powerful place to be reminded of our true selves and how He who loves us deeply sees us in all the potential of what we are to become in Jesus. Once we have received and have peace in the love received, we need to retain this truth and remind ourselves of it often until our true identity is tangible. Only then are we equipped to authentically love others and see the best in them.

God Uses Us in Big and Small Moments

When we begin to master the incredible attribute that Jesus had of loving others in the moment, it is as though a beautiful work of art has come alive. We begin to see life as a series of divine opportunities to reach out and meet others in realness and love. If only we could learn how to practice such exceptional skills as Jesus had in our conversations! Yet since He is in us and we are in Him, we have the intimate connection to go out clothed in His likeness in our calling to be light to the world, empowered to love one another effectively. In our interactions and relationships, we can have "the same mindset as Christ" (Phil. 2:5, NIV). Directed by His Spirit, we are equipped to invest in people in a meaningful way.

Often, we make loving others complicated. We know loving others is dear to the heart of God, and it is our responsibility as believers. Still, there remains the question: Are we able? Do we bless our Father by the way we love? Are we reaching the goal and fulfilling the command that Jesus presented us? We value our intimacy with God, so of course, we desire to please the One we love and do what He has asked. But maybe we have searched to please Him through an action that looks big, impressive, or important, whereas God often works differently.

Likely, God is looking at the small steps of our day-to-day life. The desire to be used in the Kingdom for "big" things is great because it challenges us to reach a higher calling. Yet He will undoubtedly use our smallest choices and our moment-by-moment decisions to promote His love, to build in us deliberate actions towards the larger plan. Will we show patience, rather than irritation, when frustration comes our way? Will we take a moment of personal space with God to refresh, when we know it is needed? Will we talk with the one who is in need and look past the spoken need to see the unspoken need? Will we own up and take responsibilities seriously that we know are ours? God looks at the small, everyday stuff we do because what we do blesses His heart. So, may we not ever be so busy working towards the big that we miss the day-to-day doings. He loves to be present in those and work through them to show love to His people. The littlest of details matter deeply to God.

Subtle, Simple, Slow: Moment-by-Moment Love

God loves us in the moments—every single moment. What makes the present so rich within the frame of time is that it is here, in the now, that we experience the real and available love of God. Similarly, the present time affords an opportunity for us to actively move in love for others. God designed us to be loved by Him in particular ways through the love of others. We then have to conclude that God uses us to love other people, despite and even in our inadequacies. We are His living body to the world of His beloved creation.

In the now, God meets us, calls us, and reveals the opportunity to be life-giving light simply through our love. "Give your entire attention to what God is doing right now, and don't get worked up about what may or may not happen tomorrow" (Matt. 6:34, MSG). We experience something amazing when we live in the present moment, give Him our full attention, seek how He wants to love others through us, and when we become aware of the current opportunities as they present themselves in our interactions.

Perhaps Jesus didn't want loving others to be so complicated. He wanted it to be a way of life, a form of being—that we would be salt and light, confident that His Spirit is active and moving in us. As we abide in Him, we stay intimately connected with Jesus. His nature of love will naturally flow through us. As we live in and through Him, we allow our lives to testify to the joyful truth that Jesus is alive, and this brings hope to the world around us.

As we set out with joy, with our focus on Him for the long journey, love will come as naturally and effortlessly as breathing. We will be saturated moment by moment in love in His presence, living in intimacy as God's light in the world. As we fix our eyes on Jesus and focus on the present moment, we, in the simplicity of intimacy, shine our perfect God-light in the moment.

True Humility Loves Others Well

Over the years, I confess I have felt quite clever at times. However, at other times, I seem to lose perception of my true worth. It seems I go through periods when I either need to take on more humility or more understanding of my full value. Interestingly, when I position myself in His presence, I find what I can best describe as a peaceful walk of humbleness. When I am well aware that the Father is before me, Jesus beside me, and Holy Spirit embedded into my very being and living through me, there I discover the perfect place. In their utmost company, I find beautiful humility within the greatest company I keep, but I also find an assured and amazing identity. I am a child of the King, but He is the Mighty One to whom my heart bows in complete awe and reverence. When I am aware that I am surrounded by undeniable love, my worth is secure, and peace is certain. Living from this secret place of His presence transforms my thinking about myself, and it affects how I interact with those around me, for it positions me to be ready to love and serve others well.

When we sit in awe, aware we are loved by the Almighty who made the universe by the tip of His finger, we are in the correct position of humility. In that place, we find ourselves incredibly loved, treasured, and valued by One so beyond ourselves. We stand in wonder that we are called children of God by the Maker of this world. Our hearts take on the posture of reverence. We can live authentically. We can unpretentiously allow loving others to become our way of life.

Don't be confused: humility is not a self-disdaining state. It's not about self-dislike, and it's certainly not a form of self-contempt, for none of those are from God. True humility bows in reverence to the Maker of this whole world who places significant value on us and declares us to hold unique worth simply because He created each of us. When we recognize the importance He places on us, we see His respect for and adoration of us as His people. Humility necessitates first extending deep respect to Him, the all-glorious Almighty, and then to others. From the position of humility, we see the self as deeply valuable (as proclaimed by our God), and we see we are called to a better way and a higher standard. This calling leaves no room for foolish, selfish ambition or vain conceit. Instead, it prompts us to live with utmost, sincere honor towards Him and with love for others.

Understanding who we are grants us permission to live differently. In washing the disciples' feet, Jesus beautifully exemplified humility with love. Humility loves well and establishes a deep-hearted intimacy between the Father and us as we do acts of love in His likeness. The trait will be regularly challenged in the flesh. Yet, as we abide in the Holy Spirit, humility genuinely lived out in action is beautiful.

Love Overcomes Darkness

Each moment holds power: it has the ability to leave its imprint for light or darkness. Each moment matters: we must become aware of the ripple effect that our seemingly meaningless actions might have. Each moment can affect the Kingdom.

The effects of individual moments can go unnoticed, therefore making our choices and reactions in those moments seem rather insignificant in the grand scheme of things. But little things like taking time for someone in need, giving a word of encouragement, or reacting with patience when someone is unkind can have significant long-term impacts. Everyday actions, no matter how small, play a substantial role in our endeavors to truly love one another. To give a cup of water, say a kind word, to live graciously toward one another, all the ordinary moments have a powerful effect on those around us. To live out our lives as lights has a magnitude of effects.

We've all experienced unkindness in life, such as being slighted, treated unfairly, taken for granted. Hopefully, we have also interacted with those who are Christ's light and through them we've experienced the simple blessings that kindness brings. The smallest smile and modest, kindest word can significantly impact our souls and lay the groundwork for our next encounter with love. May these experiences fuel our hearts to encourage others and cause us to know that our decisions to act in love have a compound effect.

The unseen rewards of impacting hearts for good energize us to continue seeking to master our character, outlook, and attitudes. The power of God working through us to produce goodness in turn creates more blessings. We need to focus on the prize that glorifies Him and works towards His Kingdom. "Let your light shine before others, that they may see your good deeds and glorify your Father in heaven" (Matt. 5:16, NIV). May we be so incredibly influenced by God's love that we become known as ones who love so deeply that we bring light into every situation. Our actions both big and little can overcome darkness.

The Ripple Effect of Judging

To love others effectively, we need to see the best and believe the best of them. Our limitations to fully understanding another person's situation, restrictions, and personal struggles are huge. Our best bet to be freed from wrong thinking that hinders us from loving others well is to make the effort to see people through the perspective of God's love, His value, and joy over them.

This perspective becomes especially important with the hard-to-love people in our lives. We need to win victory over negative thoughts. Perhaps we harbor a subtle slander, or worse, we accuse them before God. As we've looked at previously, these thoughts are likely to invade our perspective when we haven't spent time with the beautiful Triune who extends the deepest of love to us. When we fail to see ourselves through the lens of the best, we put others down, hoping to build ourselves up.

We need to stand firm in the loving embrace of the Holy One, secure in our intimacy with God, where no need to put others down exists. God's love is enough to lead our hearts to freedom from judging others. The strange thing is that when we judge others, we heap judgment on ourselves—just as Jesus said (see Matt. 7:1). When we judge others, we set a high bar of standards that we unconsciously know we cannot meet. We will fall short. In judging others, we condemn ourselves.

May God free our hearts from these traps, and may we rest in the depth of His love to gain victory over our thoughts towards others. Rather than looking for opportunities to judge others, may we set ourselves instead on these goals: "Love your neighbor as yourself" (Mark 12:31, NIV); "Be kind and compassionate to one another, forgiving each other" (Eph. 4:32, NIV). May we fix our hearts with a determination to see the personhood, fullness, and value others hold in Jesus Christ.

Escaping Comparison

Another menace hinders our relationship with God when we are not secure in His love. It affects our ability to love one another: it's the hazard of living a life of comparison. In the Bible, we find a sin called *coveting* can often come from comparison: we compare our lives to others and want what they have. Perhaps most dangerous, in our culture, the sin can come out as a desire *to be coveted*. Successes, possessions, and positions are placed on display to compare, and they act as a lure into wishing one's own life looked different than their reality. We see this today in the struggles many people have. What starts as innocently sharing one's life in a public way can become a place of measuring achievements and a trap of comparison. It is a far place from Jesus' example of love, which was to love others with our all— even our very own lives. He warned us: "Beware of covetousness, for one's life does not consist in the abundance of the things he possesses" (Luke 12:15, NKJV).

We need to escape our preoccupation with the need to feel we are important and significant to others. Instead, our focus should be placed on the audience of One. This is the place where we can live free from the damaging comparison habit. There are two toxic outcomes that comparison can produce: pride and envy. What a polar opposite to love it is, living in a place that is "conceited, provoking and envying each other" (Gal. 5:25–26, NIV). Comparison robs us of enjoying our own blessings. It can make us feel shame over what others have that we do not.

We need to master the art of living free from comparison. We must find a place of living in contentment and satisfaction in where the Lord has placed us, trusting His promise of working for our good in our unique circumstances. Let us strive to excel at living a life free from comparison. As we fix our eyes on God, He allows us to experience pleasure in the gifts of love that come straight from His hand. We know that we all face hardships, challenges, and struggles, but we also know we all receive good from Our loving God.

Therefore, may we "pay careful attention to [our] own work, for then [we] will get the satisfaction of a job well done, and [we] won't need to compare [ourselves] to anyone else" (Gal. 6:4, NLT). Motivated by love from our audience of One, may we live loving others well, free from all damage of comparison.

God Loves the World

As we love as He loves, we love our world well. May we guard our perception of truth and know that God loves not only us, our church, our denomination, and Christians, but the entirety of our world. Our beloved Lord "gave his life to purchase freedom for everyone" (1 Tim. 2:5–6, NLT). God loves when our hearts are in full awareness of how far His love stretches and when we have a solid understanding that Jesus is "the Savior of all people" (1 Tim. 4:10, NIV). If there is any confusion about how immense the love of God is and how He desires us to expand the love of our hearts, we read that "He himself is the sacrifice that atones for our sins—and not only our sins but the sins of all the world" (1 John 2:2, NLT).

In this world full of unbelief, worship of different gods, and hostility towards God, it may seem strange to picture this God of love working in a particular individual's life. Yet we know from Paul's life that God works in the most unexpected of hearts for redemption. Is anything impossible for God?

As believers of truth, being sure of what we hope for can lead to a trap of pride in our hearts to think that something of us has found the truth; we can forget that it was God who brought us by His hand to our faith. In His intimate love and mercy, God saved us. His heart deeply desires reconciliation with each individual created in His very own image.

May we live lives of love for God, aware of His deep love for each created individual. Every person holds deep value: all are created in God's image. "For the grace of God has appeared that offers salvation to all people" (Titus 2:11, NIV). Our call is to live in love to remind people of our God. He intensely loves them and invites them to incredible favor, simply because He *is* their Creator.

The Honor of the Call to Love

The love we find in the heart of Paul is amazing, like that of no other individual. He said he "would be willing to be forever cursed—cut off from Christ!—if that would save [his people]" (Rom. 9:3, NLT).

We, too, have love. We know our God-given role as God's co-workers and the great commission Jesus left us. Yet love seems difficult at times. It can feel as if the responsibility is too big, this idea that we share in the call to help others understand the mystery of Christ. If we have won the battle to trust and intimately know Jesus ourselves, we are already equipped to confront the biggest fight. We are enabled to be faithful ambassadors for Christ in the world. This is not a call of burden. It's a blessing to be part of the war on the side of those who free captives, release prisoners from dungeons, open eyes of the blind, and demonstrate His righteousness to the nations (see Isa. 42:6–7).

The enemy would love to make us weary, distract us, burden us, and convince us that the call to love is too big. So we must intentionally practice the basics of our relationship, such as basking in His presence and sitting at His feet, before we go out and do the good work. We need to listen for direction from the Holy Spirit about where God is asking us to join Him and not ever go out on our own, un-abiding. In our time with Triune God, we are empowered and enabled to go out and do all we are called to do. When we are in their company, we become brave and determined to stand passionately in the name of Jesus against all battles. From there, we are ready to shine out light as ones living in faith and truth so that the whole world can see the extent of Jesus' offering and love.

How incredible that in Triune God's company, we are prepared and made ready to love one another and to give of ourselves wholeheartedly!

Section 9:

INTIMACY'S INVITATION
TO
PEACE

He who is full of peace offers us the gift of living in His likeness in His peace. Far above anything the world could offer, and much deeper than any temporal thing, God's peace comes as we rest in the promise of the calm serenity of living for Him and with Him, at all times and forever.

Peace I leave with you; my peace I give you.

~ John 14:27 (NIV)

So I greet you with the great words, grace and peace! We know the meaning of those words because Jesus Christ rescued us… God's plan is that we all experience that rescue. Glory to God forever!

~ Gal. 1:3–5 (MSG)

The Offer and Order of Peace

Triune God loves us perfectly and offers the best of gifts. They present value beyond any earthly treasure, meeting deep, often hidden needs of our heart. The irony is that we often have trouble accepting His gifts. Yet to live in the fullness of life our Beloved offers, we must accept them. Among the generous, extravagant gifts is the personal peace of God. God's peace is so very contrary to the pace, focus, and ways of this world. It provides pure restoration to our souls. In His peace, there is no place for a troubled mind or heart. This peace holds rightness and righteousness. It brings calm, quietness, and deep rest.

Living in peace may in all actuality seem so far from our present reality, yet this is one of His gifts extended to us through the Holy Spirit. He is our Advocate, sent by the Father, to remind us of all truths and teach us the way of peace (see John 14:25-27a; John 16:13). In the Triune's embrace, we find a stillness, confidence, unity, and intimacy that empowers. We need to go, bask, and sit within His presence, allowing it to fill our souls until we can go out and stand within that calm—no matter what outside circumstances suggest.

Interestingly, Jesus didn't give us the option to live in anything but peace. He said, "Do not let your hearts be troubled and do not be afraid" (John 14:27b, NIV). So, we call out to the Holy Spirit, whose very presence is peace, to fill us with His fruit of peace so that we can live in the beautiful will of our Beloved. We are promised a forever togetherness with Jesus, an embedding of the Holy Spirit into our very being, and that the Father will care for us. Within Him, there is no aloneness, apartness, or abandonment, and therefore, there is peace. Our Beloved gives the intimate gift of His peace through His incredible life-giving presence.

Protect and Fight for Peace

It is the very nature of God to be at peace! The company the Trinity shares is full of peace. Perhaps their peace rests in the perfect connectedness they share. Without effort on their part, they never lack peace. If we share in their good company and are clothed in their likeness, why don't we take our peace more seriously? If someone were to come and threaten to steal or destroy something or someone of value to us, we would put up a good fight. Yet, by the way we allow chaos, busyness, and restlessness to toss us around and prevent us from living in tranquility, one would hardly know we value peace. If we were to examine its value under a heavenly lens, we would never allow the negativity, complaining, and commotion in our lives. Stillness, paring back, meditating on God's truth, and working towards calm would become our lifestyle of choice. We would obey the Triune's direction: "Do not let your hearts be troubled."

Wouldn't it be great if we refused to excuse life patterns that prevent us from sharing in His fruit, His nature, His likeness? They would simply not be an option for us. Instead, we would take time to carefully consider the source of any restlessness and then deal with it until it lined up with His offer of peace. When God sees we are serious about pursuing peace, He extends His hand, offering us the strength and ability to receive peace beyond imagination. When we ask, a prayer for peace is a prayer He is delighted to answer. No matter what our life circumstances are, He wants us close, under

His protection. The Lord delights to have us align ourselves in His victory for this treasure of His peace, which in turn leads us closer to Him.

Peaceful Perspective

The peace of God holds incredible potential for altering our perspective. It allows us to see Him, ourselves, and our lives through His God-lens, whereas apart from the influence of peace, our view is distorted. Under His truth-perception, we can see clearly who we truly are, what our identity is, and what our capabilities are.

Consider, for instance, our perception of our strength. Due to our circumstances, we may have inaccurate thinking patterns or be prone to the enemy's suggestions. Under their influence, we then believe we are weak and frail. Yet, our Lord sees us in Jesus. Therefore, despite our feelings, we are valuable, stable, and strong. It's guaranteed: if we take the time to ask His thoughts on the matter, He delights to show us how much strength He sees in us. We are in Him, and His strength never fails. His says we can do all things through Christ who strengthens us (Phil. 4:13) and that nothing is impossible for those who believe (Mark 9:23).

As Peter did, Jesus knows when we are with Him, we can walk on water. We need to trust Him and step out to see His reality unfold in whatever personal spiritual waters He calls us to. We first simply step out. Then, with diligence, we keep our eyes fixed on Him, continuing to trust Him with our minds at peace. As the Holy Spirit dwells and lives in us, we have Jesus living through us. The intimacy we find in them enables us to face all possibilities with calmness, sureness, and confidence. In our experiences of brokenness, weakness, and hurt, we have the promise of His perfect mending, strengthening, and healing. We have His pledge of their availability. He will work through undesirable circumstances for good.

Our "yes" to intimacy's invitation to enter the deepest place of peace begins our development in seeing life and all that comes at us from a very different perspective from how we once thought. Our "yes" brings His perspective to all sorts of areas of our reality, including our strength in Him.

This view mends our broken identities to transform us to His intended creation under His incredible peace.

Divine Power to Please Him

In my Introduction, I say I have been blessed to experience intimacy with God. I am so thankful and humbled. But I also see the responsibility that comes with that intimacy. "When someone has been given much, much will be required" (Luke 12:48, NLT). I often feel like I should be living out a better walk with the Lord with all that I have been given. The problem is that even though I know God to be real and full of love, and I want to do my best for Him, I still fail. Independence and sin still get into my life. It is frustrating when I know I've been given much and know better. What a blessing of peace to find in scripture that in everything, every area of my life, Triune God takes care of it, including my relationship and journey with Him. In divine power, I can stand in the promise that in knowing our Lord intimately, I have the assurance of His divine intervention. God will direct me to a life that will please Him, and He will enable me to live out all that is required.

How good God truly is! He takes care of every area of our lives, including our walk with Him and our spirituality. Our journey, our spiritual walk, our very relationship with Him can be confusing at times because it can seem to depend on our best efforts, focused will, and discipline. Yet, even here, God blesses us with the deepest peace in explaining He is the One who is in control of our journey, and He is happy to work it to perfection.

> *His divine power has given us everything we need for a godly life through our knowledge of him who called us by his own glory and goodness.*
>
> ~ 2 Pet. 1:3 (NIV)

Joining with Jesus and His promises and experiencing intimacy with God is all we need to live the full, godly life that is already ours in Him. Self-striving can cease, and the fear of not being enough can be declared false.

We have permission to lay at his feet any struggle that robs our rest. God loves to show us His goodness is so great that He has taken care of every area of our life, including our relationship and journey with Him.

Is this not always the case, God reminding us of His perfect goodness and power over every situation in our lives? We only need to embrace His Spirit and stand in trust in Him—no room for apartness, only space for complete, intimate interdependence. Living for the Kingdom, faithfulness to the call, growing to our full potential—all are promises straight from the hands of our Beloved. He is committed to us and provides all the help we need, right at our fingertips.

So, may we accept the invitation to something greater than we have been living. Boldly confessing and turning away from independence, self-sufficiency, and self-effort, may we run into the welcoming, mighty arms of God. We can then stand in His promises. We are assured the divine intervention and power we need to direct us to the life that will most please Him.

Divine Direction

We have a mighty Father who promises to navigate our journeys. The peace that comes from following His direction should never go unrecognized. The Father's invitation comes with exciting revelation of our purpose in the Kingdom! How incredible it is that we are invited into His lasting, eternal work, that we join with the Creator of the world, our Father God. Yet within the exhilarating knowledge that we have such a significant role, we have incredible peace. He specifically and intentionally lays down the precise path where He wants to use us.

If we have not yet found that path, may we ask like a child, with persistence, until our Father answers. We do not need to be discouraged if we don't yet know exactly where He is calling because He is at work in every circumstance of our lives. He continually shapes us to perfection for His future call. This sculpting has been in motion from the beginning. God takes our circumstances, challenges, strengths, interests, and all the billions of wonderfully unique ways He has made us and brings them all together for His will.

Our Designer placed our heart's passion in us. The Holy Spirit has given us our gifts, and Jesus has modeled how to be faithful to all the Father's asking and how to bring love into every action. We are invited as beloved children, as co-workers, to intimately join with the always-producing Triune God. The Holy Spirit promises direction for every step of the way, and as we abide in Him, He will give us success in our tasks.

> *I will guide you along the best pathway for your life. I will advise you and watch over you.*
>
> ~ *Psalm 32:8 (NLT)*

Knowing that He directs our life path, our job is relatively simple: we need to receive His peace and follow Him.

The "Not Yet" Season

Perhaps we have earnestly sought God's direction and calling and feel like He has been silent on the matter. Although we are passionate to know our call, the path seems unclear. In this state, peace may be absent, and we will likely have a sense of restlessness over our unanswered prayer. In these times, we can lay our frustrations before God and focus on obedience to those things we already know are our responsibility as Christians.

In the Kingdom, we are clothed in His likeness; we are light and fruit bearers. That we desire to know His specific calling for us? That in itself is a testimony of the Holy Spirit's workings. Stepping into trusting His timing and direction is essential. We can stand in assurance that each of us at some point is given a gift to glorify the Father. His ways are deep and not always understood immediately. May we be confidently resolute in the knowledge that we live for His glory, His Kingdom. We are in relationship with the Almighty Triune God, and He reveals all things in perfect timing. May we not give way to the great accuser's lies and allow seemingly unfruitful periods to erode our deep relational roots with the Father. Instead, we ask Holy Spirit to open our eyes to see all the ways He is already working in us and through us. As He opens our eyes, we will begin to see the revealing of His calling where our passion and talents lay.

Until the call is clear, we know God always desires more one-on-one time with us. In that time, we can find encouragement. In that place, we build on our relationship with the Triune. We press in, we listen, and ask for more. As we abide, we are blessed. Our intimate relationship grows until clarity comes with such power that the direction God has called us to is undeniable. Peace will flood our hearts as we wait upon the Lord, hopeful in all the ways He is using our lives and trusting the promised gift.

Peace in Precision

There comes the point in every believer's walk where there is a still deeper offer of peace. When we know our specific gifts and calling, something extraordinary settles in our hearts. There is peace in the knowledge that as believers, we are "like living stones...being built up as a spiritual house" (1 Pet. 2:5, ESV). We are each a significant living stone in this incredible building. We hold value in, are essential to, and have a specific purpose for the Kingdom.

The church is a spiritual house. In it, we have a particular call on our lives. We should place high importance on discovering this call. It is the Father's delight that we search out this mystery: "It is the glory of God to conceal a matter; to search out a matter is the glory of kings" (Prov. 25:2, NIV). The unfolding of the mystery of God's call on our life can be found in our intimate connection with Him. The Father leads us to focus on His will for our lives. He reveals His secret, and God's joy is full. He delights in giving us good gifts. How much greater is His joy as He gives us the specific call on our life for joining in the Kingdom work?

Until then, while we may show great love for others, we must ask what mountains He wants us to move. What part should we play in the Kingdom equation? There are seed planters, growers, harvesters, and more: we all have a unique, God-given spiritual gift. As our calling becomes more defined, our attempts to reach the world can become less broad and more focused. To make a substantial impact, the more we concentrate on our precise, God-given role, the better. That is what He equips us for, and that is where we will be most effective.

What an incredible breakthrough it is when we hear a crystal-clear voice in the quietness and stillness where we listen. It is Triune's delight to reveal His specific plan to us. In that incredible place, restful peace comes to us when we join their beautiful, detailed, intrinsic asking, blessing us precision that brings peace!

Restlessness: Love's Response When We Don't Live Out Our Gift

When our calling from God is clear, but we fail to obey, we lose our peace. Jonah is the perfect example of one whose peace was devastated when he chose to ignore God's direction. The Lord gave Jonah an important message to deliver to the Ninevites. However, Jonah got up and went in the opposite direction, attempting to escape the Lord and His request. His choice led him to some very uncomfortable places.

He landed in the stomach of a large fish. These are Jonah's words:

> *From deep in the realm of the dead I called for help, and you listened to my cry. You hurled me into the depths, into the very heart of the seas.*
>
> ~ *Jon. 2:2–3 (NIV)*

If we neglect God's specific call or gifting, we will feel the weight of God on us as heavy as it was on Jonah. Ignoring a calling undermines the potential that the Triune has lovingly lavished on us. However, in His supreme goodness, God will bless us with deep restlessness. Motivated by love, the Father uses the stark opposite of peace to nudge us to stay on track with His best plan.

Walking in obedience to the call blesses us with incredible peace, but that flooding of peace will disperse if we question the call, "for God's gifts and his call are irrevocable" (Rom. 11:29, NIV). There is no room for questioning. Just as Jesus, salvation, and the Holy Spirit were freely given, our calling is set aside as holy and sacred. Our loving Lord solidifies our calling like a promise. No matter what, the call remains, even if we fail. No matter what, we need to obey, even if we don't feel we are gifted for the call. The Lord safeguards what He requires. His wisdom, knowledge, and understanding of our abilities are greater than our own.

So, even if we take only small steps to begin, may we move forward in faithfulness. He will then trust us with more. With determination, may we stand in faith in our callings. We can ask for strength, help, and further revelation each step of the way. We can trust we will bear fruit. We are here to testify to His name in little and big workings. We can lean on the promise that He is working out His perfect plan and purpose in our lives.

His Request Comes with His Power

Not only are we invited into the wondrous Kingdom workings of God, but we are also, in fact, promised power from on high. For with God, all things are possible! Paradoxically, our natural human resistance can assure us of His call. Why? God takes joy in asking us to step out of our comfort zones and do things we find difficult. To do them, we have to trust Him. Therefore, the risks we take can draw us closer to Him, as we have to rely on Him in the seemingly impossible.

In response to His request, we may find ourselves fearful, yet it is His joy to cast fear out and replace it with love. It is altogether His working, His power, His Kingdom, His glory. We are not responsible for the outcome, only for joining in intimate relationship and stepping out in obedience to His lead. After obeying God in His asking, no matter how the circumstances may look, we can rest assured that He in His power can accomplish exactly what He desires through us.

> *You will always harvest what you plant... Those who live to please the Spirit will harvest everlasting life from the Spirit. So let's not get tired of doing what is good. At just the right time we will reap a harvest of blessing if we don't give up.*
>
> ~ Gal. 6:7–9 (NLT)

In his journey to spread the truth of Jesus, even the apostle Paul felt utterly inadequate to present the message. He was scared to death, yet the message was successful: "God's Spirit and God's power did it" (1 Cor. 2:4, MSG). God spoke through Paul to reach hearts and accomplish the work.

God empowered Paul to speak the truth, and God empowered the people to accept it and believe. The people responded not to Paul but to God's power.

Even given God's most challenging requests, we can have incredible peace because His great power works through Holy Spirit within us. This is a peace that produces joy as we join Triune God, who always accomplishes what they set out to do.

Life's Love Mission

It is by now no secret that God's highest priority is intimacy. For in all His asking, we are told we can do the most amazing things—physically, mentally, spiritually—but if we lack love, we are nothing. Our Father's overriding stance in all matters is love, and we find incredible peace as we share in the Kingdom's overall mission to love and treasure God and others.

The scriptures say in the end times people will be "lovers of themselves" (2 Tim. 3:2, NIV). This is contrary to the call to love. It is not a good love for oneself, in which one correctly sees his or her value to God. Instead, it's a love for self at the expense of others' well-being. Surely every generation comes up against those who don't value others and live with an unhealthy and damaging love of self. Likely, this is why Jesus treasured love so profoundly, for it magnifies something opposite from the world who tries to live without Him.

When we love, that love has power. We can argue with people, present convincing, logical arguments, do miracles, and speak wonders, but it is genuine, authentic, deep love that can actually move mountains and open space for others to find the invitation to accept the love of Jesus. By sharing love, we extend our experience with the Triune to others, and we invite them to this life-giving water for the soul. Love is our life mission, above even our gifting or call. It keeps us anchored in the deepest peace because it's the underlay of all His asking.

How crucial it is for us to come into the loving company of Triune God, who kindly and graciously fills us so we can be faithful to the highest calling on our lives: *to love*. He will teach us the way of love as He fills us with His love.

This is peace: to live a life of love.

God as Our Prize

In all our ambitions and all our God-given passions, may our love for Triune God remain our highest goal. It is impossible to experience peace when we step away from intimate joining with the Father. Unfortunately, there is a fine line between our heart's loyal motive to stay on task in following God and our work itself. We need to know if our efforts are motivated by Kingdom building or if the worldly goal to achieve something has become our drive. It's so very important to stick close to God.

> *I am the vine; you are the branches. If you remain in me and I in you, you will bear much fruit; apart from me, you can do nothing.*
>
> ~ *John 15:5 (NIV)*

May we keep our eyes on the prize of dearly pleasing the One we love. Wherever our efforts are focused, may our heart's desire be sealed for an increasing measure of growth in our love relationship with Triune God. Through relational love for God, our lives and the Kingdom move forward. Restlessness will come if we get off track. Even subtle shifts, such as if our focus begins favoring our selves and our capabilities, can hinder our fruit-bearing ability.

Yet when we are established in God's love for us and in our love and commitment for Him, we can move mountains. The mountains, however, need to be God's mountains, not our own. Through time and connection with Him, we can listen to God to figure out what these mountains are.

We have permission to ask God to purify our affection for Him alone. He would love to meet us in that request. It is well worth taking the time to analyze what we are pursuing in Kingdom life and to test whether our hearts remain on track. No distractions are allowed. There can be no self-ambition and no recognition-seeking. No "me-kingdom" can be permitted at the root of our pursuit. Instead, may we have only stable peace which results from our sealed focus on intimacy with God.

New Law, New Peace, New Invitation

How wonderful when we embrace with excitement the grand invitation to join our Father in His beautiful Kingdom work, where the old has gone, and the new has most surely come. We are invited into living the new covenant in Jesus. The curtain was torn in two, and we are invited into the most profound God-dwelling relationship. In the freedom of the new covenant, we find the peace of God.

May we guard against returning to old ways. There is no longer the pressure of *dos* and *don'ts*, for it is our joy to obey. All of the law of heaviness is lifted. If we were to return to striving in our own strength, we would find the opposite of peace. Attempts to reach perfection will only frustrate us. On our own, perfection is unattainable. Thankfully, our sweet Jesus came to earth to bring freedom, relationship, acceptance, and salvation. New law, new peace, new invitation.

In turn, we strive to live a good life under His Spirit as a thanksgiving offering for all He has done for us. He does not want us to allow the enemy to rob us of our prized freedom and peace: after all, He died for it. How common for us His children to take on so much we have little to no space for our beloved God. Love, peace, joy, and patience are no ordinary virtues to be slighted or ignored. Rather they are benchmarks that help us evaluate which covenant we are living in.

If restlessness, busyness, chaos, and impatience are our norm, then we have to ask: Are we in the place God wants us? The treasured fruits of the Spirit are just that—fruits our lives need to bear. These fruits prepare us to be the people of heavenly places and positions we will hold. Considering all the blessings of the new covenant, let us set out to embrace the generous invitation to join the Father in the place where peace reigns.

This is the divine path of beautiful, intimate peace: His way, His strength, His Holy Spirit active and alive, dwelling in us.

Marking Moments of Genuine Peace

It's vital for us to recognize the distinct places where we experience God's greatest peace—the places where encounters with the Divine feel intensely thick around us. Because we are uniquely created, these places will likely be individualized to each of us, and they will change throughout the seasons. Taking time to reflect on our day can help us recognize the moments or places when we felt at peace.

Conscious awareness of those moments can help us gain perspective regarding where we genuinely encounter God. We will often say we meet Him in our quiet times, in reading scripture, or in prayer, and yet maybe we need to look beyond the routine to find the unexpected moments relational connection with God occurred. For instance, worship creates a place like no other where connection can provide a sense of literal presence at His feet. Ironically, the most authentic connection will not likely come from studying the Word or reading a devotional. It will simply come in sitting with God and talking and listening. We will encounter new joys as we further unravel the mystery of His presence.

Perhaps a genuine encounter occurred when we shared our day with Him like we would with a friend. It may come in a moment when we are suddenly aware He is sitting by our side. It may come in reading His Word: a verse may stand out as if it were a personal love letter directly addressed to us. The Lord loves companionship with us, His created. This has always been His desire. Spiritual disciplines can be beneficial, for sure, but we can fall into the trap of doing rituals or seeking knowledge above being in His presence.

Almighty God is not one bit ordinary. The realness of His presence is always extraordinary when we engage with His incredible love. May that purest of love offered to us daily bring the unexplainable peace of His presence that wraps around us and is sealed on our hearts.

The Reality of Our Identity

We have a high bar set for us as followers of Jesus. Yet we "have been given... exceedingly great and precious promises, that through these [we] may be partakers of the divine nature" (2 Pet. 1:4, NKJV). We know that apart from Him, we can do nothing, yet joined with Him, anything is possible. If we could only clearly see how we are clothed in His likeness and bear His image!

The bar is set high for a significant reason. With the incredible challenge before us, we can't go out independently. When we come to the end of ourselves and our abilities, our independence having failed us, there is more space for God to work in our lives. This keeps us humble.

Who knew I was in an identity crisis? I had memorized, meditated, and even taught these truths to others. But the revelation Jesus gave that I am clothed in His likeness was incredible. It brought the truth I knew in my mind into my heart. The strength I knew I didn't have on my own, the kindness I felt I failed to show, the battles I wasn't sure I could win, I realized that in being completely connected to God and joined with His Spirit, I could do it, and in many ways I already did.

His mighty Spirit in me, His strength, His nature makes it all possible. The bar is set high for a significant reason. No independence is allowed: instead, what is required is a humble, intimate connection with God. He does the heavy lifting. His promise that I am a "partaker of the divine nature" made my identity solid. And that is who we are - we are one with Him in spirit.

Interestingly, God asks us to be perfect as He is perfect (Matt. 5:48). Perhaps at first, this will seem impossible. However, He also says that everything we do can be done in His strength. To clarify: He does not ask us to do the impossible, the perfect, on our own. It is His mighty Spirit in us, His strength, His nature that makes perfection possible. He does the heavy lifting to establish us into what He wants us to be.

However, we have to live in the peace of understanding and trusting who we are in Christ. If we can reach the place of believing the incredible promise that we are "partakers of the divine nature," our identity becomes solid. We know who we are, and we believe in the Holy Spirit's presence and power upon our lives to bring the deepest peace. There, we find the place of the outpouring of "grace and peace multiplied" (2 Pet. 1:2, NKJV). God transforms our perception so we can remember and recognize the victory He has already brought into our lives. In that, He calls us ones who are joined with Him and one with Him in spirit.

The person who is joined to the Lord is one spirit with him.

~*1 Cor. 6:17 (NLT)*

The Kingdom of God is Now

The peace of God is present in this simple statement: "The kingdom of heaven is at hand" (Matt. 4:17, KJV). His Kingdom has already come in us at the moment we placed our hearts' loyalty in Jesus. As we live filled by the Holy Spirit, we find His Kingdom indeed dwells in us and through us. With this in mind, our perspective on eternal matters changes. If it is heaven we long for, in that there we will be face-to-face with our best friend, the King of kings, we are offered a powerful version of that incredible closeness now. By His Spirit, we have Him living in us. This allows us to call upon God in the present, rather than just wait for heaven. Daily, we anticipate how He will have us join Him to bring open heaven to earth!

Within our waiting, there is no access for the enemy to render us un-useful. For our eyes are set on Jesus, and we believe in our calling for the here and now. It's unfortunate when we get caught up in overthinking the times and are overly concerned with the end. If we agree with the enemy's suggestions of what we should fear rather than resting in God in love, we risk placing ourselves in the traps of anxious thinking patterns, of independence and self-protectiveness. As children of the King, there is no room for this thinking, no benefit to its work. Instead, may we be found faithfully waiting on our Lord with great expectation, like the virgins—oil ready in their lamps —who were prepared to meet the bridegroom (see Matt. 25:1–13). May we be found to have great anticipation for the arrival of our King! We have great peace in the promise that we have Almighty God who is for us always, even in the end! Therefore, may we live with deep-rooted peace in our hearts, joining Him, trusting Him, and experiencing power in the truth of Jesus' love and a Holy Spirit sound-mindedness.

With our hearts set on the Kingdom of God *now*, in pursuit of moving this world closer to the awesomeness of heaven, we find peace.

Standing Faithfully in the Promises

To be filled with peace requires us to take time to remember the promises so that we can live in the favor and blessings of His offerings.

Consider the promise in Psalm 91: we will live in His shelter and rest in the Almighty's shadow. This is a picture of intimately close dwelling, peace, protection, and provision. We are invited into His very presence. It is up to us to believe and accept the offer.

God promises to take all our burdens so that we don't have to carry their weight. "Cast your cares on the LORD, and he will sustain you" (Psalm 55:22, NIV). Yet His peace only comes through our deliberate practice of taking proper time with Jesus. In that time, we can surrender the heavy load we carry.

God promises we can be filled with peace that "surpasses all understanding" (Phil. 4:7, NKJV). To find and stand in faith for that peace, the reality of the Triune's Presence in our life has to be alive in us. Intimacy is vital. Spending time—real time—simply being in the Almighty's presence, that is the secret.

To stand in peace and believe His promises, we need to be convinced of His reality. It takes a genuine encounter with our beloved Triune God to believe in His existence, and it takes earnest searching to find His presence where peace dwells. We are incredibly blessed that He extends such rich promises, peace, and His presence to us. If we genuinely come to Him, we will receive much, for He is the good Shepherd of our souls. He loves when we depend on Him to do all that He does and give all that He offers. He feels blessed when we trust Him to lead us spiritually.

When we come to Him seeking genuine connection, He teaches us. When we bask in His dwelling and receive His promises, He equips us with the most profound peace.

Joined in Purpose

God is peaceful. His intimacy runs deep. He longs for us to join Him in the peace that rests in hearts filled with passion for His Kingdom. The Kingdom of God was Jesus' focus, as its application brings peace, joy, and Spirit-filled living. As we align our souls with these gifts and take in love, peace surrounds us. When we put our efforts into what truly matters, the Eternal One floods us with peace. When He returns, may Jesus, our Master, be so pleased to find us ready, working as a joined body of believers, committed to His absolute glory and praise. "The real believers are the ones the Spirit of God leads to work away at this ministry, filling the air with Christ's praise as we do it" (Phil. 3:3, MSG).

We never have to shoulder responsibility on our own. We are favored within a love relationship as co-workers to build the Kingdom, to produce fruit. We are blessed to live in the beloved Triune's peaceful company with the Almighty. Mundane or ordinary living is not for us; each day is a gift. All of us have a purpose-filled call, and we are promised power from on high in it. There simply is no room for boredom. There are authorities in the unseen world to battle. We are called to carry the scent of Jesus into every situation and live a fruitful life.

So, may we show joy in our calling as co-workers. May we be filled with excitement, leaving no room for anything other than living with our eyes open "wide in wonder and belief" (Matt. 6:22, MSG), always asking Him for greater revelation. The intimate, pursuing love of our God is nothing short of amazing. Sharing in His Kingdom work solidifies the personal call on our lives and blesses us with a meaningful life, which in turn brings layer upon layer of peace.

Section 10:

GUARDIANS

OF

INTIMACY

In our pursuit of God, He calls us to guard the sacred gem of intimacy. In response, the enemy works overtime to interfere. Because intimacy with God powerfully moves us into all His will, the deceiver continually challenges the relationship. But Jesus came to destroy the enemy's work (see 1 John 3:8). With this truth in mind, may we do all we can do to stand, join in the battle, and be wise guards of intimacy.

> *Truth, righteousness, peace, faith, and salvation are more than words. Learn how to apply them. You'll need them throughout your life. God's Word is an indispensable weapon.*
>
> *~ Eph. 6:14–17 (MSG)*

> *They have conquered him by the blood of the Lamb and by the word of their testimony, for they loved not their lives even unto death.*
>
> *~ Rev. 12:11 (ESV)*

Guards of the Most-High Treasure

Once we have established in our hearts that we possess the treasure of intimacy with God, how do we safeguard it? How do we step up to be warriors for the Kingdom? Likely we will start by standing against things that disrupt our relationship and, in turn, compromise all other divine workings.

If the enemy can have us see our love relationship with God as something that is negotiable, then he reaches a critical foundation for all else that follows. Therefore, we must intentionally strengthen our resolve to be all we can be for the One we love and who calls us. We must learn to be aware of anything that interrupts our intimate relationship with the Triune God. There are lies we must identify, and we must ensure that truth is solidly established in our souls. Assured victory is the promise, for the ultimate battle has already been won. The last chapter is complete.

For everything in between, we have reassurance that the very One who created the universe loves us. He is the Almighty by our side and nothing can stop Him. The Lord longs for us to remain close to Him so that we continually grow stronger in love. He constantly works in us to protect our treasured intimate relationship. So, may we guard our hearts and our time with Him to tend to our souls. Then the foundation of truth in us can become healthy, our love certain, and the time we have spent with Triune will be evident. Our lives will naturally display the fruits of the Spirit. How wonderful to find ourselves standing in this hopeful place.

> *We have it all together with God because of our Master Jesus. And that's not all: We throw open our doors to God and discover at the same moment that he has already thrown open his door to us. We find ourselves standing where we always hoped we might stand—out in the wide-open spaces of God's grace and glory, standing tall and shouting our praise.*
>
> ~ *Rom. 5:1–2 (MSG)*

With this discovery, we will stand guard over the greatest treasure we share in the absolute best of company with our God. We will fight anything that gets in our way!

God Pursues Those Who Deny Him

God loves a tender heart that responds to His generous offerings. The one who knows Him believes the truths He sets out and stands in agreement, and understands the principles of how He presents life, humankind, and relationship with Him. On the flip side, God also loves the heart that says, "I don't need God. I can do it on my own, and I want my own way."

Even this one was created in His image! Triune God is patient with those influenced by worldly perspectives. He knows their hearts have not yet accepted the power of the truth and what He offers. What comes across as rejection of God, harsh sin, and at times even spiteful or vindictive behavior, Jesus says, "Forgive them, for they do not know what they are doing" (Luke 23:34, NIV). God remains patient even when the rebellious heart's posture (not knowing God, living in sin, and rejecting Him) goes against everything God requires for intimate connection. The Triune's love for us is even more powerful than any rejection of Him. In His mighty love, He will go after the lost one every time (see Matt. 18:14). He will stop at nothing. He remains persistent in drawing people to His profound love.

By its nature, sin holds the natural consequence of separation from Holy God. The freedom Jesus bought on the cross is the bridge back to the relationship. His desire is, of course, that we would not allow the love of the world to take hold of us, for it competes against the truest and richest of love offerings. "If anyone loves the world, love for the Father is not in them" (1 John 2:15, NIV).

As guards of the truth, may we be assured that pursuing Him is worth it all, above any worldly way. How wonderful when we become solid in the truth that His love runs deep in us for each person. We can guard the intimacy we've experienced by remembering His love extends out to reach every heart.

Battle Sin, Then Accusations

We all sin: it is part of our inherited, Adamic potential. Sin separates us from God, yet in Christ, we are reconciled by His love and sacrifice. Our Jesus-inheritance sets us free and provides perfect righteousness within our humanness.

> *Through Christ Jesus the law of the Spirit who gives life has set you free from the law of sin and death.*
>
> ~ *Rom. 8:2 (NIV)*

So, if we said *yes* to Jesus, not only are we loved as a treasured part of His creation, but we have also received full forgiveness for sin. We are made new: our old is gone, the new has come. The enemy would love to have us believe that when we sin as Christians, this sin remains part of who we are, rather than have us focused on the truth that sin is merely now what we battle against (see Rom. 7).

Of course, we love Triune God. We do not cherish sin. We know its consequences—that it is a "major disruption of God's order" (1 John 3:4, MSG). Holy Spirit works to bring us to awareness and conviction that we, His beloved, are called to live a much better way. As guards of treasured intimacy with Him, we have no room to leave anything hidden or out of order. Yet we are works in progress. So, in love, He shows us areas in our lives that need further alignment in Him. As they come into alignment, He brings us into completion.

May we never be worn down by the great accuser. We know who he is and what he does. He accuses us before God and accuses us to ourselves, trying to bring shame and guilt and to steal our truest identity. This is what we need to fight against. We need to battle out the sin in us first, but we need to battle out the accusations as well. We can succeed because we have overcome by the blood of the lamb.

In our connected relationship with God, we desire more closeness—we have no room for sin's lies. We resolve to guard intimacy.

The Pharisaical Heart-Posture

One way to guard our intimacy is to root out a damaging heart-posture that obviously displeased Jesus. On earth, our Lord was tender, full of mercy, love, patience, and kindness. However, the Pharisees' heart-attitude of religious superiority stuck a thorn into intimacy. It left such a sting that Jesus was adamant regarding the need to stay far away from their ways (see Matt. 16:6).

Godliness apart from intimacy can only disrupt our relationship with God. The religious leaders of Jesus' day took the idea of following God, which is about connection, faithfulness, and intimacy, and converted it into rules, principles, and laws. It troubled Jesus that those who had the treasured Word of God allowed pride, looking important, and honor for themselves to dictate their actions.

On the flip side, Jesus loves when we stay genuinely connected with the Truth, who is a person, and look to Him to live lives of love. The Pharisees, unhappy with themselves (an inevitable trap from seeking man's approval), imposed rules and laws on others. In essence, they "tie[d] up heavy, cumbersome loads and put them on other people's shoulders" (Matt. 23:4, NIV). Perhaps because they had no real relationship with God, they thought that judging others for their failures would make themselves feel better, or that they might gain divine approval by pointing out where others were falling short.

This is not how Jesus works. God's heart-posture toward people focuses not on assigning shame but on justice, mercy, and faithfulness. His loving way points us toward relying on Him and what He does for us, not on whether we follow stringent requirements. If we are self-indulgent, greedy, impose heavy-handed expectations (laws) on others, and are righteous in our own eyes, we will displease the Lord. The intimacy He invites us to entirely frees us from all accusation against us and also frees us from the insufferable trap of judging or faulting others.

As Jesus instructed, may we fiercely guard our hearts against the ways of the Pharisees by avoiding a formulaic, list-based religion. May we live humbly and mercifully with love ever leading us forward.

Humbled by Love's Great Offer of Spirit

One truth needs to be guarded above all else. One sealed promise is treasured over all others: that is the precious truth that we are most sincerely and deeply loved. May we never shy away from the sheer fact that God adores us, delights in us, loves us as His dear children. This love holds all we could ever want and all we will ever need, for it is a pledge that we will forever belong to and be accepted by our very own Creator. The fact that we are loved by God may seem elementary. Yet this truth will be continuously attacked, for the opposition knows challenging the love of God has the potential to destroy its power.

Jesus, crucified, is the symbol of the great extent of God's love. The image deeply embeds the truth in us forever, lest we forget the cross. The gift of the Holy Spirit then helps guard the promise of love. With God's generous gift of the Holy Spirit in us, we are blessed with help to understand and remain in love.

> God affirms us, making us a sure thing in Christ, putting his Yes within us. By his Spirit he has stamped us with his eternal pledge—a sure beginning of what he is destined to complete.
>
> ~ 2 Cor. 1:21–22 (MSG)

He helps us stand in the truths of His promises of love, His affirmation, and our belonging. Those will see us through until we are safely in His arms for eternity. So, if we feel tempted to promote ourselves to gain worldly recognition from others, we should know we need none. We have already been declared excellent: God says we are worthy of Him living with us, in us.

May we guard our intimacy with Him by not chasing after worldly affirmation. We already have the best affirmation possible, and we can rest in the love of His presence. The real, living almighty Divine lives in us. All we have left to do is to live our lives as a humble thanksgiving offering.

May we bask in the truth that the most important gifts—His extravagant love and presence—are already ours. They are worth guarding with our best efforts, and the powerful Spirit of God is by our side to help us.

What He Does for Us, Not What We Do for Him

As guards of intimacy, we need to stand in the certainty that Triune God, infinite in power, is wholly and intentionally focused on relationship. Being sincerely enjoined in the Triune's great company and engaging in the Kingdom work we are called to creates incomparable joy within us. However, our self-perception can subtly shift if how useful we feel becomes linked to our sense of worth. It is a place where we find ourselves focused on performance, others' expectations, or where we attempt to earn people's or the Divine's acceptance. We need to guard against this thinking, for the invitation to join Triune's company far surpasses anything else. Abiding and enjoying their company is our focus, not working to please others or looking self-important.

Nor can we settle into the trap of becoming a slave to what we think we can do for God. It has always been about what He can do for us—He is the giver of salvation, the giver of Holy Spirit, giver of His own nature. God is never in this relationship wondering what we can do for Him as if He has some need, is limited, or unable to do things Himself. He loves lavishing us with gifts, potential, possibility, and opportunities for Kingdom work because when we accept His gifts, we join Him hand-in-hand. It is not results, work, or sacrifice that He is after. Rather, He is after the abiding. So, He clarifies that when we are not joined with Him, we can do nothing. Again, this is not to impose control, shame us, or show who's in charge. It is an invitation into remembering His heart's desire for our company. God allows us to give back to Him, for He delights in a life that is joyful, faithful, and lovingly focused on pleasing Him (see 2 Cor. 5:9).

How happy He is when we genuinely enjoy abiding and working in our Beloved Triune's great company and when we rest in all they have done for us.

Usefulness. I had no idea how important this feeling is. Then I got cancer. I was shocked by how much the treatments affected my daily life. I knew there would be loss—loss of health, energy, ability, and beauty. So much is taken. But I experienced a loss that I never expected, and it struck me the most—a feeling of being useful. The days I felt really sick, I wasn't able to do much at all. I hadn't realized how even simple, typical daily responsibilities contribute to one's feeling of value.

Throughout diagnosis and treatment, I felt so much love and care from those around me. I had incredible family, friends, and even complete strangers step in to help with appointments, care of the house, and meals. My son, who was ten months old at the time, was a delight, and my husband and I were blessed with two sets of loving grandparents to help. Of course, I was still a wife, mother, daughter, and friend. But the lack of energy I experienced and my inability to do things that I felt contributed to meaningfulness was a big struggle. On certain days, there was little I could do except just be, rest, and let my body fight the disease. I am thankful that memorizing scripture had been a regular part of my routine for years before the diagnosis. That left me in a good place of having God's truths going through my mind.

But I felt my practical usefulness was gone. Yet, in the sacred place of simply being, of resting, and of focusing on healing, I was met with profound, beautiful, real love. God was saying to me, You don't feel capable, beautiful, healthy, or useful. But I don't love you for any of those reasons. I love you because I made you, you are mine, and I don't need you to do a thing. I'll take care of it all. In this season when I was positioned to simply be with God as my best company, I met the revelation that relationship with Him is all I truly need.

Guards of the Fruit: A Time for Awe, Not Curiosity

Pure curiosity can be wonderful for a season. We'll find times we are particularly eager to grow and learn about God. He loves when we are enthusiastic about all that He has to show us, that we want to be tended, grow, and reach new understanding. Excitement over new discoveries in Him will always be part of our spiritual journey.

However, when a particular aspect of Triune God and His Kingdom is revealed to us, we must shift from childlike learning to mature follow-through. Hearing God's voice call us to new understanding, to hold faith on a matter that seems impossible, or even to believe in a miracle may challenge our obedience. But when He requests that we step out in a new direction, ministry, or mission, there will be a multitude of fruits when we fulfill what He asks of us. We demonstrate reverence, awe, and respect for what we've learned when we transfer it from knowledge to actually living it out. Such an active application of the knowledge we have gained is part of true intimacy. If we guard what we have learned, we allow Holy Spirit to fill us with the fruit of faithfulness, and then we are equipped to carry out our beloved Triune's asking.

It will not always be easy. At times it will be immensely difficult, but just as we will never be ashamed of our Lord, may we also never be ashamed of what He asks of us. His love is so thick, the secret things He shares so wonderful, yet when He asks for follow through on our part, sometimes that tests our heart's affections. Will we do what He asks?

At times we may feel too vulnerable or uncomfortable to do what the Lord asks. We might think, "What will people think if I say or do this?" Yet, we are not like the Pharisees who demand a sign (Matt. 12:38). Nor are we like those who put miraculous signs on trial. With great humility, we can ask for the Holy Spirit to reveal mysteries. We can focus on experiencing the greater Presence of our first love. We deeply desire to have Triune God and their love revealed, their reality glorified. So, when His Presence or the miraculous is put on display, the response we need to have at that point is not one of curiosity or questioning. Rather we should engage in complete, sheer awe of what we are witnessing. It is not time to wonder, "Is this real?" When His power is revealed, and we are in the presence of the extraordinary and unexplainable, He requires a faith response more like Mary's than Zechariah's.

In Luke 1, we see Mary and Zechariah each had an angel visit and a message given. Zechariah responded with unbelief, and he was struck silent for a time (vv. 18–20). Whereas even though Mary was "thoroughly shaken" by the angel's visit and words (v. 29), her ultimate response was, "Yes, I see it all now: I'm the Lord's maid, ready to serve. Let it be with me just as you say" (v. 38, MSG). Mary's is the type of faith response the Lord desires from us.

So, may we step out in obedience and demonstrate our loyalty as mature workers of all revealed secrets, faithfully doing all He asks. In doing His will, we guard our intimacy with Him and build our relationship.

Guards of Personal Words Given

Triune God knows all the happenings of our lives. He is aware of our complete spiritual journey: all that has been given to us, every promised word spoken, and each blessing extended. Our stories are precious, as are the places we have journeyed to with the Lord. They are to be protected, guarded, and remembered, as they testify to our Beloved's presence and faithfulness and the things He's done for us.

We are also, of course, given many incredible promises throughout the scriptures. Yet it would seem if we don't take the time to slow down and hear God give us a personal word that speaks into our identity, chances are we will always question our character and distinctive self in Christ. God longs for us to be secure in all He has given, to know well His personalized plans, callings, and desires for us. He wants us to come into "all the gifts and benefits that come from" Him (1 Cor. 1:3, MSG). However, the love offered, the pure righteousness, and the high calling need to become like a tangible gift that we would know that it is most truly ours. We can memorize and meditate on these truths. We can even teach them to others. But until the truths come to us in a personal way, they may never become sealed as our identity.

It takes intimacy to seek God out for His personalized words and promises. It takes resolve to believe that He delights to interact with us and bless us with words of love, direction, and encouragement. We need to deeply believe in His good and loving nature. He is happy to meet with us, speak to us, and gift us with personal words, promises, and experiences with Him.

So, may we pray for spiritual eyes to be open and for ears tuned in to His sweet whispers. May we allow Him to irreversibly transform us through the most authentic of personal encounters. Then may we be fierce believers in and guards of the precious, personalized words He gives.

Guards of Our True, Purposed Selves

Perhaps we believe we don't know our purpose. We haven't yet found what God is personally asking of us. We may feel burdened by not knowing our passion. Yet, as mighty sons and daughters of the Most-High King, the truth is we have a deep call and purpose for our lives. Each one of us is invited into intimate joining with Triune God in Kingdom work. We bear fruit and carry light through the Holy Spirit in us: these are a daily and moment-by-moment part of His sacred asking. We join with centuries of followers as we strive to say,

> I am well on my way, reaching out for Christ, who has so wondrously reached out for me. …I've got my eye on the goal, where God is beckoning us onward—to Jesus. I'm off and running, and I'm not turning back.

> ~ Phil. 3:12–14 (MSG)

With noble ambition, may we guard against distraction, the mundane, and weariness to press on towards the goal.

The enemy loves to get us focused on ourselves. He builds our self-image and convinces us to satisfy ourselves through producing and earning what the world tells us to work for. Yet our souls know the truth. The deepest of life secrets include that in putting ourselves last, pouring out for others, and joining Triune God, we find the fullness of life. The mission we are invited to is eternal, life-changing work. Of course, this is why it is continuously challenged. Therefore, we will guard our purpose and call well when we remember who we are and what we are working towards in our time with the Lord. Diligently, we will seek what it is the Father is doing and join Him. Our call will be precisely certain in some seasons, but thankfully the big picture always remains, and we can pour into it every day.

So, may we stand guard, remembering who so lovingly calls us to join Him. May we take deep delight that we have the honor to participate in mighty, eternal, Kingdom-building responsibilities.

We Hear His Voice

To guard our intimacy, we need to believe that we are dearly loved, and that God speaks to us, though it may take practice to hear. As He is so highly relational, how could we expect anything less from the One who regards intimacy as a priority? Even if we feel as if we have not heard His voice, Jesus tells us the truth: "My sheep recognize my voice. I know them, and they follow me. I give them real and eternal life" (John 10:27–28, MSG). How important that we guard the sacred truth that the Lord speaks to us.

Other things will speak into our lives by various means, so we must diligently guard the voice of Our Triune God above all others. It all begins in believing the words of Jesus—that we can hear. When we believe, we can then intentionally position ourselves to become attentive to the many ways He speaks. His written word, a still small voice, the word of another may be highlighted to us: He speaks in endless ways to move our hearts. We can begin by recognizing how He is already speaking and accept how He currently is revealing Himself.

When we begin hearing, in whatever manner, we can ask for more. God loves to be asked. We should reject the notion that we are not hearing, for Triune God is never truly silent. He has endless things He to say. To battle the great deceiver, who loves to bring confusion, we must believe and listen to God. We are blessed by His promise of protection, care, and ultimate victory (see John 10:25–30, MSG.)

So, may we practice discerning the distinct voice of the Shepherd. We can set our sights on being so deep in the embrace with Triune God that we would say, as Jesus did, "I and the Father are one heart and mind" (John 10:30, MSG). May we have divine strength to be fierce guards of the truth that God speaks, He leads, and we know His voice.

Start-Overs

Perhaps we have deep regret over not following through with a leading or great asking from God. We feel deep silence from God and desperately want to hear His voice of crystal-like water. Whether we failed to follow through with what He's asked, responded in disbelief or even in deliberate sin, God is so incredible! When we turn direction and come to Him, He is always ready to give us a fresh start. The power of the love of God can draw our hearts back to His chosen path. May we guard the truth and fight against anything that stands in the way of believing in our capacity for returning when we feel off track.

Our God is the author of new beginnings. "Great is his faithfulness; his mercies begin afresh each morning" (Lam. 3:23, NLT). It may be that if we have never yet come to accept Him, up until now, we have experienced life-long separation. Or perhaps we have spent years ignoring His directed requests. Or maybe we have been authentically connected with God daily, but yesterday we chose to live in the flesh rather than the Spirit. No matter the circumstance, God in His great love always waits for us no matter what interrupted our intimacy.

Our Savior knows every scenario, which is why so much covered in scripture about His time on earth illustrates His genuine love for start-overs. The lost sheep, the prodigal son (Luke 15), and the thief on the cross (Luke 23:40–43) are all beautiful illustrations of His intense love that never wants to let go. From the moment interruption to intimacy occurs (no matter what it is), He has already begun His strategic plan to rescue us and give us a fresh start. His mercy waits to meet us so that we can change course.

May we guard this precious truth of our Lord's nature and promise. He patiently waits for us and will help us walk His new path.

Guard Against Distractions

God calls us each to a best-planned path. This path uses our past experiences, personalities, gifts, talents, and even our weaknesses to create a masterpiece of Kingdom art. The Father wants us to seek out this mysterious plan.

Triune God loves the deepened intimacy we form with Him when we join Him in Kingdom works. When He unravels details of how He has made us, sees us, and how He powerfully wants to use us, joy follows, and closeness between Him and us increases.

We must guard the mystery of the calling that He reveals. We must protect and guard the plan from the distractions that the enemy will plant to get us off track from God's best for us. We will face obstacles from competing demands. There is always good to do, but where He specifically calls us is the best. When God in His greatness and holiness has stepped out and presented something to us, we must consider it with respect and seriousness. If we ignore what He asks, we are likely to feel frustrated and be left without further direction or leading. Obedience shows respect and honor, which is a tribute to the One we love. It symbolizes our connection and the joining of purpose and will. Whether in little things He is leading us with from scripture, regarding a big decision, or in particular directions He has impressed upon our hearts, we need to respond.

Jesus' instruction to his disciples is still relevant to us now:

> *Pay close attention to what you hear. The closer you listen, the more understanding you will be given—and you will receive even more.*

> ~ *Mark 4:24 (NLT)*

To guard intimacy is to guard His asking where He has blessed us with the beautiful invitation to join Him in Kingdom working. So, may we come against all that tries to divert and distract us from our mission.

The Promise of Glory to Come

One of the powerful truths we must guard is that when hard times come, Jesus promises to be by our side. Rather than an assurance of the absence of trouble, we have something greater in the pledge of His presence and divine, ultimate victory. The Lord of peace Himself gives us "peace at all times and in every situation" (2 Thess. 3:16, NLT). We are told not to see trials as strange or unusual (1 Pet. 4:12, NLT). Struggle is a universal experience. Yet, in our trials, we are honored with the promise that we are never alone. He is faithfully by our side.

The Lord strategically uses trouble we face to work towards a better purpose. In a way that would never happen in the absence of struggle, He diligently seeks to build intimacy with us as He offers to be our helper, healer, strength, and deliverer. Heartbreak, battles, and even sin force us to choose between two very different directions: Will we draw closer to God, or will we distance ourselves from the intimacy He offers? We must guard against each strife that might cause our soul to labor outside His will. We must let every struggle act as a bridge to build more intimacy, more trust, more Christ in us. That bridge can lead us closer to our true identity.

"God causes everything to work together for the good of those who love God" (Rom. 8:28, NLT).

Someone gave me those words during a difficult season to encourage me, and they did. However, I also know these words can feel frustratingly empty in the lowest moments of hardship because we can't always see the good in the present. The promise of good can be hard to trust. It implies that we must look into the future for hope to help us through. So now I do. I envision the best possible.

The enemy loves to place the what-ifs of all the bad possibilities before us. So, over the years, I've practiced flipping them. What if this brokenness pulls me further into God? What if the struggle builds my character with greater humility? What if this difficult persevering in the challenge produces a blessing for my God in the end? With the hardships that have come my way, I've learned to look forward and imagine some of the possible good that can come.

It helps to know the powerful promise that God is working for good in all trouble that comes our way. (But, don't necessarily tell me this of my current struggle. I may not quite believe it yet! However, hopefully soon, I will fight to start seeing the possible good that may come.)

We need to guard our belief that God works to produce something purposeful and good in all life's circumstances. Indeed, He works in a way that He never could if the difficult circumstances didn't exist. It may take us days, years, decades, or even until eternity, but we will see the fruits which come from struggle. Our intertwined intimacy with God's purposes extends us hope that we who share in the hard times will share in the good times (see Rom. 8:15–17).

May we guard the truth through trials we face. God is at work, and we can join Him!

> *Be glad that you are in the very thick of what Christ experienced. This is a spiritual refining process, with glory just around the corner.*
>
> ~ *1 Pet. 4:13 (MSG)*

Guards of Joy

Jesus had invited us into the fullness of life, in the relational offering of joining the best of company in Triune God. In this intimate extending alone, we have been offered the deepest joy. Jesus told us to be fruitful. Joy should be the natural product of our lives, and we should guard that joy. When we live full of joy, we are a natural, brilliant light for the Lord, testifying to His goodness. In joining with Jesus, we have a surplus of promises and unshakeable joy in the great assurances of Triune God. Joy is a trust in certainties.

Many natural, normal life events can give us a sense of contentment. We might think of landmark life events we experience with family and friends, personal successes, promotions or accomplishing goals or dreams. Yet the contentment we feel from events like a graduation, a new job, a promotion, a new purchase, a trip, a wedding, a birth or reaching retirement can pass as quickly. True joy stems from deep intimacy, and it withstands obstacles. When we hold real joy, it is powerful, life-changing, and atmosphere-changing, in that it contains the promise for something far beyond what the world offers. Even the best natural offerings that give us a sense of happiness cannot remain forever: the satisfaction they give is likely to fade. Children grow up and move away, loved ones pass, the best of health will fail, and we will age and retire from skills and positions we worked so hard for.

In the absence of earthly security, our soul's most authentic longing is met in the permanency of His abundant presence. The best of natural circumstances are, in the end, counterfeit in their offerings. Only through permanent, solid, unchanging, and trustworthy intimate connection is true, deep joy found. We are offered solid joy in the One who abundantly, extravagantly loves us. Therefore, not only do we need to protect this joy, but we must also not put off living in this joy, for "the joy of the LORD is [our] strength" (Neh. 8:10, KJV).

May we guard the joy by standing firm in all promises, living in His love that is entirely sufficient, sustainable, and eternally lasting. We are blessed to live in the light and the joy of our Lord!

Silence and Stillness

Silence, stillness, and aloneness can be exceedingly difficult at times, yet this state of being is essential for our spirit. To be in His Presence requires a certain amount of solitude that ironically remedies any threat of loneliness we face. We must come to a place of recognizing the reality of His constant presence, which is too often drowned out by the noise of life. Until we connect in stillness with the truth that Jesus is by our side every moment, it will be difficult to take that reality with us into the everyday busyness and noise of life.

We can view times of silence as empty and lonely or as opportunities for Divine encounter. During solitude, the enemy loves to distract us with self-focused negativity: he'll imply that we are isolated and lonesome. However, rather than a disruption to community and belonging, God may have provided this time for a specific purpose. Perhaps it's meant as a season of great companionship in which we focus solely on our relationship with Him.

Though Triune desires us to have genuine connected friendships and true fellowship with others, these relationships have earthbound limits. Beyond earthly connections, we need God's constant, watchful presence that never leaves us, thoroughly knows and understands us, and is involved in every detail of our lives. Our heart desires full awareness of His presence. May loneliness never have power over us or force us into seclusion. May it rather serve to remind us that "honor and majesty surround him, strength and joy fill his dwelling" (1 Chron. 16:27, NLT). He beckons us each moment to bask in His presence and to know we are never alone: we are in intimacy's embrace.

We are with Him in quietness. There He whispers secret truths we must guard in our hearts: He is near, and when all is said and done in this life, we will be "crowned with everlasting joy" (Isa. 35:10, NLT).

Guards of Goodness

As followers of Jesus, we possess rich, life-giving gifts. Each day holds goodness and promise for the future. We need to protect what Jesus has given us. We have an enemy, and the enemy's plan is to kill, steal, destroy (John 10:10) as well as to accuse and deceive. While we possess amazing promises, the itinerary of our opposition is to attack this goodness. We need to stand in our promises and be firm in our identity, always remembering who we are. We have a Mighty Father, and we are beloved children of the All-Powerful King. Jesus won back all authority and holds ultimate power. The Father extends us the right to live as His children, and our inheritance in Him equips us to guard the goodness. Unfortunately, sometimes we get weary, and the enemy sneaks in worry, unforgiveness, weariness, or sin, which we accept as "normal." We give it permission.

To defend our position as true warriors, we must step out and guard the full goodness that the Lord pours over us. "God rises on you, his sunrise glory breaks over you. Nations will come to your light, kings to your sunburst brightness" (Isa. 60:2–3, MSG). Evil cannot remain when we find ourselves in the presence of the Holy One.

The Kingdom of God is now. As His disciples were trained to heal the sick and cast out demons, may we also operate in His name and authority against all that comes against us. What awesome news we have to bring: freedom, pardon, healing. As bearers of light and goodness, we accept no hell, imprisonment, or accusations. The enemy may bring it, but it is commanded in Jesus' name to go. Jesus' presence is that good!

The goodness, glory, and intimate love of God stand with us always. Heaven's army surrounds us, so all enemies against us will flee. We will stand guard over the goodness and accept nothing less.

Know Whose Authority and Presence We Are Under

Under the greatness of God, we have all we need to escape misconceptions that might tempt us off track. We must guard knowing under whose authority we rest. Our Lord designed us to be strong, confident, assured, and bold through who we are in Christ. It is not noble to embrace self-doubt, discouragement, or question the ability He has given us.

When the Lord is trying to tell me something, I find repetition often comes my way. It is how He gets my attention. This week, scriptures kept coming up on the same theme: everything seemed to point to God's invitation, His plan, His will, His Spirit, His story. As I let these truths settle deep into my heart, I was reminded of His great authority. I have a Father, perfect in goodness, who holds all power and direct knowledge of my life. That is incredible! I am honored that He invites and includes me in what He is doing in His great story. In whatever ways He asks me to step out, He handpicks my path and always leads me to the next step. It is my desire to obey and live in the joy of pleasing God. So this is my prayer: "Father, help me to see what You are up to. Help me be on my feet, aligned, listening, carrying out all that You ask with Holy Spirit's help. Lord, truly, my great triumph is that I have the joy of your presence and that You have authority over me."

Jesus extended great offerings to His closest friends who joined Him in Kingdom work. They were sent out and they found themselves doing incredible things in His name. Jesus responded enthusiastically to their victories and blessed them with protection against enemy assaults. However, He told them this:

> The great triumph is not in your authority over evil, but in God's authority over you and presence with you.
>
> ~ Luke 10:20 (MSG)

We must guard the sacred place of knowing whose authority is over us, whose presence we are blessed to have. As we do, we will have the favor of stepping out in authority in our Kingdom working. We will also escape the worries the world would toss to us in its attempts to interrupt our intimacy. If we entertain the concerns of life, they will cause us to question God's provision, protection, and best interest over our lives. They will challenge the surrendered heart, causing us to question the ability, integrity, and involvement of the One we trust.

We need to stand guard over the safety which comes with living under His authority and in His presence. Our big, mighty God is in charge, can fix anything, and provides all we need. We can live in the deepest of peace that He is Most High and at His command, evil must flee. He holds the cares of this world, and we can take peace in knowing that "the world and its desires pass away, but whoever does the will of God lives forever" (1 John 2:17, NIV).

Let us guard our hearts to remain in His presence and under His authority. Then, our lives will be shaped by His will that lasts forever.

Guards Against Believing We Can Understand It All

Our God is so incredibly intimate, involved, and personal. That He is also so big, mighty, mysterious, and powerful should always capture our awe. And while He has blessed us with incredible minds that can learn, process, and understand so much through logic, reasoning, and rational sense, He remains above us.

> *"For my thoughts are not your thoughts,*
> *neither are your ways my ways,"*
> *declares the LORD.*

> ~ *Isa. 55:8 (NIV)*

He is not after head-knowledge. He wants our hearts to know the relationship. Rules, laws, measurably "right" and "wrong" things? He undid that way of measuring life when He took all sin upon Himself at the cross. The offer of mercy, grace, and love was what remained. It is an unexplainable exchange. He simply loves us that much. We need to guard against thinking we can actually ever fully understand our big, awesome, full of love God! Instead, may we fully trust the truth He has extended, the mystery He unveils, and His great, irrevocable love offering.

Of course, we can never grasp that goodness on our own. God has made it too big for human understanding. We have but two things we can do that He directed us to, to come to this acceptance. Firstly, we go to Him with the humbleness of a child, knowing we can't on our own ever grasp all this. Secondly, we don't have to do it on our own. As with all things good, He has made it so that we have to have Holy Spirit do it through us. Holy Spirit alone can lead us into all truths. As we ask and He does, all of a sudden, the rest won't matter so much anymore. What matters is the joy of delighting in the mighty, mysterious, beyond-all-our-boxes presence of God.

So, we guard the truth that our God is far beyond human comprehension. We stand in joy that He delights to reveal Himself. We are in awe, aware that we can never fully understand the awesome, complex, loving mystery of the Divine.

Guards of Passion

Jesus said: "Love the Lord your God with all your passion and prayer and muscle and intelligence" (Luke 10:27, MSG). If we are aware of God's intimate heart for us, how could we give Him anything less than our all? He is our passion and our prize. So how is it then that the enemy is so clever to trick us at times into devoting a part of our heart to an alternate love? If we find a passion for success and are admired by others for something we do or create; if we enjoy a hobby or pastime, we need to test these "loves" to see if they are competing with our true passion. Of course, working toward success, achievements, and even pastimes are part of life. Yet when these become focal points of our work, strength, or time, we need to be aware. Our Lord's place of priority always needs to be guarded.

The call, the asking of Jesus is so big that He wants it to be our all. He wants us to take whatever is dear to us—whatever plan or person or thing —and surrender it to the greatest call to go and be His disciple (see Luke 14:33). Our world values achievements, success, and activity. Yet what if we made the Kingdom our passion, to know and love God more, to pursue His heart's desire as our heart's desire? What if we set to focus our achievements, involvement, and activities all in the direction of potential opportunities to build further into His desires? How amazing would it be if in our work ambitions, our extra time, and our families, all were in line with the purpose of meeting His desires? Those things we spend time on (which in our world often go unnoticed, undervalued, and without acknowledgment) are often the things the Lord looks down on with delight. He loves to see us spend extended time with Him, enjoying His company, praising, and interceding. The time we spend pursuing loving people, building relationships, and serving others on earth may never win us an award, promotion, or medal.

But where we pour our time reflects our hearts. As we guard our time and spend it as He directs, as we are determinedly focused on worthy passions, we are promised honor in the unseen world.

Stand Guard Over Truth

So, may we take all these truths to heart, all that our beloved Triune God has revealed to us, and guard them with the utmost protection. "Blessed are those who hear God's Word and guard it with their lives!" (Luke 11:28, MSG). May we live in incredible peace, for we have chosen the best. We will enjoy His intimate company as we sit at His feet, and it won't be taken from us (see Luke 10:41–42). We are not alone in our ambition to guard these truths, for Triune God surrounds us with Heaven's army's help and all the armor we need to fight the good fight of faith. Our intimacy deepens as we fight for truth and as we prioritize the relationship. He loves it when we make this our life priority and fight fiercely against anything that tries to interrupt our intimate relationship.

It is an honor that we are to completely rely on Him and live with Him dwelling in us through Holy Spirit. How blessed we are to be given the focus to live for an audience of One. He has made our heart His home. What intimate offerings! But may we make no mistake. Jesus said, "This is war, and there is no neutral ground. If you're not on my side, you're the enemy; if you're not helping, you're making things worse" (Luke 11:23, MSG). The truth, the relationship, the Kingdom of God, and living for it all must be guarded and protected. The great accuser on earth does not cease, but in Jesus, we have certain victory. The offer, the welcome into love, is our most treasured possession. So, may we live like it! "Make every effort to respond to God's promises" (2 Pet. 1:5, NLT).

These promises are the clothing that protects us. They reveal God's generous, intimate nature and heart towards us. They are worth the fight to safeguard.

Section 11:

INTIMACY INTERRUPTED — WARFARE AND LIES

The truth that we have an enemy is an absolute. One of his weapons of choice is lies. However, the greater truth is that we have a victorious Savior who fought and defeated this enemy. We are wise to make ourselves aware of the enemy's schemes, details, and workings so that we can know how to stand in victory here and now to protect our intimate relationship with God.

This is no afternoon athletic contest that we'll walk away from and forget about in a couple of hours. This is for keeps, a life-or-death fight to the finish against the Devil and all his angels.

~ Eph. 6:12 (MSG)

Be alert and of sober mind. Your enemy the devil prowls around like a roaring lion looking for someone to devour. Resist him, standing firm in the faith.

~ 1 Pet. 5:8–9 (NIV)

Wise Warriors Stand in Truth

Under love, we have a reason for colossal hope because the Lord works in each and every battle, drawing us closer to Him. A strong intimacy builds itself in times of trouble. This is an intimacy that could never achieve the same power in warfare's absence. When trouble and hardship come, a promise is whispered to the faithful: *He will use that which was intended to be used against us to work for good* (see Gen. 50:20). In certain battle seasons, our call is to simply stand guard in His promises and allow our Mighty Lord to fight for us (see Exod. 14:14). These times build our confidence in the Father's fierce love that always stands up for us.

However, there are other seasons in which He calls us to battle—to exercise the power and authority that Jesus won on the cross for us. As mature children, He calls us to stand in His likeness. After all, He built it into us, and He calls us to fight from the position of victory that He has already won. As we stand in the intimate place of intense participation in battle, we must see our position through spiritual eyes. We take up the armor He offers and fight (Eph. 6:10–18). We stretch ourselves to be confidently composed in Triune's mighty presence.

Regardless of the type of battle, whether we stand still or join in, we are never alone: we have the Father before us, Jesus beside us, and Holy Spirit within us in the center of all wars. Arrows of accusation hurtled our way are meant for our destruction. However, our Lord can turn each and every arrow around into His purposes for good.

May we be wise warriors. The battle is never without purpose, so we stand firm in the Triune's victorious company, and we take a bold, sure stance, knowing well who we are and who battles with and for us every time.

Battling as Jesus Did

It can seem desirable to ignore or avoid warfare. However, simply not paying attention to or denying its existence does not change the reality of the battle. Absolutely, our focus should always be on God, not the enemy. If we overly focus on battles of darkness, we can divert too much of our attention to the enemy of God rather than concentrating on the more deserving Triune God. However, being aware of the enemy's methods and plans benefits us. The Word directs us to be alert, to stand firm and strong against the enemy's schemes, and not to be complacent on the matter of warfare. Truly we have power from the Divine and need to use it. "For though we live in the world, we do not wage war as the world does. The weapons we fight with are not the weapons of the world" (2 Cor. 10:3–4, NIV).

On earth as a man, Jesus did not shrink away from interaction with evil spirits because His heart was full of love. He knew His beloved people needed to be equipped properly to be effective in their efforts against the enemy's schemes. As followers, we are called to do the things that Jesus did. We learn what to do by studying the life He lived and practicing the actions He performed in His name and likeness for His glory. As His beloved followers, we are included with the disciples in His calling to "heal the sick, cleanse the lepers, raise the dead, [and] cast out demons" (Matt. 10:8, NKJV).

We do ourselves no favor but rather disrupt our intimate connection with God when we choose our feelings over the truth regarding spiritual warfare surrounding us. Indeed, our relationship with Him deepens when we understand the reality of spiritual warfare and when we engage with our

Lord in His battle plan. How precious to Him when we, as His warrior children, link arm-in-arm with Him in the victorious battle of Kingdom work in the here and now. With Jesus as our example and with His mighty power and strength working in us, we do not need to be afraid, and we can rest assured that our great, triumphant God wins every battle.

The Enemy's Pointed Arrows

The enemy has his sharpened arrows. He aims at the heart of God, and he aims at His treasured possession, at us, God's beloved. Why? To hurt the Lord. The enemy seeks to disrupt, disconnect, and wage war on our relationship with God. He will lie (John 8:44) and attempt to take away the truth (Matt. 13:19) to prevent intimacy from growing to all it can be. When we examine the arrows, we find each has been precisely sharpened to attack the foundation of love. These arrows come in the form of lies. The enemy will present us questions such as, *If God really loved you, why would He allow this hardship to occur,* or *Why won't He intervene for you in this area of need?* Each one is intended to cause us to doubt our love, for the enemy knows that those who are firmly attached to and in a healthy relationship with God are powerful and effective.

We are to be fully armored in truth, ready to take our stand against the enemy's schemes (Eph. 6:11). Our intimate relationship with our Father is our prized possession. So as His beloved, clothed in his likeness, as mighty warrior sons and daughters of the Most High King, we will be ready. We will take the time to know where we have adopted compromised thinking influenced by the enemy, for not every idea that comes to us is always our own. We will devote the time needed to recognize any areas in our relationship with God which might be at risk. We should ask: what lies are present today?

Every lie is rooted in the first lie from the Garden: that we cannot truly trust God, that His love is not secure or enough, that there is something good He is holding back from us. All lies challenge the truth of what we know about God. The enemy will confront God's nature, reality, demands, words, consequences, and decisions, all with the end goal of causing us to deny His love and existence. Left to its own, our human understanding could never comprehend and grip all the ways of the One who made the entire universe —but we are not left on our own. God knows the trials we will encounter through the enemy's tests, so He equips us with all we need to fight for the truth. True love tested only becomes more robust. Whatever the attack, God only allows it to grow the relationship into one which is solid and unshakable, in which we flourish with the One we trust.

Warfare Over the Word

One of the enemy's primary targets is the Word of the Lord. If lies against God's love for us are ineffective, the enemy's next tactic is to make allegations against the Word (the Bible) because it is so deeply tied to Jesus. The bond between Jesus and the Word is a powerfully interlaced mystery of oneness.

> *In the beginning was the Word, and the Word was with God, and the Word was God. He was with God in the beginning. Through him all things were made; without him nothing was made that has been made. In him was life, and that life was the light of all mankind.*

> *~ John 1:1–4 (NIV)*

If the enemy can mislead us into questioning our source of truth in the Word, then the love we have received can be put into question, too. Even within certain Christian cultures some believe the Bible is simply the opinion of those who followed God. Others say Bible stories are simply meant to help us live a better life. Some say it was all made up, because people simply needed something to believe in. How very far from reality are all those thoughts: in all actuality, the Bible is tied so deeply with the Creator of our world that it is said: "the Word was with God, and the Word was God."

Lies will come—some subtle, others more obvious. The enemy is cunning and devious and will often find our soft spot—a place where we hold potential to compromise. Perhaps we are struggling to forgive someone. The enemy may begin by suggesting that forgiveness is not *always* required, that there are exceptions. However, if we begin to question the truth of a particular scripture, we begin down the path of allowing ourselves permission to give in to temptation. Whatever specific scripture the enemy can cause us to doubt, can have compounding effects of causing us to see the full Word of God as questionable.

These lies present us with the idea that the Bible is less reliable than we thought it to be. In these times, we must remember the enemy's highly-focused plan to destroy our love bond with God. We must also remember that if the Lord created the earth and galaxies by His fingertips, surely He holds the ability and power to provide us with a book of love and instruction for life that reveals who we are and who He is. Our Lord is that big and can be trusted, as can His given Word.

Thankfully, God made our world with beautifully interwoven truths that present themselves in creation, history, archeology, and fulfilled prophecies that testify to the Bible's certainty. However, the best, most colossal weight of evidence for the Bible's reliability rests in the wonder of living out the truth of the Word for ourselves. It is an intimate testimony to our very soul to "taste and see that the LORD [and His Word] is good" (Psalm 34:8, NIV). As we live in the truths of the Word, we find the following to be concretely evident:

> Every scripture is God-breathed (given by His inspiration) and profitable for instruction... [and] for training in righteousness (in holy living, in conformity to God's will in thought, purpose, and action).
>
> ~ 2 Tim. 3:16 (AMPC)

When we live out God's ways, we find a sense of peace and fullness that is the opposite of the chaos and messiness of life lived apart from Him. The fruit of living in the Lord and His Word is evidence of His power and the truth of the Bible.

So let us stand guard over our thinking about the graciously given, wondrous Word of God. Let us treasure the Word for all its incredible worth, truth, and instruction for living.

The Lie: We Can Understand All God's Ways

If we believe we can fully understand God, we are deeply mistaken. To believe that our understanding is fully mature, that we see perfectly, or that our knowledge is complete, is not only a lie, but it can cause us very quickly to fall into the enemy's trap of believing we can demand answers of the King of kings.

Oddly, we tend to believe we enter into this rather entitled attitude of questioning God from a place of love. From a place of compassion in our hearts, we might begin what seems a reasonable examination of God concerning matters of the workings of justice, His reasoning behind suffering and even eternal consequences. In the name of "love" for our neighbor, we question God: How could He allow circumstances that are unfit or unfair? But in doing so, we cross a line and place God on trial. This approach stems from believing the lie that we can fully understand God and His workings.

Yet scripture marks out the truth from God's perspective: "For as the sky soars high above earth, so the way I work surpasses the way you work, and the way I think is beyond the way you think" (Isa. 55:9, MSG). Certainly, there are challenges in understanding a difficult truth, such as that of the existence of eternal consequences. Yet who are we to question how the One perfect in love decides to motivate (or even intimidate) us for us to discover the wonder of His most loyal love? For He will have nothing less than a genuine relationship of choice. If His method of persuasion seems extreme, it is simply because His love is extreme. If in our sinfulness we want the best for those we love, how much more are the desires of our fully loving, without-sin God pointed towards the working of good for all?

May we resist the enemy's lie and enter into fully trusting our mysterious and good God. May we surrender with complete faith to God's every motive, move, decision, and even consequence. It is a blessing that we get to try to know the Lord better, but it is a lie that we can ever fully understand Almighty God.

The Lie: Struggles Mean God Cannot Be Good

Trouble is assured in the world. The enemy, who is the orchestrator of much of our misfortune and grief, will likely twist whatever hurts us to suggest it comes from the hand of God. Yet the true agenda—that God is good, and every good thing is from Him (James 1:17)—remains. The enemy, though, is out to deceive, destroy, and bring death into our lives, bodies, and circumstances. Our Lord works for us to have "real and eternal life, more and better life than [we] ever dreamed of" (John 10:10, MSG). The lie is that hard times come from God, and therefore, He cannot be good. If we can't be convinced of that, then the lie transforms to a second lie. God may be good, but since we have struggled, that means God does not have the heart, ability, power, or authority to take care of us.

The truths need to be understood; the lies, stood against. The fall of man, the sin of humankind, the enemy's destructive plans to harm are the sources of trouble. God's goodness is certain, He never does evil, and He absolutely holds all ability in all things. Even though at times He allows difficult circumstances, some beyond our understanding, He promises even the hardships will be redeemed and used for good.

> *Pure gold put in the fire comes out of it proved, pure; genuine faith put through this suffering comes out proved genuine. When Jesus wraps this all up, it's your faith, not your gold, that God will have on display as evidence of his victory.*
>
> ~ *1 Pet. 1:7–8 (MSG)*

Even more importantly, God's goodness stands strong and is confirmed by His constant presence. Our trust, hope, and belief in this are vital. Our Lord's words say, "I will not forget you! See, I have engraved you on the palms of my hands" (Isa. 49:15–16, NIV). When we face struggles, we can actively practice trusting these assurances from God: "'I will never fail you. I will never abandon you.' So we can say with confidence, 'The Lord is my helper, so I will have no fear'" (Heb. 13:5–6, NLT). For it is the presence that we are after. The presence is found so vividly in trials. Jesus by our side, the Father's wisdom, the Holy Spirit's counsel and truth become real in our life as we go through hardships. We see we are not forgotten or abandoned and have real and mighty help. We hold to the promise that though we have many troubles, we can take heart, as He has overcome it all on the cross.

When we accept the significance of His promise always to be our help, we increase our faith in times of testing. For the truth is that our sense of His presence might not be as full if we never experienced any trouble. As stated in 1 Peter 1:7–8, when it is all said and done, may God have our beautiful faith on display, demonstrating His victory in our life. May we quench the lie and trust the promises. We have assurance of His goodness, and so we can trust His ability. He offers us a blessed, better-than-we-could-have-dreamed life by giving us His presence in all circumstances.

Authority in Jesus' Name

Falsehoods can threaten our intimate walk when we fail to understand our intimidator's limitations. There are many constraints on God's enemy. We tap into incredible strength when we understand both the spiritual warfare taking place against us and the restrictions placed on the enemy as he seeks to interfere with God's will and plans. Because of what Jesus accomplished on the cross, He holds all power and authority (see Matt. 28:18).

> *He sustains everything by the mighty power of his command.*
>
> ~ *Heb. 1:3 (NLT)*

This truth allows us to stand in strength, with His permission, and experience His mighty help and protection.

We are called to be witnesses and tell people about Him. We have authority in His name to proclaim the message (Luke 24:47 NLT). When we step into the fullness of confidence in Jesus, we find ourselves in a beautiful place. Within that connection and understanding, we as His children have the treasure of the Holy Spirit who comes and fills us with power from heaven (Luke 24:49).

The enemy loves to intimidate, torment, and confuse us, but the fact remains that Jesus holds authority and power. We know that they are His, and that He extends them to us, His children. We are to use our God-given power and authority for His glory. So, may we learn the skills to pick up our tools, gifts, and armor, especially concerning how these help us gain ground in the unseen warfare. May we find ourselves in a place where we can say with confident resolve: We are born of God, and the evil one cannot touch us (1 John 5:18).

In our intimate relationship with God, this is who we are, and this is our identity. We are equipped, empowered, protected, and called into mighty

Kingdom work to spread His incredible message across the earth, in the authority of His name.

Bold Confidence in Our Identity in Christ

The enemy loves to attack our confidence. If he can make us question the authenticity of our ability, worth, power, or new nature, he can transform how we see ourselves and how we believe God sees us. These lies can interrupt our relationship with God and the greater purposes to which He calls us.

However, when we stand in confidence of who we truly are in Christ, we can live in the power, love, and gifting He extends to us. Then the truth will define us. As our hearts are penetrated with our identity in Christ, we see that even in the most challenging times facing the cross, Jesus was not abandoned. His identity was in the Father who was with Him:

> *I am not alone because the Father is with me.*
>
> ~ *John 16:32 (NLT)*

Presence is the intimate hold of love that sustains our confidence. Jesus said He told us this so that we can have bold, unshakable assurance and profound peace, in that even when we face hardship, we can know He has conquered the world. So, may we learn to eradicate the timidity, weakness, shame, and lies the enemy suggests. We abide in the solid promise that we are exactly who God says we are. Like Jesus, we are never abandoned: we are always under the care of the Father. As we eliminate the lies, may we remember He has overcome the world, and in full assurance, we can rise in confidence, power, strength, and love. May this be our identity! As we walk with an accurate perception of how the Father sees us, we build upon the beautiful intimacy and stop any plan for interruption in its track.

Jesus says that we are not of the world, even as He was not (John 17:16.) Rather, miraculously through Holy Spirit, we have the Divine in us. That gives us all the confidence and boldness we could ever need.

God-Confidence, Not Self-Confidence

The enemy has managed an effective attack if He can cause us to take on confidence in ourselves apart from Jesus. The world promotes self-achievement as a beneficial trait. When we buy into the worldly view of achievement, we trust an unstable, unable, fallible power. Jesus warned against resting on what one already has: "But it's trouble ahead if you think you have it made. What you have is all you'll ever get" (Luke 6:24, MSG). What sustained Jesus' strength was His confident, assured identity in being fully loved by the Father, and we can rely on nothing less.

Boldness, power, and confidence are useful for the Kingdom when they are rooted in Jesus. Without Him as their source, they become unpleasant and foul. They take on a stench of arrogance, pride, and position-seeking, as with Saul's downfall (see 1 Sam. 15, MSG). After the people of Israel asked for a King, Saul was crowned. However, there was a turning point where he was not obeying God and was acting self-important (vv. 22–23). He cared more about pleasing the people and letting them tell him what to do over following God's instructions. In turn, God rejected him as king over Israel (vv. 24–26). The consequences Saul received for his self-importance were severe. His self-confidence led him to arrogance which caused the Lord to reject him as king. May we fervently guard our hearts against the pride God so clearly despises, but never shrink back from the strength and confidence that He desires us to live in.

In Jesus, we have more than enough and all that we need. There is nothing we need to add. No rigorous self-denial, no idolization of our own abilities or gifts—we live for His glory.

> *You're blessed when you've lost it all. God's kingdom is there for the finding. You're blessed when you're ravenously hungry. Then you're ready for the Messianic meal.*
>
> ~ *Luke 6:20–21 (MSG)*

When we reverently idolize His name alone, we can live in boldness and strength, taking up all the authority He has given us. When we adore our first love, we desire nothing more, and the enemy's war against our intimate relationship cannot succeed. We will stand in solid resolve to remain in His strength and live for His plans. Forsaking any lie and trusting in no other name, we will rely on Jesus alone. He is our confidence. We are made confident in Him.

The Lie: You Are Not Good Enough

This is the love the enemy cannot stand: "Unfailing love and truth have met together. Righteousness and peace have kissed" (Psalm 85:10, NLT). It is the truth he is out to destroy. If he can cause us to doubt our eternal promise even slightly by challenging our righteousness or peace, then he can gain critical territory. His lie is ancient, and it has been common since Eden. He whispers: *You are not truly loved. You are not truly saved. You are underserving. You are not good enough.*

God knew the accuser's influential lies would come and go to challenge His love and our ultimate salvation. So He made it fully clear that salvation is based on one thing, and one thing alone: Christ.

> *The mystery in a nutshell is just this: Christ is in you… It's that simple.*
>
> ~ Col 1:27 (MSG)

He has placed His seal of approval and ownership over us, claiming us as wholly His. We have complete confidence, not because of our ability, goodness, or work, but because we are placed securely in Him when we accept the gift with the promise. The enemy will bring his lie back around repeatedly, perhaps as a hint or even straight-out accusation: *You are not good enough to meet the mark to receive eternal life with God.* Yet, Jesus has the perfect response. While it is correct that we are not good enough, He most definitely is. In Jesus alone, we secure our salvation. We are enough in Him.

May we abide in the security of trusting Him alone and find this promise so real that we can be "confident of this, that he who began a good work in [us] will carry it on to completion until the day of Christ Jesus" (Phil. 1:6, NIV). Triune God's glory is magnified through this all. When we accept the focus, favor, and honor He extends us, God's goodness becomes recognizable and can therefore be adored by onlookers. Even without words, our life is a testimony. We live as people shining out light, in that we are loved and righteous because of Christ alone. So, may we look to Him with peace and bask in His unfailing love.

> *He dressed me up in a suit of salvation, he outfitted me in a robe of righteousness...*
> *So the Master, GOD, brings righteousness into full bloom and puts praise on display*
> *before the nations.*

~ *Isa. 61:10–11 (MSG)*

I will be the first to admit there were times when the enemy presented me with each of these lies. "You are not truly loved. You are not truly saved. You are underserving. You are not good enough." These thoughts would pop into my head, and growing up as the only Christian in a family without people to explain the truth to me, there wasn't much to combat them. They were planted from what I see now as an obvious source, the great deceiver. Thankfully, my heavenly Father was faithful and provided reinforcing sources of truth, such as a summer camp leader, a Billy Graham speech on TV, or a book to disassemble the lie. Though the ancient lie was there, the solid truth was also confirmed again and again: You are loved, you are saved. It is not about being deserving and good enough. It is about Jesus and all that He has done to save you. The enemy doesn't really have that much to work with. The ancient lie hasn't changed much. When we stand against it and call it out for the lie it is, we gain great ground. Because of Jesus and what He did, we can stand in confidence in His work in us that brings us to completion. He has dressed us in salvation and robed us in righteousness. This is the "unfailing love and truth." It is all about what He has done for us, and the enemy cannot ever take it from us.

Power of the Present

> *So do not fear, for I am with you;*
> *Do not be dismayed, for I am your God.*

~ *Isa. 41:10 (NIV)*

After we battle out the lies against our identity, we still must be aware. The accuser has further attempts at deception and confusion hidden up his sleeves. To disrupt us from doing effective Kingdom work in our new secure identity, the enemy plots to prevent us from engaging with the present. The present is a powerful place. When we fully live in it, we are free from all past regret and all fear that can be imagined in the future. When we live outside of the present, the enemy can successfully rob our gratefulness, peace, trust, and focus. Our greater purpose is vulnerable to attack if we are distracted by the temptation to dwell on our past or if the future demands our attention.

It is in the present moment that we find His presence. That is where it dwells. In the present moment, we can "approach God with freedom and confidence" (Eph. 3:12, NIV). May we fight against the subversions of past and future concerns and focus simply on where we are and what God is showing us now. The enemy will sabotage our Kingdom work by having us get stuck in the trap of the past. This is why Paul strived towards "forgetting those things which are behind and reaching forward to those things which are ahead" (Phil. 3:13, NKJV).

We can move forward and know that we have the power to do all things He calls us to as we engage in intimate presence with Him in our present moment. As we dwell in the fullness of the One we love and are in the present with Him, we will find incredible strength to take up whatever He calls us to. We can "press toward the goal for the prize of the upward call of God in Christ Jesus" (Phil. 3:14, NKJV). How wonderful that when we are hand-in-hand with our Lord, focused on the present, we can resist the warfare that tries to shift our focus. He empowers us with the endurance, attention, and concentrated effort we need to do all He places immediately before us.

Holy Spirit Moves Us Forward

It should come as no surprise that our enemy has detailed plans to aim at the power that comes through the alignment of a person fully connected with God's call and working in Holy Spirit's strength. We need to anticipate the arrows of lies directed to make us feel inadequate and weary. The more passionately focused we are on the Lord's call, the more meticulous the deceptions the enemy will use against us. When we feel accusations pointing out our insufficiencies and lack of strength, it is because the enemy knows our potential. We are a target because we hold such great Kingdom purpose.

The predominant plan of the enemy remains to break down our relational connection to the Father. He knows the powerful joy we experience as we join Jesus as coworkers, witnesses, and friends. We need to hold the following truth tightly: God's strength alone moves us forward in purpose. The strength to remain in Him does not come from ourselves. Instead, it comes entirely through Holy Spirit living through us. Holy Spirit empowers us to live in a tightly intimate connection with our first love, and that is where we find our incredible strength.

> *In him we were also chosen, having been predestined according to the plan of him who works out everything in conformity with the purpose of his will.*
>
> ~ *Eph 1:11 (NIV)*

It is His choice, His plans, His work, His will. The enemy will attempt to slow us down, but the truth of God's power sustains us. It is not us in our fleshly works or in individual attempts that we operate, but Jesus in us through the Holy Spirit accomplishes all things. We will not run out of strength, His plans for us will not fail, and His perfect purposes will prevail. Even if we don't see results immediately, our Mighty God of love "works in [us] to will and act in order to fulfill his good purpose" (Phil. 2:13, NIV).

Embracing Our New Nature

As we become strong in our Christ-identity and see success in living in our new Spirit-filled life, it's important to remember the enemy would love to bring us back around to our old ways of living. For some going back and living the way we lived before will look like self-promotion or selfishness, for others it may look like apathy or defeatism. The temptation to hold on or return to the patterns of flesh that war against our new nature can be strong. Whatever the sin—whether greed, anger, or any impurity—the enemy will do his best to have us return to the old way, even if in subtle ways at first. If that is not successful, then he will endeavor to dull the conviction, halt the confession, and stop any real repentance that changes course.

However, we can take heart. The Holy Spirit's greater force works for our complete, genuine, and remarkable transformation into being the sacred people God calls us to be. We are the holy people: He chose us. So may we break the lie and know the truth: whatever sin is trying to get a hold on us again, it is not worth it. There is absolutely no value in holding on to bitterness, resentment, or any bad behavior as followers of the King of kings. We must take on our new nature and allow ourselves to be made fully lovely through the One who fully loves us—no room must be left for the enemy to have any foothold (see Eph. 4:27).

May we believe that in Jesus we have the power to overcome and answer the call to the new way of life.

> So, chosen by God for this new life of love, dress in the wardrobe God picked out for [us]: compassion, kindness, humility, quiet strength, discipline. To be even-tempered, content with second place, quick to forgive an offense.
>
> ~ Col. 3:12–14 (MSG)

What a beautiful dwelling land He calls us to in our new identity. There, we are newly empowered to live with Holy Spirit dwelling in us and giving us His strength. May we hold strong and be determined to simply ask for a fresh filling of God when we need it. Then we will live out the incredible gift of life daily renewed in Him.

The Battle Has Been Won

We should never feel powerless in the middle of all this warfare of compelling lies. Rather, we should hold firmly to the truth that the One in us is greater than the one who is in the world. "For only as a human being could [Jesus] die, and only in dying could he break the power of the devil, who had the power of death" (Heb. 2:14, NLT). The lie that the battle has not been won is some of the enemy's most devious work. It twists peoples' perceptions and creates confusion, discord, and chaos. Yet the war has been won—it is complete and finished on the cross by our Savior. We know the battle's ultimate outcome, and we can live in full confidence and power in this accomplished victory! We are signed, sealed, and established in our new nature; we have forgiveness, redemption, and salvation. We have the honor of living already knowing the story's end, so we ought to live in faith, firmly convinced in the wondrous outcome.

May we live confident that the good and wonderful we are hoping for will occur, knowing the things we can't yet see will take place. As we live with our eyes on Jesus, we have the ultimate victory and all the promises that come with it. In the wrestling of forces for power, God has conquered all. This truth, as we believe it, causes us to rise up. We are among those who live strong, like those in the hall of faith. "They shut the mouths of lions, quenched the flames of fire… Their weakness was turned to strength. They became strong in battle and put whole armies to flight" (Heb. 11:33–34, NLT). As we step into confident faith in the promise that the aftereffect of it all has already been decided and Jesus in all His glory has won, we can become strong in our own battles and send whole armies to flight in the spiritual realm. We can stand in confidence that He has won the battle over our own lives, and the plans that He sets forth for us will come about. Each step forward, we take with sureness. How wonderful that we have the intimate company of our wonderful, triumphant Jesus on our side, promising victory!

The Lie: God Is Not Big Enough

Within the lie concerning who holds the victory is an underlying lie: that God is not big enough. Oddly, even when we genuinely believe that the battle has been won and that Jesus has triumphed, at times, we still can live in a manner that does not reflect this truth. When we begin to see our problems or our concerns over others' well-being or spiritual state as our job to fix, we indirectly demonstrate belief in the lie that God is too small, incapable of solving the problem, will not come through for a need, or that He cannot intervene. However, the truth is God is all-able. He is no less than great, glorious, and full of strength. Nothing is impossible for God.

We fall into a similar trap if we allow ourselves to entertain the idea that we know better than God. If we try to solve another's problems, it can suggest that we care for a particular individual's needs more than God. When we involve ourselves too heavily in other people's circumstances, or allow their life stress to overwhelm our life, we demonstrate that we are not allowing God to be who He truly is. It is the Lord's role to sufficiently intervene. He alone can be all things to all people. Though we should always be caring, empathic and willing to help. Triune God alone is the answer, and we need to believe this. God is big enough.

God's ways are far beyond our own, and His understanding beyond comparison. What human wisdom has surpassed our very own Maker's? What love could be as deep, high, or wide? "Blessed is the one who trusts in the LORD, whose confidence is in him" (Jer. 17:7–8, NIV). Above problems, needs, concerns, and cares, He has it all under control. He is indeed that big, and the enemy is that small. As a party balloon is to a hot-air balloon, or a pebble compared to a mountain, satan is no match to Jesus. Bold faith believes in a big God.

May we pay careful attention to how we see our God and be rooted deeply in Him. When we choose to see Him in His real, capable, loving nature, as our all-powerful, holy, big and able God, our trust in Him will distribute itself across every aspect of our lives.

Reclaiming Territory with Power

Despite how difficult the struggles in battle might look, as we move to reclaim our rightful Kingdom territory, God is generating all things good. Every inch of our character and true nature that the enemy works to wear down and destroy will be built up again strong. "They'll rebuild the old ruins, raise a new city out of the wreckage. They'll start over on the ruined cities, take the rubble left behind and make it new" (Isa. 61:4, MSG). As we believe in the authority we have in our God, there will not just be a strength similar to what we had before, but a mighty strength.

Now may we be all that He designed and wants us to be. If we have faced guilt, then may we walk not merely understanding the basics of Jesus' grace, but let us be awestruck by its immensity, and let us genuinely celebrate the love He lavishes on us. If we have faced self-doubt, let us live, instead, completely inspired by who we are in Jesus. Then, we can live in the wonder of all we can accomplish in the glorious strength of Christ living through us. If the enemy has caused us doubt, may we retaliate with striking resolve simply to believe God. Once the lie has been broken, and this area has been regained under truth, we have such great potential. How powerful the witness who faced hardship and came through proclaiming victory and hope, like the Psalmist who wrote: "Your love has always been our lives' foundation" (Psalm 89:2, MSG).

In His love, the Lord has built us up strong in truth, freedom, joy and life. We are counted as ones who can stand in whatever storms life brings, whatever challenges. We are made strong and endure because the Lord has laid the groundwork. After struggle, we will overcome, rebuild, reclaim and stand in truth. God is for us: He is mighty, and it is He who restores us. All goodness is ours, and we reclaim the land of the blessed and full life He offers. All this is possible because He is our foundation.

Jesus won, and He extends us the offer for power and full living.

> *If you work the words into your life, you are like a smart carpenter who dug deep and laid the foundation of his house on bedrock... Nothing could shake it; it was built to last.*
>
> ~ *Luke 6:48–49 (MSG)*

Physical Attacks

Attacks against our spiritual health are common, and we also face attacks against our bodies, our physical health. We must remain faithful in connecting with our Lord, and He will give us His will on the matter and His eyes for His perspective. The enemy has his plan to deceive, kill, and destroy. Yet scripture tells us that healing is not only possible through the Lord, but that He is more than able to intervene: "I will heal them; and I will reveal to them an abundance of peace and truth" (Jer. 33:6, NASB). In intimate relationship, He whispers promises that tend to our heart, emotions, even to our very soul. In this place, healing begins.

We mend as these promises transfer from the soul into the entirety of our being, including our physical bodies. "Beloved, I pray that in all respects you may prosper and be in good health, just as your soul prospers" (3 John 1:2, NASB). Our Lord's will for us is a full life; His desire is for peace and truth to infiltrate our whole lives without boundaries. As they do, there is an incredible impact on our physical health and well-being. Jesus spent much of his time on earth healing the sick; we know healing and wholeness was His heart for people. He came as Truth and as the Prince of Peace, and He beckons each of us into a sacred place of healing.

We have this scripture as well: "How impossible it is for us to understand his decisions and his ways" (Rom. 11:33, NLT). As impossible, at times, as it is for us to believe the miracle when He does heal us, it is more challenging to accept the heartache when the healing doesn't come. Yet even there, we have this hope: He works all things for good. His goodness and power stand.

The Kingdom of God Surrounds Us

The Lord desires that we reach maturity and completion, and this includes having an authentic understanding of our real dwelling in the Kingdom of God. May our spiritual awareness be so sharp that the unseen and internal reality would become greatly magnified to us, even beyond what we see in the external. If we ignore, deny, or overlook this realm, we will miss out on so many of His great offerings. Through the Holy Spirit, our spiritual eyes are open, and we are connected to the fantastic reality of the hidden, invisible realm. When we see with spiritual eyes, we experience the truth of the eternal, of heaven's army, and of our always-purposeful King who reveals His workings to us.

He says now He lets us in on His plans; they are no longer a fully concealed mystery. When we join with Him in Spirit, it becomes quickly apparent that this real God-Kingdom is in the here and now. Jesus himself drew us into this awareness that "the Kingdom of God is already among [us]" (Luke 17:21, NLT). Dwelling in our Beloved's realm of reality allows us to discover our identity, strength, might, and purpose, to live a life far beyond our perceived present circumstances. May we live for the Kingdom of God now and embrace the light. Sure of who we are and who we live for, we are established in God's mighty armor to face every lie of the enemy that seeks to destroy our sacred relationship. Courage and boldness are required to step into our full identity, but we hold authority, love, power, and divine purpose as children of God. It takes stepping into the resolve of how deeply and unwaveringly we are loved by the King of kings, and who calls us into a confident, assured, strong identity, to find this divine resolution of precisely who we are in Christ. It allows us to boldly stand in the truth, no matter what attacks may come, and remain as beautiful, striking, transforming light in this world. May we be ones that live like this.

In your majesty, ride out to victory, defending truth, humility, and justice. Go forth to perform awe-inspiring deeds.

~ *Psalm 45:4 (NLT)*

Giving Him Our All

A lie from the enemy will have us believing that complacency or half-hearted devotion is okay. This belief may show itself when we say we want to follow God and give Him some sections of our life but withhold others. Or when we say we want to live for God's Kingdom, but the truth is we are self-satisfied with defining our own life ambitions. If we have a posture of indifference, are unresponsive to and unconcerned for God's plans, people and for the lost, we display a minimal effort and devotion. When we measure it against truth, lukewarm living is not acceptable. When we are aware of God's unfailing love, we will want to meet Him with upright, authentic hearts, and we will want to live in the fullness of all Triune God offers. Yet, more often than not, we become content and seem to settle into a routine where we squeeze our relationship with God into defined devotional time, prayers, and ministry. We come short of the power of a real encounter. We compartmentalize our first love, neatly fitting bits and pieces of love for Him into specific, limited times and spaces of our life and heart. Yet we are most likely to find ourselves truly happy, truly living during periods when we give the Lord our absolute all—in desire, attention, purpose, and pursuit. Anything short of that, and we cannot be fully satisfied.

The foolish style of living—of allowing little pockets of time in which we seek others' approval, build up pride in ourselves, and seek Him only minimally—will always stunt beautiful, full living. "The way to life—to God! —is vigorous and requires total attention" (Matt 7:14, MSG). The proper God-way leaves no room for half-hearted seeking, feeble devotion, or sluggish faith. These will only frustrate us because we can't shortchange

God. The godly way to life is robust and energetic, heartily enthusiastic, and it fully believes in the worth of our pursuit, for He is our first love.

So, in this world and our everything, may we stand up for our God and love Him with our resolved, absolute all, with no holding back. Then, there in that place is a beautiful promise, in that this is what He is waiting to find. We've seen the verse before, but it bears repeating here: "For the eyes of the LORD range throughout the earth to strengthen those whose hearts are fully committed to him" (2 Chron. 16:9, NIV). Our Lord's heart loves the faithful one who seeks Him in everything, so much so that His eyes search the earth to find these very people to help and strengthen them. Indeed, we know our Lord Jesus gave us absolutely everything. He held nothing back, not even His very life. May our hearts, too, be so very generous to our God. May we, like Jesus, give the Father our all.

Weapons Against Warfare

Our God is mighty in power, and in His all-knowingness, our God is aware of every one of the enemy's schemes and lies. Of course, He is completely in tune with all that we will require to govern the battle. Our incredibly gracious Lord, who brings love into all matters and always desires an intimate connection with us, transforms times of opposition to draw us even closer to Him. There is no place for us to be impartial or independent when the enemy attacks. Rather there is a full relational connection need to be with our Father. We must rely on our attachment to the Most High who promises all the best help. His strength to make us strong depends on His victory that allows us to fight and win.

> *Be prepared. You're up against far more than you can handle on your own. Take all the help you can get, every weapon God has issued.*
>
> ~ *Eph. 6:13–18 (MSG)*

In each conflict, there is an opportunity for us to fully depend on His gifts of armor. So, may we, with thanksgiving, take up all that He has offered in truth, righteousness, peace, faith, salvation, and Spirit. We must surround ourselves with the facts that align with the battle's existence, never ignorant, and never trying to fight on our own. We cannot be complacent towards the enemy who looks to destroy, nor should we on our own try to resist him. Instead, we rely on the unstoppable, unbeatable strength of the Lord. He makes us strong and calls us more than enough to conquer the one who comes against us. There is no neutral ground on earth. Yet God will take every opportunity, each attack, all the struggle and transform it powerfully under the placement of His good and perfect purposes. We must be caught in the reality that almighty, wondrous, victorious God is by our side. As we stand firm, deeper layers of intimacy form through our alliance with God. He provides our armor, He protects us, and He is always there with us in each confrontation.

Holy Spirit, Divine Weapon of Transformation

The most treasured of all defenses, the mysterious and powerful tool that will help us overcome it all, is the Holy Spirit's supply for every battle we face in life. This is no ordinary weapon, for this divine allocation empowers us to transform our lives. Our Heavenly Father has clothed us in all His wonderful attributes, and He shapes us in His purpose. It is our identity, and we need to familiarize ourselves with the power and authority at work in and through us, by His Holy Spirit, to be well-equipped to take on all He involves us in. He is our assurance, our help, and the testifier of all truth of Jesus. He is faithful to keep us on track.

It is no simple call this immersion with Christ; engaging in the Kingdom is often very complicated. Kingdom pursuits can face fierce attacks. Yet Paul says, "Keep putting into practice all that you learned and received from me —everything you heard from me and saw me doing. Then the God of peace will be with you" (Phil. 4:9, NLT). The only way we could ever possibly hope to join into Kingdom practices is to be changed into His glorious image and equipped by His very Spirit. In truth, joining Kingdom purpose is impossible unless we completely embrace the relational, genuine connection from Holy Spirit. It is only in that place of relational bond that we are authentically transformed into His likeness.

Just as it was in the early church of Acts, it is the same for us now: we need to receive the power of the Holy Spirit before we go out. In the generous outpouring of the Spirit by Jesus, the potential for the impossible becomes possible through us as we step into opportunities for His glory. We are equipped to overcome any and every scheme that comes against glorious Kingdom living.

The Armor of a Personal Word

The prophetic. God speaking to us. The idea of a word of God known as rhema. There is much division within the church on the idea of whether or how one can receive personal word from God. I was skeptical. It was a revelation of new territory. Yet I knew Jesus often does things in unexpected ways to stretch our trust or remove the boxes we place Him in. I needed to trust Him even with this. So, one Christmas, I tried it out for myself. I asked Jesus for a personal word. I was scared I would receive nothing.

An image came to mind. It was of an egg, cracked, broken, and weak. The Lord said, "This is how you feel." It was true. It was the Christmas season; our house was full of people; it was the busiest time of the year. With so much going on, I felt drained. Then He gave me an image of a strong, solid, golden adorned egg. And He said, "This is how I see you, strong. 'I can do all things through Christ, who gives me strength.'" The Lord took this truth in scripture and gave it to me in a new, unexpected way that transformed me. When the enemy wears me down and tells me I am weak, I remember this promised truth from scripture in a very personal way because of the word and image God gave me. This promised word helps me and armors me.

The word remains true for all of us. He is the one who makes us strong.

The One who is most deeply intimate provides us armor by blessing our hearts with personal words to us. Throughout history of the Bible, we see that God has spoken words to His people to direct their path of life. Jesus explained the ultimate importance of God's word when He said: "Man shall not live on bread alone, but on every word *[rhema]* that comes from the mouth of God" (Matt 4:4, NIV, addition mine).

The Bible contains promises, warnings, and direction. They are the amazing truths of God's provision, protection and guidance throughout life.

In scripture, we are told to arm ourselves with the belt of truth around our waist (Eph. 6:14), and we find the truths contain amazing promises of our God to combat all sorts of lies.

It is essential that we hold these promises with serious intent and unwavering belief, for they are the tools He says we will use in warfare, and we must have faith in their power. "His faithful promises are your armor and protection" (Psalm 91:4, NLT). We can know these promises by heart, but if we never have a personal experience that solidifies a truth as our own, the promises remain like mere theory to us. However, God wants us to wear the promises as our own.

In quiet times with God, when we His sheep listen to His voice (John 10:27), personal words come to us for encouragement, to build our identity, instruct us and give us direction. We test, of course, that they align with scripture. When they do and we accept them, they provide a thick, armor-like protection. We can take up "the sword of the Spirit, which is the word [rhema] of God" (Eph. 6:17). Rhema is the Greek word for utterance of God. Personal words of God are part of how the Holy Spirit moves upon our hearts and how we receive direct teaching from God Himself (John 6:45). Our armor is strengthened in incredible ways when we receive divine direction and distinct, specific words from the Lord.

Each personal word of God is sacred, supports us in battle and empowers us for victory. Perhaps He will speak of our strength, remind us of the reality of our protection, or the truth of His ever-presence. When we receive an intimate, personal word from God, it holds a wondrously unique ability to defeat all sorts of lies. In fact, Paul encouraged Timothy to rely on the personal words of God he'd had: "Timothy, my son, I am giving you this command in keeping with the prophecies once made about you, so that by recalling them you may fight the battle well" (1 Tim. 1:18, NIV).

May we humbly seek God for these most precious life-giving words. We should draw close and ask Him for personal words, pictures, or insights to transform the biblical truths we know into mighty, individualized reality. The Holy Spirit holds the power to take scripture and bring it to life as a beautiful gift and a piece of armor made tangible to our own experiences. These personal signs and wonders of God's particular direction move us into the confidence we need to stand firm against any and every lie that battles against us and our intimacy.

Protecting the Sacred Treasures

If one's intimate relationship with God is the highest of all treasures, then it should come as no surprise that the enemy's warfare efforts are highly stacked and specifically set against our precious bond. Since the beginning, the enemy's every lie and scheme has had the underlying pursuit to destroy intimacy with God, yet we have many mighty weapons. The Holy Spirit is at the top of our list of powerful defenses, for it is by Him that we are led into the precious space of all truths of Jesus. God has placed beautiful truths in our hearts and minds, and He supernaturally protects them through the indwelling of the sacred Spirit. We are under tremendous blessing and have the great advantage that we have the presence of Almighty God. He sends out His light and truth to guide us to the holy mountain, to the place where He lives (Psalm 43:3). Where else could we be safer from attack than under the shelter of God? We find there light, truth, and Spirit, and all we need to fight against all that wars against us and against the holy, intimate relationship. We have boldly entered heaven's Most Holy Place, all because of the incredible sacrificial love of Jesus (see Heb. 10:19–20).

It is an incredible, sacred honor to receive this invitation into His divine presence to experience the utmost favor of love's connection. We are to enter in holiness through the perfect sacrifice that found its completion in Christ. Jesus has fought, won, conquered, and holds all victory, and He offers us full, harmonious union with Him. In belonging to Christ, we also have a sacred place of dwelling with the Holy Spirit, which establishes us in triumph over our enemy in the final picture. He who is mightier and bigger holds all power and authority and can stand up to anything that comes against us.

We have all we need in Him; the holy place is key. His presence allows us to stand in truth and resist the lies. He guards our intimate relationship, and we have all that we need to overcome!

Found Standing Firm

Ignorance will not change the battles we are up against, and understanding truth is key to our defense and victory. Any warrior knows it is wise to try to comprehend the tactics of the enemy. Whether the enemy is warring against God's character, our identity, or our call, we know who is on our side, fighting side by side with us. Whether we face oppositions towards our physical or spiritual lives, false perceptions of the past or the future, we know well who our Beloved is and where our help comes from. Our God is big enough; it is He who reclaims, redeems, and holds victory. Holy Spirit moves us forward, and our new identity and nature are certain through the work of Jesus on the cross. He has reclaimed us to live for Kingdom, and we have the weapons, the promises, and the indwelling Holy Spirit, which provides all the confidence we could ever need.

Though at times deeply unpleasant, each battle holds incredible potential to draw us deeper and further into the thick layers of intimacy with God. In hardship, we have company so faithful, and we will be in awe of their loyalty. In impossible situations, we will be blown away by the power and strength we find that shows up for us when there seems no way out, simply because of the mighty company we keep as our own. Lies that once seemed so compelling and which began to influence our thinking will be torn down one by one. Truth will be rebuilt in our souls until we stand on the firm foundation of unshakable and endless promises. We have Triune God's faithful strength and the capacity of heaven's armies' steadfast help by our side in whatever battle we face. The gem of God-connection, of intimacy's bond, is our power; it equips and prepares us for all that comes our way. It whispers the promise: *After the battle, we will be found standing firm* (see Eph. 6:13, NLT).

Section 12:

BUILDING
DEEPER
INTIMACY

Having grown deeply in our understanding of our most loving King and His heart of love for us, how can we not be moved to devote ourselves to being builders of intimacy? With this desire, we ask the Lord to teach us the way. We seek to learn the secrets of all we can do to construct a life for the greatest possible relationship with the Divine.

> *Then he picked us up and set us down in highest heaven in company with Jesus, our Messiah. Now God has us where he wants us, with all the time in this world and the next to shower grace and kindness upon us in Christ Jesus. Saving is all his idea, and all his work. All we do is trust him enough to let him do it. It's God's gift from start to finish!*

> *Eph. 2:6–8 (MSG)*

> *The Kingdom of Heaven is like a mustard seed planted in a field. It is the smallest of all seeds, but it becomes the largest of garden plants; it grows into a tree, and birds come and make nests in its branches.*

> *Matt. 13:31–32 (NLT)*

Devoted Intimacy Builders

The intimacy Triune God extends to us is incredible and inspires us to something extraordinary. To us, His beloved, His invitation is such a delight, it's fully life-giving and undoubtedly the only thing our soul needs even more than physical life itself. So, of course, the Spirit begs to ask the question, how can we join with God's heart? How can we be mighty builders of intimacy and strive to meet His love with love? We know to protect this love: it is essential to fight off the lies that battle against the Kingdom of love. Yet beyond this, what heart posture can we take to make ourselves pliable to His moving, receptive to His affections, equipped to give our Beloved our all and meet Him in the intimacy He offers? This is our heart's desire and His heart's want.

Perhaps the secret rests in the knowledge that it is all His work. He picks us up, sets us right, and He draws us into His goodness. His incredible company makes us want to be good. It is certainly all Him— yet surely, we can give Him something. His giving inspires us to be dedicated intimacy builders in return.

Perhaps this scripture will provide us with some direction: "The person in right standing before God through loyal and steady believing is fully alive, really alive" (Hab. 2:4, MSG). The secret of being an intimacy builder may be in simply trusting in Him, in steadily believing in our right standing that comes from only Him, and in having faith that He will provide for our intimacy by leading us forward. Having a pure heart, authentically seeking to please the Father, and believing He will come through—perhaps this trust is all that's required.

So, we are blessed to take the next step, and then another, trusting God will meet us there. We ask His Holy Spirit to make us fully alive, believing that He works and provides all we need to be builders of the intimacy!

Clothed in His Likeness

When we understand that we have been molded into God's likeness, our intimacy can grow. We were made in His image and we live in the very nature of God. How deep our Father's affections go, that He sees us as His beloved children. Like the best of fathers treats his children, we are God's pride and delight. He loves it when we want to grow strong in our understanding of who He truly is. Triune God works to build us into nothing less than to be like them, in divine nature. With Jesus by our side and Holy Spirit living in us, Triune God's excellent traits can develop in us. Jesus desires this so much that He wants us clothed in Him and living in His armor of light (see Rom. 13:11–14). So, when we think of God's amazing traits—that He is peaceful, confident, able, and full of life—may we know these are the same traits He wants in us.

Jesus is our perfect role model and example. He shows us extravagant love, kindness, and joy, and He wants to mold these traits into us. As we faithfully live these and the fruits of the Spirit out in our lives, not only do they produce testimony to the world, but they simultaneously draw us closer to Him. Triune God wants us clothed in the same strength as Jesus. Timidity is not an option. We must know the power, authority, and boldness our Lord displays. He calls us to live this out in His likeness. Jesus Himself said that we were to do even greater things than what He did on earth.

We are faithful builders of intimacy when we seek a life that reflects His likeness. When we eagerly look to have Him build His nature into the fibers of our character, heart, and actions, we come closest to having our lives wholly and beautifully "defined by Christ" (Col. 3:11, MSG).

With Unity, Love the Body

The only attire that will cover us and prepare us to fill the deep heart desires of the Triune is to live clothed in His likeness. As we are enveloped in His likeness, our intimacy increases. We are called to live with the body of believers in the same unity the Trinity has together as Father, Son, and Spirit. Jesus prayed, "The goal is for all of them to become one heart and mind" (John 17:21, MSG). Our hearts must become pure and so full of the love we've received that we then pour that incredible love out, embracing both believers and soon-to-be believers alike. His heart is that we would receive His love and then come humbly before Him in all dealings with the body so that we would reciprocate the same love toward them that we have experienced in the Godhead.

It delights Triune's heart to see us living in the way that they live, free from tiresome foolishness that often burdens human relationships—comparison, competitiveness, judging, imposing expectations, enforcing rules. Disappointingly, this is what often results from our flesh-attempts to deal with our God-family. However far from His ways we stray, the Holy Spirit will empower us to transform and extend the love we receive from Triune to the body. The Triune's hearts are always good towards each other and pure. So, may we build our intimacy with God by testing our motives, purpose, and workings to insist that they align with the Lord's incredible grace. Whether we are leaders or new believers, we are all His servants, and we need to reach out to those who don't yet follow.

> Isn't everything you have and everything you are sheer gifts from God? So, what's the point of all this comparing and competing? You already have all you need. You already have more access to God than you can handle.

> ~ 1 Cor. 4:7–8 (MSG)

We have everything we could possibly want in Triune's affections and Holy Spirit's indwelling, so may we protect, treasure, and foster deep, united love with all in the family of believers.

Secret of Being Intentional

A picture of authentic intimacy can look like this: we seek the friendship of the Lord, have Him by our side, and remain in the Presence in all life's moments. Believing that the Lord is always with us blesses us in a permanent togetherness. The Holy Spirit literally dwells in us; this is our great reality—total Presence. Yet, there is a decision we need to make. Will we seek to authentically remain and abide in Him? Remaining is a practice rooted in lasting intimacy. It was not for any other reason than an enduring relationship that Jesus said we have to rely on them to succeed at doing anything and everything. Triune God loves our reliance on Him because it fosters a continual remaining in Him. When we remain in Him, we put ourselves in a posture to receive what we need to strengthen and enable us.

> *Let your servants see what you're best at—the ways you rule and bless your children. And let the loveliness of our Lord, our God, rest on us, confirming the work that we do.*
>
> *~ Psalm 90:16–17 (MSG)*

As this Presence rests on us, we see His rule and blessing, and our works are confirmed. It is as though in the abiding, we see God—we "see the best" of His actual intervening and the reality of our moment-by-moment friendship. There is no room for self-focus, but instead, we are consumed by the friendship that provides the Presence. As we daily have this continual increasing surrender to Holy Spirit, inviting Him to move, direct, and dwell in us, we meet our Triune's desire. With intimacy intact, we are healthy and strong in joining as one in Spirit with Him. May we abide like "the seeds in the good earth—these are the good-hearts who seize the Word and hold on no matter what, sticking with it until there's a harvest" (Luke 8:15, MSG).

What an invitation to abide in togetherness, with our eyes set on Kingdom work and harvest. When we find this beautiful place of abiding in Triune God, we have found the secret of being an intentional, wise, and serious builder of intimacy.

Obedience: Follow Through in the Asking

If we want to be builders of intimacy, we need to remain in a posture of obedience and agreement with the Lord. Throughout scripture, we find the Lord placing all sorts of requests on people, and He was eager for them to follow through. Jesus put so high a value on obedience because it uniquely demonstrates surrender, trust, and love. Jesus puts it like this: "Obedience is thicker than blood" (Luke 8:21, MSG). When we step out and follow through with what He asks, it is a great opportunity spiritually to love Him well. We are humbled that He who is all-able asks us to join Him in His working. In obedience, we demonstrate that as beloved children, we want to honor Him as our Lord. Our hearts take a posture of surrender.

We can trust our big, awesome Father has it all under control. His control is never to be feared, for, under His perfect love, we are blessed to be fearless. When we have heard His request or direction, obedience is always the way to go. Even if what He asks or directs does not make sense, we have the freedom to release it all into His hands. We have the promise of Presence wherever we go, and we also have the assurance of protection. The Holy Spirit's role in leading us in all truth secures us to move in response: He will not allow us to fail. Therefore, we can freely step out and obey all Triune God's asking.

When we died, we were set free to live for Our Lord's will. "For you died, and your life is now hidden with Christ in God" (Col. 3:3, NIV). Selfishness, worry, people-pleasing, and self-promotion have been put to death, for we live for the great audience of One. Hidden in Him, we are safe, protected, purified, and victorious to live in all of His askings. He will always lead us in the perfect way to go.

So may we stay here in this incredible place of intimacy-building obedience, joining with our first love, operating with Christ living in us.

Gauging our Response

It is crucial to follow through on what God asks of us. In intimacy, we have sought Jesus' heart's desire. Therefore, when we hear Him speak and His leading is directional, our response reflects our belief in what comes next.

If we greatly value our relationship, we will eagerly follow through with what He asks. However, if we don't meet God in His asking, the conversation may pause.

So, if we feel a silence from God, we should ask ourselves: have we followed through with His last request? After all, God is not aloof. He is constant, involved, and very personal. Once He has spoken, we may not hear more until we do as He has asked. He gives us room to meet Him in His request. Once we do, we can be assured He always has more to say.

As followers, we should routinely test our hearts to confirm we harbor no cherished sin that would introduce separation. Our next question should be, what did He last ask? If we have followed through with the last thing spoken, we can rest assured. If we sense any confusion over our direction, we can rest at His feet and persist in asking. He cherishes genuine requests. As beloved children, may we never allow the enemy ground by allowing silence to steal from our relationship.

God's requests can seem big, complicated, and almost impossible at times. But He understands our flesh's hesitation and recognizes that what He asks can leave us feeling vulnerable. However, the big requests are often a sign of His love pulling us into further intimacy. Those places of big asks offer deep soil for a fertile harvest of greater connection to Him.

May we thoroughly examine our follow-through on what He asks. His heart of love for deeper relationship is always behind His requests.

The Cross in Us Shines Out

We are made strong in intimacy when we trust who God has revealed us to be. Beyond lies, others' opinions, and the competing roles of our lives, Our Father has molded us, built us, and mentored us in our personhood. The enemy would love to have us doubt ourselves: he accuses our very nature and challenges who we are at our core. We might look back and magnify moments when we have been less than kind or lapsed in our resolve to love both God and others, and guilt may set in. Yet we are God's very own people sealed by the Holy Spirit. We operate in His kindness and His strength. So, we can know our hearts are secure because we live in His

Spirit. Our hearts' honest dwelling is preserved by God because we belong to God.

Christ embeds His cross in our very hearts, and He seals them to shine out His light. All of this is immovable because God has established it. We are who He made us to be, and we must trust He keeps our hearts and develops and matures us in our personhood. We are full of love shining out. We hold strength when we stand our ground in this reality, when we refuse to be tossed about and instead remain mighty in belief. At our core, we must know that we know that the Father sees the best in us. He defines who we are, and He says we are the light of the world. We are not to cover or suppress this light; it is not to be puffed out by others' opinions. We must faithfully let it shine for its purpose to build the Kingdom of God. These realities need to prevail over the enemy's lies, the world's opinions, and even the ideas we hold of ourselves at times.

May the Great Shepherd's be the voice we listen to, as it provides the hope of who we are in Him and how He works us to completion in love. We will believe the One who says our hearts are His, with His Spirit resting in them. When we trust our life is already united with Him and that the cross is embedded in our every fiber, we may go out in boldness and be that incredible light!

Step-by-Step Direction

Intimacy deepens the more we aim to be real and honest with God. Life alone has many challenges, and the Christian life in particular can be hard at times. Yet Triune God loves when we ask, believe, and live in dependency on them for all things. When we find ourselves in a place of confusion regarding where to go next, we can increase the depth of our intimacy with God by depending on Him more. If we lean into the difficulty we face, God will show us His workings, and we will see He reveals a map for each next step along the journey.

Our honest voice, when we relentlessly seek the divine's leading, positions us to wait upon the Father until we receive a secret, specific word of direction for our next step. As we ask and wait, we will have clarity on what He asks us to do next. When we receive what He reveals, we know that He honestly gives us only the best. He gives us the endurance to fulfill His request. Profound intimacy building takes place when we spend the time to listen to what He has to say. Our attitude and the perception we now hold aligns in total agreement with the Triune God. Now we faithfully follow the lead of what He asks, living as beloved children who want to please their Father.

Whether we are called to sacrifice in the moment, endure through suffering, or step into victory through battle, each call requires an intimate embrace of trust that displays the relationship's foundational worth. By moving in faithfulness and following His map, we declare our love for Him. Power comes from the place where we believe God's call. As we join in with Holy Spirit's Kingdom focus and working, we practice incredible faith. Foundations of courage, boldness, belief, and intentionality for seeing Jesus' purposes fulfilled are established in the core of our being.

Perhaps part of the secret to being content whatever our circumstances and to having peace that surpasses all understanding is to know that we have prayed to, asked of, waited on, and been led by Triune God. Now we find ourselves in the intimate place of knowing the great Navigator has set out our course.

Patterns of Conversations With God

Intimacy is strengthened in daily asking, believing, and relying on God with the expectation that He always shows up. However, in our relationship with God, we are after more than mere answers to our asking. We build relationship through our daily interactions. As we make them part of the rhythm of life, we please God. We present a godly request before Him, one that we are confident is already within His will. Then we wait to see the fruit.

In establishing these deep patterns of conversations with God, we sometimes have joy in seeing immediate results. This may look like finding peace in chaos or having the strength to endure a hard day. At other times, we experience immense pleasure when a long-awaited request finally comes. In the practice of believing, trust grows. In the times of waiting, faith's foundation becomes even firmer. When we are in the routine of asking, we see Him on the move frequently, and we experience the joy of recognizing how the living God interacts with us as He extends help and direction. We trust Him more as we see that in all reality, He really hears us. He often wants us to ask so that He can give, for He knows that makes Him more real to us.

It is the non-asking, the silence from us, that creates a divide. "You do not have, because you do not ask God" (James 4:2, NIV). Some place little expectation on God, perhaps thinking that is a humble position to take. We may think our need is too little, or that He is too important to ask, or that He doesn't get involved. But these are human thoughts. By not expecting much of God, and by not asking, we miss a crucial opportunity to grow closer to Him. He tells us to ask, and He knows we need to ask.

While the everyday demand to lay our hearts before God can seem overwhelming, this is "the confidence we have in approaching God: that if we ask anything according to his will, he hears us. And if we know that he hears us—whatever we ask—we know that we have what we asked of him" (1 John 5:14–15, NIV). Intimacy forms in ongoing interactions, and interaction blesses our relationship with astonishing realness that God hears, cares and gives what is needed. For when we reach out to the Lord and ask for Him to make himself or His love even more real to us, we have confidence that this request is already in line with His will, and He will answer every time. The reality that He will reveal to us, the Presence we will sense as we ask and believe, builds an incredible experience of intimacy.

Full-Out Belief

There comes the point where we need to make some critical decisions about our relationship with God. We can study about God, learn about Him, experience Him, work with Him, and even be in an intimate and close relationship with Him, but will we believe Him? Not just parts of what we know to be true, but the fullness of God, His words, His asking, His promises, and even His call—will we believe?

We see this in Abraham's life. After growing into a well-aged man without a proper heir, the Lord came to Abraham in a vision.

[The LORD] took him outside and said, "Look up at the sky and count the stars—if indeed you can count them."

Then he said to him, "So shall your offspring be."

Abram believed the LORD, and he credited it to him as righteousness.

~ Gen. 15:5–6 (NIV)

Abraham's belief in God resulted in a powerful faith commitment, which built a dedicated relationship. Deep down, the truth is there. Anything less than fully committed belief shortchanges God and us from all that this relationship and life is intended to be. Without complete confidence in what He says, the affection He has for us, in the Kingdom we are called to live for, this life and our closeness to God will be interrupted if not dead.

As it does in any relationship, there comes the question: do we completely trust this one—in this case, this One we call God and Friend? Do we believe in all we know about Him to be real? We can read, meditate, memorize, and even teach truths about God and His character, but something deeper is required. We must operate from a place of sureness and hope. This sureness comes not in leaning on our own understanding, science, politics, or popular church culture, but solely and loyally on God's truth and His words. When we find the place where we relinquish all unbelief, we step into living a full-out, one hundred percent, burning hot, all eggs in the basket, *Yes!* to God.

In this position of richest intimacy, we take on the exceptional faith that makes us truly alive, where human understanding is set aside for Spirit understanding and our minds are set on Kingdom single-mindedness. In childlike, pure commitment, without hesitancies or timidities that get in our way, we stand surrendered to radiant belief in the One we love.

Power and the Key of Faith

Faith is a key that opens all sorts of blessings, including power, protection, and provision. Perhaps that is why without faith, it is impossible to please God. There is a lot of work to be done on this earth. He uses us as His hands and feet, He gives us gifts, and He calls us. If we lack certainty in His truths and promises and question Him every step of the way, our progress will be stifled. Yet when we faithfully join Him as co-workers in His kingdom work, we receive power, provision, and protection.

A Christ-follower seeking power may at first feel hesitant. The enemy would love us to stay weak and not exercise God's gift of power. Our model, Jesus, though, did not shrink back from the power extended to Him. He displayed His power with remarkable humility. We must live in this power, to "fight the good fight" (1 Tim. 6:12). We depend on His power to fight, and we are promised all we need of it from the Holy Spirit.

It takes spiritual understanding and courage to ask for God's power, provision, and protection, but it builds such profound intimacy when we do. As we take up the great and mighty protection God offers, we become equipped and effective. We are promised incredible armor and heaven's army's help, with the assurance that nothing will occur to us that doesn't pass through His say. So, may we have faith in our Almighty's guard over us! There is no provision we need that He lacks; every good thing is from His hand. Our God is full of goodness, our God has an "abundant storehouse" (Deut. 28:12, CSB), and He is excessively generous.

Throughout scripture, God asks difficult things of His people that require faith, sureness, strength, courage, and yes, even power. He asks for big tasks, yet makes great promises, so we must rely on our big God. When His children depend on Him for the incredible power, the fierce protection, and abundant provision only He can give, He gives freely, and greater intimacy results.

Recognizing God's Affection and Attention

God wants us to genuinely seek to understand intimacy, even if His full glory is beyond our sight. While Kingdom work with God is fantastic, we will find something we long for even more deeply. When we receive it, it fuels an even greater passion for more Kingdom work. It occurs when we enter into the reality that the eyes of our Beloved are on us, and we hold His focus. With this understanding, we become authentically absent of any egotistical, self-centered, prideful desire, motive, or ambition. When we are set on abiding in intimacy with Him, we humbly recognize we are under His affection and His attention.

As I grew up, I observed many amazing parents—my own parents, parents of friends, schoolmates and others in the community around me. None were flawless; all had imperfections. Now, as a parent myself, I see those flaws as simply part of being human. But I noticed certain parents who really gave their children full attention, while others prioritized regular check-in times. I saw some who you could tell adored their children and others that were protective in a good way. Certain parents exemplified what it looks like to stand up for a child in difficulty. Others did random acts of kindness, and their kids knew they could always depend on them. Some incorporated regular family meals together or time serving others together, and other families just had plain old fun together, and that was their priority.

So, I took all these admirable traits I saw in others, and when I became a parent, I set out to incorporate them in how my family looks and how I wanted to strive to be as a parent. Even though I don't always attain the ideals and what I do is done imperfectly, I aim for those admirable traits.

As I've observed parent behaviors, I've noticed that the most admirable traits line up with how our loving heavenly Father interacts with us, His family and His children. Yet He does all the above well with perfection. We are the object of His focus, the apple of His eye; we are the ones God adores and delights in because we are His beloved children. The Lord is reliable, protective, and stands up for us. He knows how to have fun. We are always welcome to check-in and come to His table to spend time together. As the best possible parent, He blesses us with great attention and affection.

The intimacy Moses experienced with God in the tent of meeting gives us a glimpse of what God desires. In Exodus 33:11, we read that inside the tent of meeting, "the LORD would speak to Moses face to face, as one speaks to a friend" (NIV). There is no picture here of a removed, aloof God, but rather we see a snapshot of Moses' deep connection with Almighty God as a friend—and they are in conversation with one another, no less. What honor we carry to be counted among those who are "GODaffirmers [who] find themselves loved every time they turn around" (Psalm 32:10, MSG).

Jesus opened this powerful Presence for us all, and it was Triune God's idea, plan, and longing for us to receive His gift of powerful closeness and embracing friendship. It is given, not earned, and it can move mountains when it is practiced and accepted. For the Presence we stand in is astronomical. And it is God's plan for us to be in this place, for our intimacy with Him deepens when we understand that His focus is on us.

> GOD's *business in putting things right;*
> *he loves getting the lines straight,*
>
> *Setting us straight. Once we're standing tall,*
> *we can look him straight in the eye.*
>
> ~ *Psalm 11:7 (MSG)*

Praise be to Jesus. He has set us straight already and released worthiness over us. We can stand tall and see the Father's loving eyes focused on us.

Power in Him

What favor we have, knowing God's eyes are on us! He is aware of every detail. What potential for love and intimacy we have entered. May we never doubt that God sees us, watches us, and wants us to live in Him, for Him, and with Him. Within this deep love, He understands we will fail at times, and we will not be all we know He wants us to be. He meets us there with more love. As the best of parents have seemingly endless patience for a child who is learning something new, so the Father has this love for us. He already sees us perfect in the end picture, complete in Christ.

He wants to enjoy the journey with us and for us to enjoy it with Him. As we grow in maturity, we practice an increasing discipline to intentionally, constantly set our sight on Him. He loves the intimacy-building potential that comes at each turn in our path. Our Lord is the overseer of our lives. With all wisdom, understanding, and leading, He extends His hand to us when we ask. As a loving Father to His children, He passes blessing with perfect direction on to us. We can rest because we don't have to look to other's opinions, our own expectations of ourselves, or popular culture—we hold every freedom in Christ and have the favor of resting in His approval alone. From the position of being focused on His desires, we can trust He leads us to excellence.

Where the Lord leads is not always easy, but the Holy Spirit is with us as we journey. The path before us is distinct and intentionally paved in love, and Jesus promises to walk along beside us. We are never alone: we have their great company. "We have this treasure in earthen vessels, that the excellence of the power may be of God and not of us" (2 Cor. 4:7, NKJV). So, may we go and be radiant light for our God as His vessels, excellent in His power, shining out for Him in love.

A Childlike Place of Praise

How pure and lovely it is to place ourselves at the feet of Jesus in adoration, worship, and praise, to surrender, to admire, and give our all just for God. "His love is the wonder of the world" (Psalm 31:21, MSG), yet many miss the wonder. For those who know Him personally, it is a delight to be at His feet and praise Him with all we've got. "Invent your own song to him" (Psalm 33:3, MSG). Heartfelt, sincere, and generous giving to God is unquestionably a gateway into Presence and a way to form intimacy. It can come as a gentle whisper of worship to the Holy One. At other times, we might make a shout of joyous celebration, a dance, a "gift of laughter" (Psalm 100:2, MSG). When we present a creative, one-of-a-kind gift of worship to God, we bless His heart with our sincere, childlike loving efforts. God is so good to us. He's worthy of all our efforts to worship Him at every turn. How could we give Him anything less?

Worship is pure because it is all about Him. Above even thanksgiving, it wins in the purity of its offering, for it is not dependent on anything He has given us. It is a celebration and declaration of who He is, not just what He has given. "For God is sheer beauty, all-generous in love, loyal always and ever" (Psalm 100:5, MSG). In the place of worship, we fully give God the highest praise; we set our eyes fully on Him. Worship is a love offering in which we voice our delight in who He is. God gives us the gift of worship so that we might have an outlet to give something back to Him.

When we tap into it, we find that worship runs through the course of every fiber of our very being because we were created to celebrate, honor, and delight in the Creator. He is the One who gives us life, love, and our every breath; He is the One we adore. So, we shall sing, laugh, dance, take great joy and delight in worshiping God with all we have because He is worthy. It takes no other reason than that! From the place of worship, we more deeply enter the depths of the most wondrous of intimacies.

Living Out Our Calling, Using Our Gifts

God has given each of you a gift from his great variety of spiritual gifts. Use them well to serve one another... Do it with all the strength and energy that God supplies.

~ *1 Pet. 4:10–11 (NLT)*

It blesses God's heart when we use the gifts and talents He has so generously given. We harbor a false humility if we think we do not have a gift, for scripture clearly says otherwise. It is immature to ignore the gift God gives. Instead, we are to take it and act upon it with seriousness and maturity, giving it all we've got. For it is in the place of intimacy that God reveals the gift to us, and our appropriate response is to listen, understand, and obey. As we do, we demonstrate trust and faith. Therefore, may we build intimacy further by holding the treasures of His gifts carefully and protecting them steadfastly, never letting go. There should be no turning away from or burying our talent. Rather, let us stand in full belief that He gifts us. We can find encouragement in the apostle Peter's words: "Then everything you do will bring glory to God through Jesus Christ" (1 Pet. 4:11, NLT).

Behavior often follows a decision. It may seem odd, but a life of faith comes down to living out what you have agreed to be true. As you put your faith in action, you experience its reality: "For as he thinks in his heart, so is he" (Prov. 23:7, NKJV). Knowing this truth, may we be ever so careful about how we think and see the gifts God has given us and the call that He has placed on our life. As we commit to seeing the skills He's given as a special blessing, we see how we fit into all the working of God in this world. What an amazing position He gives us to join Him in living in and building the Kingdom of God.

So, rather than put to death our potential in Christ because we harbor some unbelief in our heart, let's commit to being all-in with our belief. No holding back, doubting ourselves, our call, or God; instead, we stand firm with all our energy and strength committed to acting in the gifting He has called us to.

Rhythms of Spiritual Practice

The rhythms of daily spiritual practice have the potential to be an excellent tool for building intimacy. However, the rhythms we adopt can become routine steps or check-off boxes, producing minimal—if any—relational connection. So, as we put different rituals into practice, we must look at why we engage in them. Once rightly positioned, a routine can provide a powerful rhythm in which we encounter God's love and where we find great Holy Spirit rest and movement forward.

For instance, if we step into a practice of memorizing scripture, what we memorize becomes a delicately knit covering of truths upon our heart that can affect our being in incomparable ways. "I have hidden your word in my heart, that I might not sin against you" (Psalm 119:11, NLT). Memorizing scripture is a powerful discipline that produces many fruits. It grows us in the Lord's truth.

Meditating on His Word is another important practice we can adopt. We are directed in scripture to meditate on God's unfailing love, on His commands, and on His majestic miracles (see Psalm 48:9, 119:48, 145:5). As we meditate on them day and night and carefully follow God's asking and direction, we are met with the promise that we will find success and do well (see Josh. 1:8). In specific, focused meditation time, we dedicate ourselves to reflecting on God's story, truth, and promises. In that process, something profound embeds in our very being.

Prayer and fasting also have an important place in our rhythms with God. When done with the right motives for Kingdom benefit, fasting holds great power and can have excellent results (see Mark 9:29 & Acts 10:30). Withholding something from ourselves while we petition God for a need mysteriously opens doors that might otherwise remain closed. When Daniel turned to God, pleading with prayer, petition, confession and fasting, scripture says that there was astonishing movement in the heavens and Daniel was given insight and understanding. These movements in the heavens began as soon as he began to pray (See Dan. 9). Prayer—whether in speaking with God as a friend, or in asking, or in petition—aligns well with the pattern God gives us to connect deeply with Him (see Eph. 6:18).

These rhythms and patterns of spiritual practice can serve as an extraordinary gateway into the most intimate presence of God. May we guard the purity of the motive behind these practices to continue and build on our authentic intimacy with God.

Power of Remaining, Asking, Believing and Doing

To remain in Him, to ask "How shall I pray?", positions us in a beautiful place of joining our Lord in dependency and surrender. To enter that place regularly creates rhythms that imitate the life pattern Jesus had with His Father. Jesus' dependence on the Father ultimately produced incredible victory on the cross. The practice of remaining in Him, praying in dependence, and living in surrender are powerful builders of intimacy. When we align with the Father, joined with Him, we can have immense confidence to ask what He places on our hearts.

> *If you remain in me and my words remain in you, you may ask for anything you want, and it will be granted! When you produce much fruit, you are my true disciples. This brings great glory to my Father.*
>
> ~ *John 15:7–8 (NLT)*

In joining in the Kingdom of God as disciples who desire to serve Him and produce the fruit that glorifies the Father, we are given great permission to ask. As His children, we ought to ask our Father for everything but demand nothing. Jesus knew that the motive to serve one's self-interest has the potential to get in the way. He prayed to the Father, "Not my will, but yours be done" (Luke 22:42, NIV).

When we remain in Him, walking in intimate closeness, we make requests freely and often. Paul instructs: "Pray every way you know how, for everyone you know" (1 Tim. 2:1, MSG). But this also overflows into a multitude of areas in our lives. Examples of abandoned calls for mercy, desperate pleas for God's movement, help, healing, and miracles are throughout the scriptures. These are all ways to pray. We can call for power, Holy Spirit's help, for hearts to soften, and we know our prayers are heard. His heart is moved by our prayers. He is our good Father, and even when we do not see immediate answers, we are blessed when we wait and believe.

Our God is able, and nothing is impossible for Him (see Gen. 18:14). Even when our human eyes cannot see, we can ask God to open our spiritual eyes to remove any disbelief and help us to move forward in trust. As when Jesus walked on water and extended His hand to Peter to come to Him, may we too respond and get out of the boat to endeavor into the seemingly impossible. Peter had remained in the company of Jesus. Peter asked, and then he believed.

> *"Lord, if it's you," Peter replied, "tell me to come to you on the water."*
> *"Come," [Jesus] said.*
> *Then Peter got down out of the boat, walked on the water and came toward Jesus.*
>
> ~ *Matt. 14:28–29 (NIV)*

So when the Lord extends us His hand and asks us to come, may we get out and exercise our faith with courage and fearlessness to walk where He leads. For remaining in Him, asking, believing, and doing are powerful builders of intimacy.

Trusting His Unfailing Love

A genuine belief and commitment to trusting the unfailing love of the Lord are likely going to be the ultimate builders of intimacy that will powerfully hold together all else. For each of us, there needs to be a fierce resolve to bask in this truth of unfailing love until we come to a place where we know that we know that this factual truth is sealed on our hearts, minds, and spirits. This truth is the gospel's core, and it's interlaced throughout by all Jesus did for us on the cross. He *did* so love the world, and we have Holy Spirit to enduringly remind us of this life-changing truth. Yet we need to find the place where we step in and commit to believing, where we say in agreement that we will "trust in God's unfailing love for ever and ever" (Psalm 52:8, NIV).

Someone asked me where the shift in my life occurred, where Jesus advanced to become my Lord? I would love to say I just choose Him out of maturity, understanding, and commitment. But the truth is it happened in a very different place. It happened in brokenness.

In my late teens, I went through multiple events, which made for a difficult season like no other before or since, and the Lord met me in an amazing way. He was there; He cared for me; He put life back into me. His faithful love mended me and put a fire into me for Him being the Lord of my life, covering every inch. After that, vision for His Kingdom became sealed on my heart because I knew He was the answer to everything.

Everyone goes through seasons of brokenness. We can't escape them. But if we can help others find the source of strength and healing in Jesus, we give them a lifeline like no other. Since that time for me, I can't help but realize brokenness should not be feared, for it is a powerful tool that can move us like few other things to find the place of Him alone being the most dependable thing in our lives.

We may have come to a place of committing to Jesus, but there is a deeper place of committing to trusting that He loves us. For many, this may be the place where Jesus advances in our hearts from being Savior to also being Lord. Here we find true abandonment to place Him as King over our everything. This is likely where we have first seen His love to be the most dependable thing in our lives. This acknowledgment sometimes follows a place of facing deep pain, failure or sorrow, that is simultaneously met with the reality of faithful friend Jesus by our side when all else seems insufficient to meet the heart's needs.

> I waited and waited and waited for GOD.
>   At last he looked; finally he listened.
> He lifted me out of the ditch,
>   pulled me from deep mud.
> He stood me up on a solid rock
>   to make sure I wouldn't slip.
>
> He taught me how to sing the latest God-song,
>   a praise-song to our God.
> More and more people are seeing this:

they enter the mystery,
abandoning themselves to GOD.

~ Psalm 40:1–3 (MSG)

There is a new sureness in us when we receive the steadfast love that deeply plants the embedded seeds of truth and trust. As we wait on God, we find Him looking at us, listening, pulling us out of the mud of life, placing us safe and secure on a rock of love. Within this mystery, with a new praise song in our heart, we abandon ourselves to the Lord.

So, in the secret heart-place, to build intimacy, may we decide to trust this love which is like no other, to see it as the foundational core of truth and treasure that wins over all else.

Belief in Current and Future Rewards

It may seem strange to say that believing in the rewards of God builds intimacy. However, that seems to be the way Triune God has laid things out. "Anyone who wants to come to him must believe that God exists and that he rewards those who sincerely seek him" (Heb. 11:6, NLT). Sure, we understand the value of believing that He exists: that is understandable. Yet what about the idea that we need to believe He rewards us when we earnestly seek Him? The concept of reward seems tied with faith and belief. Perhaps trusting in the reward reveals two things about our hearts. First, it reveals which kingdom we live for, our own or His. Second, belief in reward shows what we are focused on, the seen or the unseen world. As we set our hearts on an out-of-this-world reward and diligently pour out our lives for His Kingdom, our actions clarify to Him and ourselves deep, powerful obedience. That obedience is fueled by love for our Lord and a desire to please Him alone as we live for the promise we will receive in our new life to come.

Our obedience demonstrates we stand not on the comfort and safety of this life but that we are ready to lay our lives down for the One we have chosen to live for. It is a faith that lets us be daring, brave, and bold; it is one that leads to mighty action. It puts into motion the seemingly impossible, even to the point that we will surrender our lives as we bank our full hope in promises not yet received.

Blessed are you when people insult you, persecute you and falsely say all kinds of evil against you because of me. Rejoice and be glad, because great is your reward in heaven.

~ *Matt. 5:11–12 (NIV)*

But our reward begins here and now in that we are in Divine relationship. The specifics of the heavenly rewards are not fully clear, but we have already received a great promise.

Belief in the current and future rewards provide us incredible courage to face all sorts of trials. When we have entered intimacy's embrace, we are strengthened to face whatever our Beloved asks of us here on earth. Set on living for God's Kingdom now, we will endure whatever comes our way as we hear the whispered promise that the rewards still to come are real and worth it. We live in the intimate wonder of truth that we will see our beloved Lord face to face.

Trust for All We Need

There are many ways to love God well and build a profound relationship with Him. When we truly know God's love for us and the value we have to Him, we want to present our best for our Lord. From surrender, to prayer, to giving Him our full-out belief without any doubt, each of these plays a role in how we can grow closer and experience more of Him. Interestingly, there is an unexpected and mysterious place where we find perhaps the greatest building block of our connection with God. We come to this unique, intimate dwelling place when we fully realize we cannot do it independently: we cannot even seek to build intimacy on our own. Here we make the raw, sincere confession: we need His faithful embrace to do any of it. He alone raises us up into every act of obedience. We enter with the hope to please and serve Him. "Let the Spirit renew your thoughts and attitudes. Put on your new nature, created to be like God—truly righteous and holy" (Eph. 4:23–24, NLT). What significant Spirit love!

Our God, who thought of everything, meets every need, especially the utmost heartfelt one—the necessity of always building deeper into our relationship. "Our God gives you everything you need, makes you everything you're to be" (2 Thess. 1:2, MSG). It is Him who shapes us, our habits, our spiritual practices, and our very own authenticity. The Lord's strength moves through us and accomplishes all to make us all we are to be. His very own deposited Spirit occupies within us, blessing us with the greatest possible position, beyond any human strength or standing. Our God makes us fit and able to grow to accomplish all He calls us to in maturity, so may this be our asking. How great He is to show us we are incapable of this on our own. It's yet another way He draws us into the deepest of intimacy. Even in this, we cannot go out on our own or attempt to do it without Him.

In the attempt to build on the intimacy He invites us to, we must pursue it with and through Him. Praise God, for even in this journey towards building deeper intimacy, He gives us the best of company: Himself.

MEETING OUR POTENTIAL, FINDING OUR PURPOSE

As we dwell in God's Kingdom and it becomes our reality, may we steep ourselves in everything Triune God reveals and calls us into. As we abide and align ourselves with them, they enable us to do the incredible things they ask for the greatest Kingdom purpose. What we can do as we are joined with them is unimaginable. In their intimate embrace, they empower us to faithfully live out our most significant purposes.

Steep yourself in God-reality, God-initiative, God-provisions.

~ Luke 12:31 (MSG)

Love Runs Through Us

Even with our best efforts, it can be difficult to maintain a clear perspective of our purpose. As Christians, there are many very good things we can work towards achieving. Often, above the pursuit of the best, "good" work crowds in and competes for our attention. We need to ask what is it, exactly, that we seek? Better yet, what exactly does God want us to pursue in the Christ-filled life? Likely, He won't direct us to believe better, serve better, or obey better. And although loving better might be closer to the ultimate goal, He's probably not even directing us toward that. In and of itself, a focus on love can come independently of God's heart's desire for us. Perhaps ironically, believing, serving, obeying, and loving better each holds the potential for misalignment with God's heart, in that they can become individual pursuits disconnected from God. I can serve for others' approval, obey for the virtue of obedience, and love as a principle. Yet this still stands true: if I "do not have love, I am nothing" (1 Cor. 13:2, NIV).

Thankfully, it does not say, "if I don't love others or God flawlessly, I have nothing," as we all seem relatively weak at loving perfectly. The scripture instead signals that if I do not have the meaningfully connected, complete love of God running through me, I have nothing. That is the love that comes from God and flows through us with sincerity for God and others. The truest love is found in the authentic love-hold of God that encompasses a moment-by-moment, genuine joining with Him that allows us to pour out well in love back to Him and onto others. This is exactly what God and our own hearts seek.

In that love, we reach the first goal of devotion that assembles a fertile ground of all sorts of wonders, such as loyal obedience, deepest belief, and sacrificial love. It unlocks our original purpose in Kingdom living: in all things, we are "more than conquerors *through him who loved us*" (Rom. 8:37, NIV, emphasis mine). As we operate with this love running through us, we have no limits. In the God-hold of love, we experience the greatest connection that enables us to align with all our potential for being part of God's Kingdom.

To Live in His Extravagant Glory

We have been invited to the grand experience of living life in His extravagant glory. God's full fondness and care and the wonders of His affections are revealed in the complete love story. Without God's love, we have nothing; but with His authentic, pure, connected love, we have everything. As His love transforms our perspective, it is likely to invade our entirety—how we see this world, people, relationships, work, and our role in it all. It overruns our every function. As His love becomes our reality, there is no longer room for boredom or simple living. We begin to pursue our first love and live in all He has for us.

The hunger that drives us to know God brings us into a new place. We are no longer satisfied to just know about Him. We passionately work to experience Him and live in intimate relationship with Him. We want the great encounter of the wonder of knowing God. Paul prayed this for the Ephesians:

> *I ask—ask the God of our Master, Jesus Christ, the God of glory—to make you intelligent and discerning in knowing him personally, your eyes focused and clear, so that you can see exactly what it is he is calling you to do, grasp the immensity of this glorious way of life he has for his followers, oh, the utter extravagance of his work in us who trust him—endless energy, boundless strength!*

> ~ *Eph. 1:17–19 (MSG)*

May we trust God fully and see the everyday miracles. From His unlimited resources, He makes it possible for us to move forward in His purposes. We will ask, believe, and be ready to move when He directs. As we live in the very Spirit He gives us, we are capable and perfectly equipped to join His work. Never alone, Jesus always by our side, we are ready for intense living in His magnificent glory.

He stands right before us, and therefore we can receive the full, extravagant life he offers.

Who We Are in Him Defines Us

Prior to entering into our greater purpose, we face an identity crisis. We must encounter the brilliant reality of Christ's full truth. As we first come to Jesus, we know that we are forgiven, have the promise of salvation, and are changed to live another way. Those changes alone are astonishing! However, it is remarkable how many of us followers don't take on our full identity, capability, and potential in all that God desires for us. When we see who our Father is and when we understand His nature, goodness, power, and that we are children of the King, we receive the possibility of doing the extraordinary, for we are in His likeness. He transforms us to be great in our nature, goodness, and power.

In our earthly nature, we tend to ignorantly believe that nobleness or poverty defines us. Yet in the Kingdom, our great King and Father clarifies that our true identity rests only and completely in who we are in Him. He alone defines us! He is amazing, and He is out to make us amazing people who represent Him. What lengths He has gone to to extend Himself to us. He provides the amazing connection of Christ in us!

As followers, we are told that we will do even greater things than Jesus did on earth. It requires practice to see our identity through the lens of the unimaginable. We have access to the same power that raised Jesus from the grave. How incredibly God has equipped us, how beautiful the call, how intimate the bond and relationship He yokes us in as His children. May our identity in all this fullness be firm!

So now, as children who know their identity in Him, we go out in love. We do nothing on our own: we listen to our Father, we carry out His orders, and we complete all the tasks He gives, just as we saw Jesus doing (see John 5:30). Defined by Him alone, our identity and purpose are complete.

Uniquely Called

How does knowing the wonder of our God-given identity impact our greater purpose? We are under the love that means everything, so we can be confident in who God says we are, to be all we can be, to reach our God given potential. A popular misconception is that we should not think too long about our own identity, that concentrating too long on ourselves is self-focused. Yet even though it is true—He reigns in the place of utmost honor and should always be in the proper position on the throne of our life—we do need to look at ourselves to better comprehend the role He calls us to. We must have a firm grasp on our identity. We are uniquely and wonderfully made by God, and we no longer live in the selfishness of the flesh but have been incredibly transformed to live a God-honoring life in the Spirit.

God sees it as essential for us, His beloved children, to become mature and know who we are. He loves building our resiliency. He wants us to understand not only His love but how it develops us into who we uniquely are to Him. We find ourselves working together with Him, poised and assured that we are equipped in love, readied to pursue Kingdom purposes. To effectively live out the strength, victory, freedom, and intentions that He desires for us, we must be convinced of all we are in Him. If we see our character as still in its flesh-state, our identity remains weak, and our dedication becomes feeble.

To give our full loyalty to Him, we must live from the rich inheritance of strengths, giftings, and callings He gives. When our whole life is all about Him, we can draw from His unlimited resources. He needs us to know exactly who we are: That is how we will have a strong identity to represent Him well. As we believe that we are His children, each of us unique and well-known, we become confident in the equipping that comes from His very hand for our greater purpose. We are "Christ's ambassadors" (2 Cor. 5:20).

Overcoming Fear of Excellence and Success

Even with knowledge of our identity, an abundance of resources, and our call to excellence, we may still feel intimidated, be fearful of pride, or afraid to fail. The scriptures give sad examples of people raised to greatness who then shamefully forget God. Consider Saul and Solomon. After they achieved much success, a disheartening record shows them giving into pride and turning to their own ways. However, our call to excellence still stands. The call comes from God. We cannot be afraid of or shrink back from the call to succeed, using humility as a cover for fear. When we undercut and underrepresent ourselves, whether in our mind or to others, we do no one any favor. If we do not believe in our call, responsibility, or identity in the Lord, we allow timidity to take hold, rather than stepping out in power, love and sound mind.

God knows our hearts' motives. If we allow fear to prevent us from moving into greatness, we can end up wandering in the wilderness for 40 years, as in the time of Joshua when the Israelites would not face their giants. We should allow nothing to stand in our way of seeking excellence in our God-given callings. Believing who God says we are, what we are called to, and using our gifting to glorify God—that is true success. Living in excellence in all that we work towards in humble thanks and divine dependency—this is the place of great achievement in meeting our potential. We should live as mighty lights for the Lord, not passively hidden or aloof, but shining brightly as on a hill. We should live as beautiful ones, in righteousness, as ambassadors, representatives, and examples, as children of the true King that draw others. In that place of intimacy, our true selves shine and glorify our God.

We cannot be scared that success will lead to pride and allow that fear to become a stumbling block the enemy uses to block God's great plans. Living in success means having no fear of our potential and living in hope of the fruits our faithful work will produce. Success is calling on power and love to work in us, above the draw of timidity. Success is keeping a sound mind; it is found in not allowing pride to get in the way but in doing our best with our minds fixed on honoring God.

May we trust in Him who can help us remain pleasing to Him: we can show sincere meekness within every success. As we step out in obedience and belief, He will move us into His purposes to conquer, succeed, and even do the impossible by the Mighty Spirit that moves through us. We will know without a doubt that it is Him in us that helps us be "strong in the Lord and his mighty power" (Eph. 6:10, NIV). Our Lord loves when we place ourselves in the position of doing the impossible, something out of our reach, as we must rely entirely on Him.

So, now may we take great joy in stepping out in faith, our only fear being to obey Him.

It may sound strange, but in the past, I feared excellence or success. I felt like achieving it could possibly turn my eyes off of God and onto myself. But the Lord challenged me with words like "no shrinking back." He reminded me that I should only allow one fear in my life, which is a reverent fear of Him alone. Nothing else should play a role in dictating my life.

I've also feared failure. The truth is, I love having something I'm working towards that I know I can't do on my own. I love the journey into the spiritual promise land of God. In this life, we live with Jesus. He calls us into the wide-open space of all the goodness, freedom, presence, and love. This offer to us and the journey He calls us to is worth any fight and the facing of any giant. Is it scary at times? For sure. But then we know we must step out in strength and courage, trusting our God will never fail us. For he said, "Have I not commanded you? Be strong and courageous. Do not be afraid, do not be discouraged, for the LORD your God will be with you wherever you go" (Josh. 1:9, NIV).

So obediently, I follow through, and when I do, I find God's loyalty comes through. I press on. I have read about ancestors wandering in the wilderness for 40 years who didn't get to enter the promise land because they feared giants more than they feared God. That's my confession. I feared the excellence that could lead to pride, the possibility of failure, and the giants. But then I take courage and reject fear. I move forward in faith because I know there is only one true, mighty, beautiful thing to fear—God alone.

No Shrinking Back

Under perfect divine delight, we come to a place of beautiful understanding of being truly loved. Obeying the call to live in excellence and to be light, filled with His likeness, can be both exhilarating and frightening. The divine invitation is amazing: in it, we can see our role in Kingdom building, with all the potential God puts at our fingertips. Yet, pride in the role we might play and how others might admire us in that role can sneak in. Fear of the ugliness of that pride can be enough to freeze us, and it can seize all our attempts to live in all He calls us to be.

When we find success in living in our Kingdom identity, the enemy will always be quick to accuse us of pride. Pride is the destructive sin the enemy fell into when he faced his fall. Yet, there is a simple beauty in the power that rests in the love of God. For when we have found the safe, free, lovely place of truly knowing we are loved by God, we have our hearts sealed on one desire alone: to love Him back. In this place, we have sincere, heart-filled love that nearly explodes with the desire to worship, love, and honor God.

But this desire cannot come if we doubt, question, or mistrust the Triune's love. Trust and rest in His love is key. Under truest love, when we love God full-heartedly, we are in a safe place to spread our wings and be all-in, with excellence for God with *no shrinking back*. Under divine love and full of love for the Divine, we have no self-ambition left, no building of our own image, no ugly pride. Our full passion becomes making known how great He is.

So, we become willing to step into the greatness of being ones who strive to represent the likeness of God. We call, ask, and seek to live fully, all to glorify Him. We strive to be equipped with whatever gifts are needed to manifest His presence, to be examples of His amazing power and might, all with careful aim as we desire to make His name known and declared great.

There is no shrinking back! In love, we step into all He desires and calls us to in greatness and excellence for His name.

Declaring Truth

What better example do we have of a seemingly impossible purpose or call that requires the supernatural strength of God than our call to faithfully testify of the truth of the gospel? Just as those in Acts were entrusted with the message of grace, we are to live a life set apart and to guard the pure truth. We must live in a manner that represents the Gospel message and present our lives as those truly working to feed and care for His beloved sheep. May this call to safeguard the greatest of messages never be taken lightly, and may we never shrink back from declaring its truth. Paul said there is one message: "the necessity of repenting from sin and turning to God, and of having faith in our Lord Jesus" (Acts 20:21, NLT). Let us be found faithful, unlike those who Paul warned want to distort the gospel's meaning.

God has extended tremendous trust in assigning us the noble task of being defenders of truth. As warriors for the Kingdom, we are called to nurture, proclaim, and protect these God-principles of believing in the love of God, repentance, and salvation in Christ. These life-giving ways of embracing Jesus as Savior and Lord and then living a life of love and kindness towards others hold the power! May we live aware of how our lives continually affect all around us: moment-by-moment, we declare a powerful message. With committed hearts, we will diligently seek the help of the Spirit to live beautifully with our Lord, with the hope that the testimony of our life speaks His truth. It is a worthy aim to strive for our lives to reflect being a true disciple, witnessing by our way of love. What honor we have to be guards of the sacred love letter. We have experienced the joy of turning our old lives in for the new life that Jesus gives.

Now may we move into all of God's asking, declaring truth by living beautiful lives marked by grace, truth, and loveliness that results from the intimate connection with the Almighty!

Evangelize—A Life that Loves and Declares

To intentionally pursue the reconciliation of beloved hearts separated from God is a purpose and honor beyond comparison. Most certainly, God could do whatever He likes, by whichever means, but out of His intimate heart and intentions, He has extended the highest of honors by inviting us to Kingdom work. At times we might carefully invest in a relationship with others or openly share our testimony. We might also believe in and rely on God for incredible gifts in the Spirit to minister to others. Each holds a place of honor, joining God in Kingdom work.

Most certainly, to have any lasting effect, each effort to reach out for hearts first requires a close, intimate connection with Triune God. There is no half-belief here, no room for doubt. To be fully invested as a co-worker, we have to fully commit our steps in the work of the unseen realm. To pour ourselves all into this greater purpose, we must be wholly convinced of God's faithfulness. When we commit entirely without looking back, the potential for abundant fulfillment is incredible.

We have indeed found a treasure when we are satisfied in pursuing something so worthy. In this place, we diligently seek His heart and ask to be effective in reaching people. The search for His will creates a beautiful oneness between the Maker and created. He leads us to meet people in their individually designed, needed approach. He divinely intervenes that we can plant, water, or harvest in joint pursuit with Him to expand the family of God. He makes a promise that lifts any feeling of burden: "God makes the seed grow" (1 Cor. 3:7, NLT).

We are not merely living in the here-and-now world of what is seen. Our time here is short, so may we set our passion for joining with the Father to restore, make new, and tell the good news that brings true life. His heart is set on love, and our hearts genuinely join in the greatest of pursuits—to declare His name by whatever means to transform hearts and lives.

Keeping Our Eyes on Jesus

Once we have committed to living for the Kingdom's greater purpose, the enemy will weary, burden, distract, and even at times bore us all in an attempt to get us off track. We need to take measures to ensure our heart's pure loyalty and holy passions remain.

Therefore, since we are surrounded by such a huge crowd of witnesses to the life of faith, let us strip off every weight that slows us down, especially the sin that so easily trips us up. And let us run with endurance the race God has set before us.

~ Heb. 12:1 (NLT)

It is the grand race of all races, the ultimate battle, the one thing alone worth living and dying for, that we might stay in a close, loving, intimate connection with our Lord. What beautiful commitment and pursuit we display when we stand to live in obedience to the One who loves us so. Are we going to trip? Of course. Will we have moments of weakness, exhaustion, and defeat? Without question. The enemy puts a lot of energy into overthrowing the pursuits of the child committed to the Father's will—the mission is that valuable.

Thankfully, we are never alone in these pursuits. We are promised His forever-presence, and the indwelling of Holy Spirit power is at work in us, guiding, strengthening, and helping us along the way. Awareness of the battle is key, so we will be ready. We must run; we must fight. Whether sin, burden, weariness, boredom, or distraction, we have not fought so hard that it cost our lifeblood (see Heb. 12:4, NIV & NLT). We do not fool God in our lack of effort, and He needs us to give our best and all. So, where do we find the constant, enduring strength to run, fight, and live holy? "We do this by keeping our eyes on Jesus, the champion who initiates and perfects our faith" (Heb. 12:2, NLT). Living in the shelter of our intimate God, eyes fixed on Him, is essentially the only way to win the race, to have victory in this battle. Our hearts' motive must remain focused and dedicated to the One we love. It is in being in this deepest of relationships with its foundation of love that will help us stay the course to reach our greatest potential.

Divinely Armored, Confident Warriors

As we are armored in power with the secret to success, may we go out in joy as confident warriors with our sights set immovably on Jesus. As His beloved children, God has purposed each of us with a unique call within His grand plans. We now have only to set out to fulfill His asking. We seek to carry out all that He intends us to, filled with belief and experiencing the joy of togetherness with Him. We remember well as we journey that we don't do any of this on our own: we operate only in the strength of the Spirit in whom we are perfectly equipped. It will take something from us for sure: we must sincerely embrace the fullness of the truth of all that Jesus accomplished on the cross. He disarmed rulers and authorities, allowing us to live free from this world's spiritual powers (see Col. 2:15 & 20, NLT).

What rich equipping we are promised as armor. This armor solidifies the intimate ties which attach us firmly with our King. We have promise upon promise from the Lord that "overwhelming victory is ours" (Rom. 8:37, NLT). The Father in intimate love equips us daily with armor sufficient to fight against all accusations, untruths, and temptations. How blessed we are as His people. We have the promise of His strength and guidance as we go into any of His askings. May we be counted among those who...

> ...understand the incredible greatness of God's power for us who believe him. This is the same mighty power that raised Christ from the dead and seated him in the place of honor at God's right hand in the heavenly realms.
>
> ~ Eph. 1:19–20 (NLT)

We are His people. Strong and mighty in Him, we will do all the good works He has called us to. So we step out in anticipation, eager to move mountains with the faith and assured confidence He has given us, for we have the sureness that He has placed us in the exact position and purposes He wills. We can therefore move forward as confident warriors.

His Constant Presence

If there is one strength that will allow us to continue in our greater purpose more powerfully than any other, it is in dwelling in our Lord's constant and good company. Whatever great objectives we pursue under the call of our intimate God, this is what will sustain us, enable us, and empower us. Yet we must be aware this can't just be in our mind's understanding, but it must be carved on the fiber of our heart, and we must have an authentic awareness of the reality that we exist in the actual presence of our God. His promise is forever and uncompromised: He goes before us, always is with us, and never leaves us (see Deut. 31:8). We have the choice to live in this by faith and fully embrace it.

For me, the truth of God's constant presence is what I needed solidly established in my life before I could fully step out into the things God was asking of me. God knew I needed the promise of the best of company by my side forever. It makes any of His asking worth it. The security of having the Lord with me did many things. It allowed me to step out in courage when He asked challenging requests. It kept me away from false pursuits because I wanted to live instead to glorify my best friend, Jesus. His presence with me helps me stay focused on the purposes He asks of me. This best of company gives me hope to spread the word about Jesus. I truly believe that if Jesus is by the side of any person, it is the power that will move them into the absolute best. God's very own company is the strength that allows us to continue into our greatest purposes. I can say with confidence that in the place of divine intimacy, relationship changes everything.

This paradise-place of constant Presence is our soul's fulfillment. His company is not a temporary stop or simply a run-to state in times of trouble for us, but our spirits' continual dwelling spot of existence. Heavenly Father's presence is always before us. It stands in a yoked status with our Savior Jesus in His unfailing companionship. As temples of the living God, we trust the indwelling, constant empowerment of Holy Spirit. This is who we are! These are no simple truths. There is extraordinary living available in the beloved's identity, as never-abandoned children of God. What rich inheritance and beautiful hope that extends us the confident, mature, and increasing faith to go out and meet our full potential in the purposes He calls us to.

May we discipline ourselves to live fully for the One who has made Himself stunningly, fully present to us. May we master our perspective and see everything through the lens of authentic dwelling in His shadow. What power it has to help us understand His concrete presence with us and transform our thinking of ourselves, others, and God Himself. The never-leaving, intertwined Presence is the secret power that allows us to step fully into greater purposes.

Established in Passion

Finding the sweet embrace of tender love and living in the most astounding purpose of God's tight grip is a blessing. The promise is priceless. By remaining in truth, we stay in the wonderful company of the Triune (see 1 John 2:24), where we are engaged with the source of life that makes us increasingly fruitful. Abiding in and obeying Him assures our hearts that we are truly His. What freedom and blessing we stand in! We are loved, we are His, and He remains with us. May this be sealed on our hearts, and may we live passionately, never turning away from it.

There will be seasons when our passion flows freely, faith feels solid, and living for the Kingdom comes easily. Yet if we face any pressure, we may feel complacency beckon, the lukewarm set in, and with it, a sense of disconnect. The enemy can get us stuck in this place. He will present our lives as measurable by our work standards, thereby distracting us from focusing on our relationship with God. The deceiver will work overtime to keep us from our greatest call. By implanting feelings of separation from God, the enemy can be very effective at making us feel apart, worthless, or alone.

When we sense these disturbing feelings, we should remember: we are called to work on our salvation with fear and trembling (Phil. 2:12). So, to keep our relationship with God robust and devoted, we can prioritize our efforts and focus on returning love to God. We can honestly examine ourselves regularly to keep giving our all and our excellence to our Lord, the One who gave His very life for us.

When we seek to remain in the place of fiery, passionate love for our God, joy follows. In this pure, good location, may we be counted among those who continue in committed faith and are declared "established and firm" (Col. 1:23, NIV). Let us keep our eyes alive, with laser-sharp focus, on our greatest call to passion.

God-Led and Going Strong

There are defining moments when God's hand leads us with detailed, undeniable exactness. Think of Moses with the burning bush, Noah directed to build an ark, or the disciples when Jesus said, "Come, follow me." Any confirmation in a calling, a specific direction for our life path, the discovery of a spiritual gift—all represent defining moments when life changes. In those times, as we step out in faith and follow His lead, we receive incredible favor in the potential for beautiful connectedness. When we carry out the plans God deposits on our hearts with eagerness and perseverance, it is pure joy. The excitement of being called and the evidence of fruit encourages our endurance. Yet when excitement passes and fruits are few, we need to not grow weary in the call.

Faith becomes essential when we don't see results. We need a fundamental resolve to carry out His leading, no matter what. Power rests in Jesus Christ, and our intimacy is built as we find strength in and through Him. The measure of our belief is a powerful tool: we must trust we live in Him who equips us with all we need to do His will and produce that which pleases His heart (see Heb. 13:21, NLT).

It requires solid trust and belief to accept that God has called, God has led, and we are exactly where He wants us to be. The same intimate guidance that got us where we are is still available to lead us on. If we listen closely, we will hear His promise and continued direction that everything will be fine, that we don't need to change our plans, for Mighty Triune God, our very own family, is with us. This is the place of true contentment to keep on going, even when it seems impossible. We can trust His leading and embrace the rich company and love that is always with us.

May we keep going strong, led each step of the way by God, moving forward in our greatest purpose: "So take a new grip with your tired hands and strengthen your weak knees. Mark out a straight path for your feet" (Heb. 12:12–13, NLT). How blessed we are to have the connectedness that allows us to rest in Him. He leads us moment by moment in that straight path to all the purposeful spaces that please Him. This is the place our intimate hearts long for—to simply please Him.

The Simplicity of Effortless Companionship

God has a calling, gifting, and Kingdom-building purpose for us. Yet these are not precisely in what or how we find the fullness of living. As noble and satisfying as it is to live out all God has assigned to us as ministers in the form of upright pursuits, we will miss the most significant experience of intimacy if we believe those pursuits are solely what we are here to do. Since the beginning, God has always desired to have fellowship with His created (1 John 1:1–3). When our efforts and focus are on what we can do for God, we compromise our relationship.

He desires to restore our highly-favored relationship. He wants us to concentrate on simply being with Him and on enjoying Him in effortless companionship. He wants us to take in his divine company and be still, listen, and allow Him to show us what's new on His heart. Yet we often choose what's second-best: we get caught up in being "important" or "useful" and neglect our relational side with God, which should be of first importance. Because we do, there will be periods when we will feel stagnant in the Kingdom. In response, we can allow the feeling to frustrate us or use it as a reminder of that which is more important.

This is a longing of our Lord: the beauty of simple camaraderie with Him. It's not in seeking knowledge, experience, or results—it's in spending time with Him. Is this not why we work so hard to help restore His lost people to our Father? That they would know Him and His love? It certainly is not so that they would go work so hard Kingdom building that they neglect the tender, beautifully restored relationship they gained with God.

So, when we face blocked effectiveness in ministry, we can take joy in remembering that God loves us so profoundly that He longs not for what we can do for Him; rather, He longs first for relationship with us.

Why Are We Still Here?

We are the beloved, ransomed, forgiven children of God. Bought with a promise, we stand in deepest intimacy, eternally in the presence of our Lord. We long to dwell in beautiful, forever closeness. When we feel its absence, we can be left exhausted and feel the weight of a pressing question. Why are we still here?

To move forward in all our God-given potential, we must address the unrelenting matter of purpose. Just as our heart longs for His presence, He whose name is Love longs even more heavily for us to be with Him. We can absolutely rest assured that our still being here on earth is for great reason. We are purposed to be His light, reflect His nature, and testify to His truth for the eternal aim of glorifying the One we love. The Holy Spirit works through us to complete the will of the Father. To die is gain, to be more fully with the one we love, and to live is Christ (see Phil. 1:21). Therefore, empowered by our new nature, we focus on being Jesus-affirmers through our transformed Spirit-filled lives.

> *"You are my witnesses," declares the LORD, "and my servant whom I have chosen,*
> *so that you may know and believe me and understand that I am he."*
>
> ~ *Isa. 43:10 (NIV)*

We have rich blessings here to sustain us; we are chosen as His very own people; we know Him, believe Him, and understand His good purposes. May we remain in these eternal truths and pray that they would be experienced "on earth as it is in heaven," all with the utmost desire to share the deep, satisfying life in Christ.

As for now, till our sweet Lord calls us to our eternal home, we are to remain in the body. May we not waste an ounce of strength on any lesser purpose than living in the intimate call of our Beloved. With hearts aimed at reaching all our potential, we will be found faithful in waiting, living fully, and loving our treasured Lord and King.

Love's Purpose

> *So keep at your work, this faith and love rooted in Christ, exactly as I set it out for*
> *you. It's as sound as the day you first heard it from me. Guard this precious thing*
> *placed in your custody by the Holy Spirit who works in us.*
>
> ~ *2 Tim. 1:13–14 (MSG)*

The heart of our Maker is incredible. We are drawn to the truth that our created purpose above all is to love and be loved. He has clearly laid out the primary importance that we are to love Him with all our heart, all our soul, all our mind, and all our strength (Mark 12:30). So, may we meet Him in all His asking and seal this purpose into everything we do, to present this life of ours as a gift of thanksgiving offering.

However, we cannot escape the most pressing of all other purposes: our need to allow ourselves first to be loved. Love must be given and reciprocated in any genuine intimate relationship. The truth is, we cannot fully love God until we place ourselves in the position of truly being loved by Him. At times, to try to love Him can be much easier in the doing than in allowing Him to love us in the resting. Yet this is His offering, His desire, His prayer for us. Our feet must be firmly planted in this love. So, as our Beloved says,

> *The LORD will take delight in you, and your land will be married. As a young man marries a young woman, so will your Builder marry you; as a bridegroom rejoices over his bride, so will your God rejoice over you.*

> *~ Isa. 62:4–5 (NIV)*

Can we accept this goodness to be true? Will we meet Him and allow this love that delights over us, rejoices in us, builds us, and marries us to flood and fill up our souls? For it is in that place that we truly join Him, step-by-step in all our doing. Here, we love Him. Here we have our true being. Here we are most useful to Him, for His love empowers us to love all others well. There is nothing like intimately joining with Triune God.

Here in this place, we reach our greatest eternal purpose.

Printed in Great Britain
by Amazon